Promoting Third-World Development and Food Security

Promoting Third-World Development and Food Security

CX

Edited by
Luther G. Tweeten
and Donald G. McClelland

Westport, Connecticut
London

Library of Congress Cataloging-in-Publication Data

Promoting third-world development and food security / edited by Luther
    G. Tweeten and Donald G. McClelland.
        p.   cm.
    Includes bibliographical references and index.
    ISBN 0–275–95815–9 (alk. paper)
        1. Agriculture—Economic aspects—Developing countries.
    2. Agricultural assistance—Developing countries.   3. Developing
    countries—Economic conditions.   I. Tweeten, Luther G.
    II. McClelland, Donald G.
    HD1417.P766   1997
    338.1′09172′4—dc21   96–47613

British Library Cataloguing in Publication Data is available.

Library of Congress Catalog Card Number: 96–47613
ISBN: 0–275–95815–9

First published in 1997

Praeger Publishers, 88 Post Road West, Westport, CT 06881
An imprint of Greenwood Publishing Group, Inc.

Printed in the United States of America

(∞)™

The paper used in this book complies with the
Permanent Paper Standard issued by the National
Information Standards Organization (Z39.48–1984).

10 9 8 7 6 5 4 3 2 1

Copyright Acknowledgments

The editors and publisher gratefully acknowledge permission to reprint the following:

Chapter 4, "Issues of Infrastructural Development" by Raisuddin Ahmed and Cynthia Donovan, is a
modified version of Raisuddin Ahmed and Cynthia Donovan, *Issues of Infrastructural Development:
A Synthesis of the Literature*, Occasional Paper (Washington, D.C.: International Food Policy Research Institute, 1992). Reprinted by permission of the International Food Policy Research Institute.

Figure 4.1 reprinted from T. R. Lakshmanan, "Infrastructure and Economic Transformation," in A. E.
Andersson, D. Batten, B. Johansson, and P. Nijkamp, eds., *Advances in Spatial Theory and Dynamics*, copyright © 1992, with kind permission from Elsevier Science–NL, Sara Burgerhartstraat 25,
1055 KV Amsterdam, The Netherlands.

Figure 9.2 originally appeared in International Food Policy Research Institute, *IFPRI 1990 Report*
(Washington, D.C.: International Food Policy Research Institute, 1990). Reprinted by permission of
the International Food Policy Research Institute.

Contents

Tables and Figures

FIGURES

Preface

Some 800 million people are chronically food insecure, rarely getting enough to eat for a productive and healthy life. The chief cause of food insecurity is general poverty in developing countries. The cure for poverty is broad-based sustainable economic development. Because three-fourths of people in poor developing countries are employed in agriculture, the long road to development begins with increasing agricultural productivity. This book provides the most comprehensive coverage and in-depth evaluation to date of the payoff from public intervention to promote food security and agricultural development.

In his closing remarks to the 1995 IFPRI conference entitled *A 2020 Vision for Food, Agriculture, and the Environment*,   Keith Bezanson, President of the International Development Research Center, stated that

there is a crying need for priorities and for a basis on which to decide priorities. The task is to identify those investments that will yield that combination, that configuration, of action that would result in the highest return, given that resources are certain to be constrained. The most significant weakness in the IFPRI process to date is that we have not addressed the issue of priorities or the means to arrive at them. That is clearly a most serious dilemma and must be addressed if the 2020 Vision is even to have a chance of succeeding.

The chapters in this book document the payoffs from alternative means to promote economic development and set priorities for an overall development strategy.

With an end to the Cold War and spectacular economic progress of many once-poor nations, many Americans have turned their attention away from international assistance. Foreign aid is under greater scrutiny than at any time since World War II. Many individuals and agencies want to know how best to foster economic development and food security. The public wants to look carefully at what works and wants to prune what does not work. Practitioners and policymakers dealing with food security and development want information to focus on successful strategies—thereby making for better results, public relations, and support. This review and synthesis is especially instructive in sorting out proper roles for the private and public sectors, noting effective public strategies that complement and stimulate the private sector rather than crowd it out.

The principal audience for this book is students of Third World economic development, be they professors, government officials, persons in classrooms, informed laypersons, aid donors, or aid practitioners. Because agriculture is such a large component of Third World economies, the audience extends to all individuals and agencies interested in Third World food security and general economic development.

The U.S. Agency for International Development (USAID) has devoted substantial resources to investments in Third World agriculture, probably the largest single component of U.S. foreign assistance. Several of the chapters in this book are the product of an extensive review of USAID agricultural development strategies carried out by the agency's Center for Development Information and Evaluation. The reviews were prepared mostly by experts outside of USAID. All chapters draw on development experience from numerous sources, including USAID. Comments of Bruce Johnston, Per Pinstrup-Andersen, and James Shaffer were very helpful; they are in no way responsible for shortcomings of any chapters.

We are grateful for help in preparing this manuscript. Renée Drury and Wendi Stachler processed and formatted the manuscript. Support from the U.S. Agency for International Development and Ohio State University was critical to the authors of the chapters. However, we emphasize that the views expressed in this book are those of the authors and are not necessarily those of the aforementioned agencies or individuals.

Luther G. Tweeten and Donald G. McClelland

Promoting Third-World Development and Food Security

1

Investments in Agriculture: Synthesis and Overview

Donald G. McClelland

INTRODUCTION

American economic assistance to developing countries at 0.1 percent of gross domestic product (GDP) ranks near the lowest among industrial nations and is about one-tenth that of several countries in northern Europe. Despite this, American foreign assistance budgets continue to be cut. Poverty, hunger, and pestilence still plague large numbers of people in developing countries. Failure to respond to critical needs traces to several sources:

1. *Many developing nations, especially in Asia, are making substantial economic progress.* Once they were targets of development assistance; now they no longer need it, and some are aiding other economies. Several formerly impoverished countries in East and Southeast Asia are now middle-income countries. Foreign economic assistance helped create the emerging markets of Brazil, Chile, Korea, Mexico, and Taiwan. They are now major commercial importers of American agricultural products. However, hundreds of millions of people in Africa, South Asia, and elsewhere remain poor and food insecure. Other factors help to explain our reduced foreign assistance.
2. *An end to the Cold War.* Americans once viewed developing countries as the principal economic battlefield in the struggle between democracy and communism. With that battle won following the collapse of the Soviet Union, many conclude it is time to bring the "troops" home. The United States is now directing considerable foreign assistance to the former Soviet Union and East Bloc countries. This assistance, motivated by the need to help former Second World nations make the difficult transition to democratic capitalism, competes with aid to Third World countries.
3. *Budget stringency.* The domestic political constituency for foreign economic assistance has never been large. That portion of the constituency supporting humanitarian assistance seldom gets much beyond short-term food aid and emergency assistance to

examine long-term development assistance. The budget of any program without a sizable political constituency is a tempting target for cuts.

4. *Ignorance*. In opinion polls, Americans overestimate the nation's outlays for foreign economic assistance. Indeed, when asked what the nation *should give*, they respond with a number well in excess of actual assistance.

5. *Ineffectiveness of assistance*. A fifth concern is that foreign economic assistance has been ineffective. It is argued that payoffs in Third World economic progress have been small from outlays of foreign assistance. Further, it is argued that too little is known about how to invest for economic progress so that foreign economic assistance can work.

This book addresses the fifth concern. It examines the empirical evidence on payoffs from various types of foreign aid investments. Results reveal which aid strategies have paid off, and they give direction for future economic assistance designed to achieve sustainable economic development and food security.

The focus is on agriculture because agriculture provides the major economic engine and employment base of poor countries. Without agricultural development, most poor countries are unable to progress. This book identifies priorities for moving agriculture forward. It suggests the conditions under which investments in agricultural development have been successful and unsuccessful in contributing to agricultural growth in developing countries. *Agriculture* is broadly defined as those activities (traditionally funded under section 103 of the Foreign Assistance Act) in support of rural nonfarm production as well as agricultural production. These activities can be conveniently organized into five subsectors.

1. *Policy reform and planning* (budget support for agricultural policy reform, analytical capacity building)
2. *Technology development and diffusion* (agricultural research, agricultural education, agricultural extension)
3. *Rural infrastructure* (rural roads, rural electrification, irrigation)
4. *Agricultural services* (agricultural credit, input and output marketing, crop storage)
5. *Asset distribution and access* (land tenure and land reform, land use and land settlement)

Successful agricultural development normally requires (1) an economic policy framework that is conducive to agricultural growth and in which farming can be profitable; (2) agricultural technology applicable to particular soil, water, and climatic conditions; (3) roads and related rural infrastructure to transport agricultural inputs (such as seeds and fertilizers) and to market agricultural outputs; (4) key agricultural services (such as credit, marketing, storage, and processing); and (5) secure tenure arrangements to encourage investment in land and other agricultural assets.[1]

Donors have obligated substantial resources to support agricultural development in low-income countries during the past twenty years (and more). During six years of the 1980s, USAID investments in agriculture (excluding natural resources and the environment) exceeded $1 billion annually (including resources from both the Development Assistance Account and the Economic Support Fund). As a proportion of total Development Assistance, support for agriculture has changed substantially over the years. In 1973 when the "New Directions" legislation was enacted, Agency investments in "food production and nutrition" made up 26 percent of total Development Assistance; in 1974, 35 percent; and in 1975, an estimated 54 percent (U.S. Agency for International Development [henceforth USAID] 1975). From 1975 to 1985, USAID investments in agriculture averaged 55 percent of total Development Assistance. In 1985 they decreased to less than 50 percent for the first time since 1975; and in 1990 they decreased to less than 40 percent. They remain at or below that level today.

The composition of USAID investments in agriculture has also changed over time. Figure 1.1 shows that total funding for agriculture has declined in recent years, from $806 million in fiscal year (FY) 1989 to $418 million in FY 1994. Table 1.1 shows the percentage of total USAID and World Bank funds going to the agriculture sector over the same six-year period. For USAID, agriculture's share of total funding has been declining fairly steadily, from 14 percent to 6 percent of total funding. For the World Bank, agriculture's share has increased to 19 percent from 16 percent.

This chapter seeks to answer six questions (McClelland, 1996):

1. Is there a logical sequence for investing in the five agricultural subsectors?
2. Has successful agricultural development occurred in the absence of investments in one or more of the five areas?
3. Under what conditions have investments in each of the subsectors been relatively successful or resulted in a relatively high economic rate of return?
4. Is the private sector best suited to invest in certain areas (such as agriculture services), and is the public sector best suited to invest in other areas (such as rural infrastructure)?
5. Among the various agencies that implement agriculture activities, including nongovernmental organizations (NGOs), are some better suited in certain areas than others?
6. Does the United States have a comparative advantage over others in providing agricultural assistance in some areas?

This chapter assumes that agricultural growth is essential to sustainable economic development in most low-income developing countries. Thus, these six questions concern the composition of investments in agriculture, not the importance of agriculture investments relative to alternative (nonagriculture) investments. Although most of the issues concern the role of the public sector, which among other things must provide the enabling policy environment and the essential "public goods" to allow the private sector to operate effectively, most development professionals agree that successful agricultural development must rely primarily on the market and that most investment decisions will have to be made by the private sector.

Figure 1.1.
Allocation of USAID Agriculture Resources by Subsector, FYs 1989–1994[a]
($ Millions)

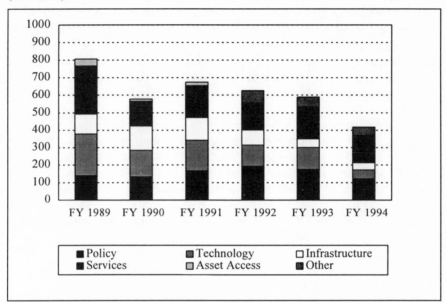

Source: USAID
[a]The five subsectors are aggregations of investments in specific activities tracked by USAID. "Other" refers to investments in crop, livestock, and fisheries production, activities which were funded before FY 1992 but not tracked as such.

THE FIVE ELEMENTS OF AGRICULTURAL DEVELOPMENT

Element One: Agricultural Policy Reform and Planning

This first element of agricultural development is generally pursued through two major kinds of investments: (1) "balance-of-payments support" (capital transfers) to encourage or support economic policy reform and (2) technical assistance and training in economic planning and policy analysis (see Simons and Kent, Chapter 2 of this book).

Balance-of-payments support consists of cash or commodities provided to host country governments to support their efforts to liberalize economic policies, including agricultural policies. The objective of such support is both to leverage significant changes in economic policies and to cushion against the adverse and often politically unpopular short-term effects of these changes. Technical assistance and training for planning and policy analysis have commonly supported policy analysis units established in ministries of agriculture, planning, and finance. The objective of such units is to provide agriculture, planning, and finance. The objective of such units is to provide decision makers with comprehensive policy options derived from improved analytical expertise.

Table 1.1.
Allocation of USAID and World Bank Resources to Agriculture, FYs 1989–1994 (in $ Millions and as a Percentage of Total Economic Assistance)

	FY 1989	FY 1990	FY 1991	FY 1992	FY 1993	FY 1994
USAID						
Agriculture allocation	806	577	674	626	589	418
Total economic assistance	5,900	6,684	7,353	6,572	6,776	6,641
Percent of total	14	9	9	10	9	6
World Bank						
Agriculture allocation	3,490	3,656	3,707	3,894	3,267	3,907
Total lending	22,367	20,702	22,685	21,706	23,696	20,836
Percent of total	16	18	16	18	14	19

Source: USAID, *Congressional Presentation* FYs 1992, 1993, and 1994; and World Bank, *Annual Report* 1991, p. 179; 1993, p. 165; and 1994, p. 147.

Donor attempts to induce economic policy changes in developing countries with capital transfers are described in various ways. Some observers have characterized these programs as "trading cash for policy reform"; others emphasize that such transfers make reforms easier by cushioning populations from the negative side effects of economic changes. Generally, adjustment operations that cushion or ease incipient or ongoing reforms have met with more success than those that attempted to buy new reforms. Similarly, policy dialogue has met with more success than policy conditionality.

Some adjustment operations concentrate on macroeconomic reforms that indirectly affect agriculture. An example is adjustments in the foreign exchange rate that shift the terms of trade agriculture. Other operations focus directly on agriculture, such as lifting agricultural price controls. The International Monetary Fund (IMF) and the World Bank provide the major portion of adjustment assistance in macroeconomic affairs; adjustment assistance specific to agriculture is provided by the World Bank and to a lesser extent by USAID. USAID has been the lead donor in establishing and developing planning and policy analysis units.

Historical Context

Policy dialogue and policy conditionality have been in the limelight over the past dozen years or so. But donor conditionality extends back well before 1980, especially in India and Latin America.

In India, American officials in 1965 "thought that Indian [agricultural] policies needed changing and that it was appropriate to use transfers, especially of the nonproject kind, to encourage such changes" (Lewis n.d., 15). Accordingly, the U.S. government demonstrated its disapproval of India's approach to agriculture by withholding Public Law (PL) 480 food assistance, upon which India depended. Only after that nation formally adopted a new agricultural strategy along the lines suggested by U.S. officials did President Johnson authorize release of PL 480 food assistance and resumption of nonproject lending (with a $50 million fertilizer loan). In retrospect, it is clear that agricultural policy reforms in India were important and that their adoption owes much to U.S. pressure. But India's leaders resented being pressured into reform, especially because the PL 480 shipments that were withheld were crucial during the drought years of the mid-1960s (Lewis n.d., 29).

In some ways, the experience in Latin America with the Alliance for Progress parallels that of India. However, most of the conditionality associated with the Alliance supported stabilization measures and other macroeconomic reforms; agriculture was addressed only indirectly. According to most observers, the results were poor. Berg (1991, 216), for example, notes that "few traces of the exercise were visible by the end of the decade." Heller and Wionczek (1988, 134) state that the "Alliance experience can be interpreted as an overwhelming repudiation of the general efficacy of the assumption [that conditionality can work]."

Disappointment with the unpopular (though effective) Indian experience and the Alliance's macroeconomic (and thus indirect) focus prompted donors to shift away from conditionality and toward specific investment projects in the 1970s (Weintraub 1989, 24). Indeed, most projects during this decade "were conventionally designed to work within rather than to change the domestic policy environment" (Food and Agriculture Organization [henceforth FAO] 1989, 33).

The project mode, however, had revealed its limitations by the end of the decade. By 1980 donors began to reach a consensus that the policy environment was so negative in so many developing countries that it was necessary to engage in policy dialogue to promote reform and adjustment. The World Bank developed new loan instruments for this function: Structural adjustment loans (SALs) were used for the first time in 1980, and sectoral adjustment loans (SECALs), in 1983. The IMF increased its conditional lending to developing countries through its Structural Adjustment Facility and Enhanced Structural Adjustment Facility.

USAID began turning its attention to free markets and the economic policies necessary to make them work. Despite the disappointing experience with policy conditionality in India and under the Alliance for Progress, USAID again began to provide policy-conditioned assistance, much of it addressing agricultural issues.

Results of USAID Adjustment Operations

Since 1960 USAID has invested $2.7 billion in 221 agricultural policy reform and planning activities worldwide. About three-fourths of the activities have been small projects designed to develop capacity in policy analysis and planning. Such projects accounted for about $660 million of total expenditure. A much greater proportion of expenditures, about $2 billion (including PL 480 food aid), was committed to conditionality programs (including "hybrid" projects that addressed both planning and policy reform) (Tilney and Block 1988, 1991).

Numerous evaluations examined by Simons and Kent in Chapter 2 report mixed results. But on the whole, USAID support was successful and accelerated liberalization of agriculture in those countries where the government was genuinely committed to reforms.

Results of World Bank Adjustment Operations

The World Bank has invested more than $5 billion in agricultural sector adjustment loans over the past decade or so that stress policy conditionality. In addition, the Bank has invested more than $15 billion in structural adjustment loans since 1980. Sixty percent of them contain conditionality related to agricultural pricing (Knudsen and Nash 1991).

Most literature on World Bank adjustment loans in agriculture indicates that results have been fair to good (see Chapter 2). Knudsen and Nash's work shows that 68 percent of agricultural pricing conditionalities have been met. McCleary (1991) reports that about 60 percent of the policy changes agreed to as conditions of SALs and SECALs were fully implemented. Among the areas where implementation was most successful were agricultural pricing policies and exchange rate policies, which are critical to improving agricultural terms of trade. Cleaver (1988, 49) indicates that, on average, reforms pay dividends. Aggregate agricultural production was significantly higher in adjusting countries than in other countries. This suggests that, overall, "where policy is good or improving, performance is also good or improving."

Still, as Islam (1991) points out, most studies deal insufficiently with the impact of these reforms on agricultural performance. Instead, they focus on whether the reforms were implemented. Lele (1991) concludes that the World Bank has had limited success in persuading countries to undertake changes when their leaders were opposed.

Results of USAID Planning and Policy Analysis Activities

Over the past thirty years, USAID has been the principal bilateral donor funding projects to help build local capacity in agricultural planning and policy analysis. From 1979 through 1984, USAID sponsored at least 129 agricultural policy and planning projects with total funding of $475 million (of which USAID contributed $278 million).[2] The projects were designed to provide the analytical basis for policy reform (as distinct from financial support of policy reform) as well as to strengthen institutions.

Institution building. The evaluation literature identifies six factors that have contributed to successful institution building in planning and policy analysis projects: (1) project staff, both expatriate and host country, are competent; (2) incentives are in place to recruit and retain qualified host country staff; (3) the right kind of training, including on-the-job training, is provided, and well-qualified trainees are selected; (4) physical equipment, such as computers, is provided; (5) the analytical work addresses the country's policy needs; and (6) results of the analyses are widely disseminated.

Too often these factors are not present. In identifying expatriate staff, donors often give too much emphasis to technical skills and too little to teaching and management ability. Host countries often select counterparts on personal or political, rather than professional, grounds. Civil service pay scales are not high enough to attract and retain qualified analysts. Trainees are often selected not on their qualifications but through influence. On-the-job training may be inadequate, a circumstance that perpetuates dependence on expatriate personnel.

Policy reform. The evaluation literature identifies four factors that actually induce policy change: (1) the host country supports the change; (2) the analysis meets the needs of the policymakers by addressing immediate policy issues and by providing direct, practical, implementable recommendations; (3) the policy analysis unit is situated close to senior decision makers; and (4) the policy advisers perform high-quality analysis and have credibility with and access to policymakers.

Sometimes these factors are not present. Because governmental leaders often resist analyses that challenge or expose the limitations of existing policies, the analyses are unlikely to produce short-term results. Large, quantitative, highly abstract modeling exercises have little pay-off in policy change because they fail to meet the tests of practicality and relevance. Policy analysis units are often isolated from the entity having prime authority in setting agricultural policies, often a ministry of finance or planning.

USAID's planning and policy analysis projects have had less success in achieving actual policy change than in achieving their institution-building objectives. Of sixty-one projects evaluated, only twenty contributed to actual changes in policies or programs (see Chapter 2). However, absence of actual policy change does not necessarily mean that the policy analysis and planning activities failed. Even with the highest-quality analysis and the best decision-maker access, policies may not change in the short term. However, when countries pursue policies inimical to economic progress and food security, economic development assistance has little or no chance for success.

Element Two: Agricultural Technology Development and Diffusion

Technology development and diffusion contributes to agricultural growth by reducing costs and/or increasing yields (see Oehmke, Chapter 3 of this book). By boosting agricultural productivity, successful technology development and diffusion enhances consumer welfare because techniques that increase the quantity of agricultural output often result in lower market prices for those products. In addition, higher agricultural productivity provides the economic base to help fund infrastructure and schools and reduces pressure to expand production on environmentally fragile land. Two types of agricultural education, the third component of the tripartite U.S. land grant model (together with research and extension), especially affect technology development and diffusion: (1) education of farmers and (2) higher education of researchers. The contribution of education is detailed in Chapter 7.

Two key indicators of the state of agricultural technology development and diffusion are: (1) changes in on-farm yields and (2) the gap between on-farm yields and potential yields. From 1960–1961 through 1990–1991, average yield increases for the major staple crops (rice, wheat, and maize) have been substantial, doubling in many parts of the world. Average yields, however, are still well below potential; that is, there is still a gap between on-farm yields and potential yields. Among developing countries, the gap appears to be greatest in Africa.

Table 1.2 shows that over the period 1960–1961 through 1990–1991, rice yields increased by 78 percent worldwide. In the Far East they more than doubled. They increased least in Africa; in fact, rice yields in the other regions of the world were higher in 1960–1961 than they were in Africa in 1990–1991. (In Cameroon, an exception, rice yields increased fourfold.) In the case of wheat, yields more than doubled, even in Africa. In Africa, though, they remain far below yield levels in other parts of the world. Finally, maize yields also increased dramatically, even in countries (such as the United States) that had already adopted hybrids before 1960. Again, Africa has shown the least progress. These yield increases are attributable largely to (1) improved varieties resulting from agricultural research, (2) development of irrigation, and (3) increased use of chemical fertilizers.

Historical Context

In most developed countries, technology transfer from researchers to farmers takes place rapidly and effectively. The primary mechanisms are public bodies such as the Cooperative Extension Service (in the United States) and private firms through their sales efforts. The process is a continuum, and it is difficult to determine where research ends and extension begins.

The situation is quite different in most developing countries, where, compared with developed countries, extension workers (1) often have little to extend and (2) must service a larger number of farm units, particularly poor farmers on small holdings. Workers are usually male, and they most often contact male members of

Table 1.2.
Average Yields (kilograms/hectare) for Rice, Wheat, and Maize, by Region, 1960–1961 and 1990–1991

	Rice		Wheat		Maize	
Region	1960–1961	1990–1991	1960–1961	1990–1991	1960–1961	1990–1991
Africa	1,120	1,602	595	1,394	900	1,174
Latin America	1,790	2,634	1,095	2,080	1,165	2,008
Far East	1,700	3,558	840	2,594	930	3,316
Near East	2,875	4,564	950	1,844	1,550	4,383
North America	3,835	6,248	1,520	2,408	3,285	7,116
World	1,980	3,516	1,230	2,526	2,055	3,712

Source: FAO, *Production Yearbook,* Vols. 15 and 45 (1961 and 1991).

farming families, even though women do much of the farming. They are usually city born and bred and have little practical knowledge of farm conditions. Funding of public extension services is often inadequate, with the result that extension workers suffer from low pay, inadequate equipment, and limited operating expenses for visiting the countryside. In contrast to developed countries, private sector firms carry out relatively little extension work.

In 1952 the United States began investing in the development of agricultural universities in developing countries. Large numbers of U.S. faculty were sent on long-term overseas assignments to host country universities to help establish or improve education and research programs. Similarly, thousands of host country faculty were sent to American universities for advanced degrees in the agricultural sciences. By 1989 such assistance had been provided to sixty-four universities in forty countries. Most of the agricultural university development projects (fifty out of sixty-four) were initiated in the 1950s and 1960s. The largest programs were undertaken in Brazil, India, Indonesia, and Nigeria (Hansen 1989).

Typically, a host country university was paired with a U.S. land grant university. Universities from thirty-six states were used as contractors, and these universities helped to instill the tripartite institutional model (research, extension, and education) common in the United States. Many of the forty countries made substantial progress. The new institutions, however, were often not able to implement the farmer-controlled land grant model, partly because it did not match the institutional models inherited under former European colonial rule (particularly from the British and French), which placed research under central government ministries of agriculture.

Impact of Investments in Agricultural Technology Development and Diffusion

Public expenditures on agricultural research in developing countries increased from $2.5 billion a year in 1971–1975 to more than $4.3 billion a year in 1981–1985 (in 1980 dollars). Expenditures have been substantially greater in the Asia/Near East region than in either the Africa or Latin America/Caribbean regions (Pardey and Roseboom 1989).

Research and extension. A single finding from the literature summarized in Chapter 3 overwhelms all others: Investments in agricultural research have generated high economic rates of return, indicating that the social benefits of the investments justify the costs in virtually all countries, for a wide variety of commodities, and under diverse agronomic and climatic conditions. Many of the rates of return range from 30 to 50 percent, indicating that interest rates of 30 to 50 percent could have been paid on public funds used to develop and (in some cases) diffuse agricultural technology while breaking even on the investment.

The findings of high returns across most countries and commodities have led most reviewers to conclude that investment in agricultural research is economically justified and essential for food security (see Chapter 3). For Africa, although most studies show that investments in agricultural research were justified, there were some exceptions. In fact, the negative rates of return found in a few studies are unique to Africa.

USAID's extension experience falls into three phases (Cummings 1989). During the first phase, in the 1950s and 1960s, extension was a high priority. USAID provided broad support and mobilized thousands of professionals to establish and expand American-style extension systems throughout the developing world. In the early 1970s, other donors, most notably the World Bank with its training and visit system, took the lead in promoting national systems. In contrast, USAID began, in the second phase, to integrate extension into rural development activities, supporting an increasing number of farming systems projects—an attempt to bridge research and extension through closer on-farm interaction with farmers.

The third phase of the Agency's extension experience began in the late 1980s. Improvements to extension systems became part of a wider agricultural development strategy that included support for policy reform, agricultural research, private sector growth, and rural resource mobilization. At long last, it had become clear that extension agents had very little useful information to offer when visiting farmers, thereby substantiating the view that research was essential. In the United States, for example, establishment of state experiment stations preceded *by decades* establishment of public extension work.

Education. Social rates of return on investments in primary, secondary, and higher education have averaged, respectively, about 25 percent, 15 percent, and 12 percent in developing countries (see Chapter 7). These rates compare favorably with returns to conventional capital investments in the private sector and to public education in developed countries. Satisfactory progress in agriculture, food security, and overall economic development depends on broad-based access to elementary schooling. Schooling of women, often neglected, is important not only for economic reasons but also to improve health and reduce birth rates.

Foreign assistance agencies have played an important role in training teachers for higher education and research. Most of the host country faculty trained by USAID returned to their home universities, which became major sources of trained personnel in the agricultural sciences. Some larger universities, such as those in India, Indonesia, and Thailand, have been able to support significant levels of applied research. In contrast, the research role of smaller universities, many located in Africa and Central America, has been much more limited.

Most universities have not been involved in significant extension roles because government line agencies have tended to guard this function for themselves. As suggested previously, however, public sector extension does not appear to have had much positive effect on the diffusion of new crop varieties. In fact, technologies that offer significant improvement in economic returns will spread quickly among farmers through example, as was the case with high-yielding varieties of wheat and rice that spread rapidly and widely in much of Asia. "The best extension agent," the saying goes, "is looking over your neighbor's fence."

Element Three: Rural Infrastructure

Infrastructure development involves creation of public goods, which often are also durable capital goods. These public capital goods normally reduce costs of other goods and services and produce social benefits and not just private benefits (see Chapter 4). As a result, use by one individual of the services provided by these public goods does not prevent other individuals from using and benefiting from the same services. The private sector normally does not provide public goods because it cannot capture monetary benefits to pay for them. Examples of public (or quasi-public) capital goods, or physical infrastructure, include public utilities (waterworks, telephone, electricity), transport facilities (roads, bridges), and health and education facilities (hospitals, schools).

Four characteristics (in addition to their public goods properties) help to distinguish infrastructure, which contributes *indirectly* to economic growth, from investments that are *directly* productive (such as fertilizer): (1) the services provided by infrastructure facilitate carrying out a wide variety of economic activities; (2) they are provided in most countries by public agencies or by private agencies subject to public control and thus are provided free of charge or at rates that are publicly regulated; (3) the services for the most part cannot be imported; and (4) investments in infrastructure tend to be indivisible or lumpy.

Impact of Investments in Rural Infrastructure

Economists and others have tried to evaluate how rural infrastructure affects agricultural production. Because infrastructure typically contributes only indirectly to economic growth, it is difficult to measure the magnitude of that contribution. (For this reason, it is also difficult to determine what level of resources should be allocated to infrastructure activities relative to directly productive activities.)

For example, rural roads make it possible (or less expensive) to distribute fertilizer and other agricultural inputs. Fertilizer, in turn, contributes directly to increased agricultural productivity and incomes. But in trying to explain why agricultural productivity and incomes increased, it is difficult to disentangle the effect of the fertilizer from the effect of the rural road that made the distribution of fertilizer possible in the first place. Rural roads also make it possible to move food from surplus to shortage areas, a contribution important for an efficient economic system and for promoting food security.

Studies reviewed by Ahmed and Donovan (see Chapter 4) found that infrastructure variables contributed to production technology choices and output increases. For example, one study (Binswanger et al. 1987), using annual data (1969–1978) for fifty-eight countries, found that increased road density results in increased fertilizer demand and increased agricultural production. Another study found that rural electrification has a direct and positive effect on well irrigation (but not on gravity-fed irrigation) and multiple cropping. In addition, availability of electricity stimulated growth of rural grain mills by enabling mills to operate in the first place and through irrigation, which contributed to increased agricultural production (which stimulated demand for milling services).

Ahmed and Hossain (1990) found that farms in villages in Bangladesh with relatively well-developed infrastructure (1) used greater amounts of fertilizer, (2) had more land under irrigation, (3) had more of their land under high-yielding varieties, (4) marketed more of their agricultural production, and (5) had 12 percent higher rural wages and wage income.

Some evaluations have estimated economic rates of return on infrastructure (see Chapter 4):

1. A Mexican roads project reported an estimated economic rate of return of 11 to 18 percent, depending on the road section analyzed. The rate of return increased to 20 percent if other "unquantified" benefits were added.
2. A rural roads project in Liberia reported economic rates of return ranging from 7.9 to 23 percent, depending on alternative construction and maintenance projections. The evaluation also found that vehicle operating costs fell by 90 percent as a result of the roads.
3. The multidonor Kenya rural access roads program showed an economic rate of return of more than 30 percent associated with labor-intensive roads (as distinct from those built with conventional capital-intensive techniques).

Taiwan and Korea share similar growth paths, although incomes have reached higher levels in Taiwan. In Taiwan about 80 percent of rural income is received from nonfarm sources, compared with less than 48 percent in Korea. This difference can be attributed in part to differences in rural electrification and rural roads in the two countries. In Taiwan, 70 percent of farm households had access to electricity, even in 1960, compared with only 13 percent in Korea. Moreover, in Taiwan, density of paved roads was 76 kilometers (per 1,000 square kilometers) in 1962 and 215 kilometers in 1972. In Korea road density was less than 10 kilometers in 1966 and less than 50 kilometers in 1975.

Element Four: Agricultural Services

Agricultural services include credit and marketing, both of agricultural inputs (such as seeds, fertilizer, pesticides, and equipment) and of agricultural commodity outputs (see Meyer and Larson, Chapter 5 of this volume). Farmers typically need agricultural credit to speed adoption of new technologies. Agricultural marketing services are needed to transport, store, package, and process inputs all the way from manufacturer to farm. Marketing services are needed as well to perform the same functions in reverse for agricultural outputs—from farm to final consumer. Unless these services are available, farmers will be unable to produce a marketable surplus.

Many developing-country governments have viewed market failure and high marketing costs as justification for intervention in agricultural credit markets as well as input and output markets. Governments nationalized many of the marketing functions, often by creating parastatals with monopoly control of a particular commodity and by passing laws to control prices and marketing margins (thus setting the stage for needed reforms discussed previously).

This began to change in the early 1980s. In agricultural credit, these changes have been manifested by fewer subsidized credit projects, less targeting of loans, more flexible interest rates, and more emphasis on savings mobilization. Moreover, emphasis has shifted from measuring the impact of credit activities on borrowers to measuring the viability of financial institutions and the performance of financial markets. As for input and output markets, many parastatal "businesses" have failed to perform efficiently and are now in various stages of bankruptcy, closure, or privatization. The private sector is now seen as having the dominant role in distributing inputs and outputs in the context of competitive markets, with the role of the state being to create an enabling environment in which the private sector has a financial incentive to operate.

USAID and World Bank Funding of Agricultural Services

USAID has a long history of supporting agricultural credit. Between 1950 and 1985, USAID channeled more than $1 billion into agricultural credit. The lion's share of credit funds went to the Latin American region. USAID marketing assistance has been oriented mainly toward the public sector (52 percent). Of 203 agricultural services projects funded by USAID during 1958–1982, twenty-four (12 percent) were "marketing only" projects; many others, though, had a marketing component.

The World Bank has been the largest external source of funds for agricultural credit projects. Overall, ninety-four countries received Bank funding for agricultural credit from FY 1948 through FY 1992. The Bank funded 683 credit projects totaling $16.5 billion (in current dollars). That represented 26 percent of the Bank's total agricultural lending during this period. Forty percent of the funds were concentrated in just three countries—India, Mexico, and Brazil. Most World Bank marketing assistance has been provided to parastatals, with small amounts to private sector firms and cooperatives. Of 402 agriculture projects supported by the World Bank from 1974 through 1985, only twelve (3 percent) had a "marketing only" objective; however, an additional 185 projects (46 percent) included marketing components.

Agricultural credit also has been important in lending programs of the regional development banks. During 1970–1982 the Inter-American Development Bank (IDB) provided more than sixty loans for agricultural credit totaling more than $1.2 billion. Additional projects included credit as a component. The IDB pipeline for 1983–1986 included thirteen loans for agricultural credit totaling $640 million plus additional loans that had credit components. The Asian Development Bank began its agricultural credit operations in 1970. By 1991 it had approved seventy-two projects totaling almost $1.4 billion.

The rationale for donor and government involvement in providing credit was that lack of access to credit kept farmers from adopting modern technologies. Such adoption required poor small farmers with meager savings to lay out cash for inputs such as fertilizer and improved seeds. This perception of unmet need for credit led policymakers and donors to increase the supply of loans, which was considered necessary to spearhead agricultural development.

The Impact of Investments in Agricultural Credit and Finance

Serious doubts about the impact of agricultural credit projects began to emerge as early as 1973 with the USAID *Spring Review of Small Farmer Credit*, and many evaluations and academic studies since then have documented their shortcomings (see Chapter 5). Credit projects can affect (1) borrowers, (2) lenders, and (3) the national economy. The fungibility of credit makes it extremely difficult to determine its impact on borrowers at the farm level. Some farmers, for example, divert farm credit to finance more lucrative nonfarm activities, especially when the loan is subsidized. Others use loan funds to substitute for their own savings, which in the absence of credit they would have used to purchase agricultural inputs. Also, subsidized credit projects have tended to worsen, rather than improve, income distribution.

If the effect of credit projects on farmers is ambiguous, their effect on lending institutions is clear. Many public development finance institutions, including specialized agricultural development banks, have failed in developing countries;

others have had to be recapitalized because of losses, and most rely on continuous subsidies. Four reasons account for their poor performance: (1) poor loan recovery; (2) high operating costs; (3) neglect of deposit mobilization; and (4) a hostile economic environment. The first factor, poor loan recovery, can be devastating for financial institutions. Lenders tend to be rewarded for making, not recovering, loans, and this leads to lax record keeping and weak collection efforts. Also, the incentive structures built into government- and donor-funded programs (as distinct from commercial operations) tend to have a negative influence on loan recovery.

The second factor, high operating costs, also hampers the financial viability of lending institutions (see Chapter 5). In Honduras, for example, lending costs for a government-owned bank using donor funds were nearly five times those of a privately owned bank using its own funds. In Sudan, the Agricultural Bank could charge only 7 to 9 percent on loans when its administrative costs averaged 10 to 15 percent.

The third factor is that deposit mobilization has been neglected. Borrowers are more likely to repay and lenders are more likely to exert more effort at recovery when the funds come from local savers rather than distant governments or donors.

Finally, some financial institutions have failed because of a hostile economic environment. Agricultural credit is not a good bet in the absence of an economic policy framework conducive to agriculture and an agricultural technology that is profitable.

Although the results of many agricultural credit projects at all three levels of potential impact (borrowers, lenders, the national economy) have been disappointing, there are a number of successful cases. Factors contributing to the more successful results include: (1) generally favorable economic conditions; (2) flexible interest rates so savers can be rewarded and financial institutions can cover their costs; and (3) emphasis on simple, traditional rural institutions that operate on a scale consistent with the routine transactions of rural people. In contrast, the failures are dominated by top-down projects designed to provide subsidized credit to targeted borrowers who are assumed to be too poor to save, so that savings mobilization is ignored. Thus, macroeconomic, financial, and agricultural policies must be reformed before interventions in rural financial markets are likely to be successful.

The Impact of Investments in Agricultural Marketing

Until recently, donors have worked primarily with public sector organizations to strengthen agricultural marketing services in developing countries. However, the performance of these organizations has been disappointing to the users, the government, and the donors (see Chapter 5). They have been plagued with high costs, poor management, misuse of funds, poor service, and large operating deficits.

The impact of investments designed to improve the efficiency of agricultural markets is intimately linked to agricultural price policy. Governments have used overvalued foreign exchange rates, price ceilings, panterritorial pricing, marketing margin controls, parastatal marketing monopolies, and other policies to reduce food costs in urban areas. But at the same time, they have reduced producer price levels. The effect has been to reduce the farmer's incentive to produce a surplus that can be sold profitably on the market.

Given this record of failure, many governments have tried to deregulate markets, promote competition, and privatize government parastatals. The key to market liberalization is to introduce policy and regulatory reforms that effectively dismantle government control of agricultural prices and reduce direct government participation in agricultural input and product markets. The government, however, has a legitimate role in providing facilities and services that are public goods, or give rise to externalities, or exhibit large economies of scale. Governments need to invest in infrastructure (such as roads and bridges, as distinct from trucks and gasoline) and market information (such as price reporting) and promote competition to improve the performance of the market system and make private markets work better.

Element Five: Asset Distribution and Access

The fifth element of agricultural development concerns agrarian structure, the institutional framework determining the distribution of and access to resources (see Lambert and Seligson, Chapter 6 of this volume). In characterizing the various types of agrarian structure and alternative interventions to reform them, the literature distinguishes among several concepts.

Land tenure consists of the legal rights and institutions that determine how land is owned and operated. *Land reform* is a basic restructuring of the land tenure system. Some analysts distinguish between land reform (redistribution of land or property rights) and *agrarian reform,* which (as distinguished here) includes both land reform and provision of ancillary rural infrastructure and agricultural services. These elements of agricultural development, many of them discussed previously, usually must accompany land reform to ensure its success.

Tenure security is the assurance of continuing access to land or related resources. Land reform is one way to improve tenure security. Other ways include *titling* programs (issuance of legal documentation to holders of plots of land) and *land registration* programs (recording of those titles by the state). Other ways to enhance access to land or otherwise modify the existing distribution of land include programs to improve the functioning of *land markets*, *land taxation* systems, and *land settlement* programs.

Small farms in developing countries tend to be more productive than large farms. As farm size decreases, farm output and employment per hectare increase. This is because small farms use land more intensively than large farms, and they apply more labor per hectare than large farms. Unfortunately, there is sometimes a tendency (or desire) to try to reproduce in developing countries the economies of scale that characterize U.S. and other Western agriculture. But such attempts ignore differences in the relative abundance of factor inputs.

A second important relationship is the association between tenure security and agricultural productivity. In principle, a farmer with more secure tenure will work the land more intensively and make long-term capital improvements because he knows he will be the beneficiary of the investments. Furthermore, fully registered titles allow the land to be used as collateral for credit. That contributes to increased investment and thus increased productivity.

Market mechanisms, as distinct from redistributive land reform, can also improve land distribution and increase productivity. The main problem with this alternative is that land markets are imperfect, especially in developing countries. Where land markets do operate efficiently, land taxation can influence land distribution and, in turn, agricultural production. At a minimum, a standard tax on all land, productive or not, should encourage owners of large, unproductive farms to sell or to become more productive. As a practical matter, though, many taxation systems are manipulated by the rich and powerful for their own benefit.

Finally, *land settlement* is an option, not for modifying the distribution of land currently in production, but rather for bringing new lands into production in countries having significant tracts of uncultivated land. Settlement of new lands typically requires infrastructure investments that generally are expensive.

Historical Context

From the end of World War II through the early 1960s, the United States promoted land reform in other countries. It was particularly effective in guiding and financing reforms in Japan, Korea, and Taiwan. The strong U.S. presence helped. The importance the United States attached to land reform is seen in the 1961 Charter of Punta del Este for the Alliance for Progress. It proposed land and tax reform as conditions for U.S. financial aid to Latin American countries. The pre-1960 reforms, including those directed by the United States in Asia, generally are viewed as the most successful. In Latin America the major pre-1960 reforms took place in Mexico (1930s), Bolivia (1952), and Cuba (1959). These were generally driven by indigenous populist forces and revolutions.

In the 1970s U.S. support for land redistribution was seen as a tool to forestall the rise of communist peasant organizations. Thus, Cold War concerns led to U.S. support of land reforms in El Salvador and Vietnam but not in Salvador Allende's Chile or Sandinista Nicaragua. Of fifty-two countries surveyed by USAID in 1980, more than half had current activities dealing with inequitable access to land. Another third had such activities in the works.

In the 1980s opponents of reform were bolstered by the lack of results of ongoing reforms in Latin America and elsewhere. Evaluations of land reform showed that successful land redistribution required costly additional investments in ancillary services and rural infrastructure to support reform beneficiaries. At the same time, U.S. foreign assistance was shifting toward macroeconomic policy reform and private enterprise development.

In the 1990s land tenure continues to be important, but from a different perspective than before. Concern about natural resource utilization and conservation has sparked a conflict between, on the one side, small farmers and landless people who need land to farm for food and, on the other, those who champion a need (less immediate than the farmers') for protected environmental zones. Also, the disintegration of the former Soviet Union has moved land tenure issues of decollectivization and privatization to the forefront of the policy agenda in Eastern and Central Europe and in the new independent states.

Impact of Investments in Asset Distribution and Access

During the last decade, several retrospective comparative studies of the effects of land reform in various countries have been published (see Chapter 6). In contrast to earlier studies, these studies suggest that anticipated positive economic effects have not been realized. The studies provide no quantitative data on the economic effects of land reform, but they do offer credible reasons for the poor performance: (1) the multiple goals of the reforms (social, political, and economic) were not compatible; (2) the beneficiaries of reforms had inadequate access to agricultural services and inputs needed to farm effectively; and (3) there was insufficient political will or strong political commitment.

Land taxation generally has not been an effective way to intensify land use or encourage land sales in developing countries. The countries typically lack the institutional infrastructure needed to assess, collect, and process the taxes. Moreover, land taxes are usually very low (often because of political pressures) and therefore do not constitute effective incentives either for current owners to use their land more intensively or to sell their land to those who might do so. And because land taxes are low, the expense of collection is generally not justified. Finally, tax collection is frequently plagued with corruption. Thus, land taxation schemes face many of the same political hurdles as redistributive land reforms.

Land settlement projects have also received donor support. But the costs per family are high and often prohibitive.

FINDINGS

Of the six key questions identified at the outset, the evaluation literature was more helpful in answering the first three (about what to do) than it was in answering the last three (about who should do it).

What to Do?

1. *There is a preferred sequencing of investments in agriculture.* The evaluation literature is clear on this. The first priority is to develop an environment in which agriculture will function. Such an environment includes at least three components: policies, technology, and infrastructure.

Policy reform and planning. The overriding priority is policies that affect agriculture, whether directly or indirectly. As the principal economic sector in most poor countries, agriculture must progress if the nation is to progress. Price policies, trade policies, fiscal policies, monetary policies, and exchange rate policies—all must provide an opportunity for the market to work for agriculture. If a threshold level of appropriate policies is not in place, it is not worthwhile for donors to contribute to other investments, nor is it worthwhile for farmers to take risks and use new technologies needed to increase production beyond subsistence levels.

Getting the *macroeconomic* policy environment right is an important first step in getting the *agricultural* policy environment right. Knudsen and Nash (1991, 131, 148) found progress on agricultural policy reform in an unstable macroeconomic situation to be rare. In fact, they found that projects implemented in a distorted, antiagriculture policy environment actually *discouraged* agricultural growth. If the *standard model* outlined in Chapter 9 is followed, most microeconomic decisions will take care of themselves and the nation will have the means (in time) to invest in infrastructure, human resources, environmental protection, and food security. Without important elements of the *standard model* in place, there is little reason for donors to provide more than humanitarian assistance.

Agricultural technology development and diffusion. Technology and infrastructure work synergistically if the proper policy environment is in place. There is no optimal sequence for investing in one or the other; rather, investments in both interact to promote each other. To promote agricultural growth, high-yielding agricultural technology must be available. Traditional technology offers little scope for substantial productivity gains. The evaluation literature indicates that countries can apply existing "high-yielding" technology that is on the shelf and borrow technology from neighboring countries. But they must have indigenous capacity to adapt technology from elsewhere to local conditions. Maintenance agricultural research designed merely to sustain existing yields (as distinct from achieving higher yields) is needed at all stages of development.

Rural infrastructure. Agriculture cannot perform well unless at least some rudimentary infrastructure is in place. Little value comes from supplying credit or modern inputs to farmers if they lack the roads, bridges, and transportation needed to acquire inputs and transport harvests to market. Subsidized credit or inputs cannot compensate for nonexistent roads or bridges.

Agricultural services. Many projects designed to provide agricultural services (typically credit or marketing services) have failed. The main reason is that the services were provided in countries that were pursuing policies heavily biased against agriculture. In addition, credit projects ran into difficulty because good technology was not available for farmers to adopt. Governments can provide business codes and regulations, but private firms deliver credit and other agribusiness services most effectively.

Asset distribution and access. The evaluation literature suggests no particular stage of development for investing to improve asset distribution or access to land. The literature does, however, make two generalizations. First, if investments to improve land distribution take place, they are typically designed to achieve a political objective, not an economic efficiency objective. Second, although political stability and equity (rather than economic considerations) drive the decision to improve distribution of assets, an economic impact, positive or negative, intended or unintended, will still result from such investments. The impact is likely to be more positive if ancillary services to support the investment are already in place—basic infrastructure, for example. Thus, investments to improve asset distribution should support agricultural development, not initiate the process.

2. *It is inconclusive whether investments in all five subsectors are essential.* Little in the literature directly addresses the counterfactual question of whether agricultural development can be achieved in the absence of investment in one or more of the five elements of agriculture. What does emerge is that a country's predisposition to agricultural development is an important condition for success— whether or not this predisposition is linked to donor investments. In particular, some level of economic and social stability is essential for agricultural progress. This is not to suggest that all elements of a supportive macroeconomic environment must be in place. For example, a number of countries, such as China and Brazil, show that agriculture can make considerable progress without optimal support. However, an egregiously unfavorable macroeconomic climate, as found in countries such as North Korea and Cuba, prevents agriculture from succeeding.

Policy reform and planning. The most successful policy reform activities have supported an ongoing program of policy change, as distinct from introducing new policies. The literature shows that attempts to introduce major new policy directions through nonproject assistance (such as cash transfers) often produced disappointing results (Wolgin 1990, ii). Similarly, successful projects occurred most frequently in those countries where reforms were already under way and were strongly supported by the countries' leadership. As indicated earlier, major policy elements of the *standard model* need to be in place *before* donors are likely to have success with efforts beyond humanitarian assistance. Investments in analytical capacity building were most effective when, among other things, there was active host country support. In contrast, countries that resisted reform had little use for even the most cogent and forceful of analyses.

Agricultural technology development and diffusion. Except for certain isolated exceptions (such as Botswana and Singapore), few countries have achieved sustained economic growth without transforming agriculture; and the agricultural transformation has generally rested squarely on intensification of land cultivation and technical change. Countries with a large land frontier have been able to increase agricultural output through acreage expansion. But once the frontier is exhausted, these relatively easy gains in output must be replaced by increasing yields on existing land. This requires improved biological and mechanical technology. Agricultural extension can have a positive effect on adoption of new crop varieties, but there is no evidence that extension is a necessary component of successful technology development and diffusion. In the Philippines, for example, farmers throughout the country use a rice variety developed, but never formally distributed, by the extension system, demonstrating that technologies that offer significant increases in economic returns will spread quickly. Other countries, such as Jordan, rely heavily on domestic private input supply firms to obtain and diffuse timely technology from around the world.

The highest priority for investing in education in developing countries is at the elementary and, to a lesser extent, secondary levels. Higher education, including higher agricultural education, is less important. There is often a presumption that an indigenous capacity to train agricultural scientists is necessary for agricultural development. However, no evidence indicates that this is a necessary condition for *technology development*, because scientific expertise can be obtained, at least in the short term, from developed countries. Too many of the brightest and talented youth of developing countries receiving graduate training in developed countries do not return home—a brain drain poor countries can ill afford.

Rural infrastructure. Agricultural growth, to the extent it occurs at all in the absence of investments in rural infrastructure, is likely to occur far less rapidly, judging from a comparison of infrastructure development in Africa and Asia.

Agricultural services. No country can achieve a *high* level of agricultural development without investments in agricultural services. The greater the level of agricultural development, the greater the variety and sophistication of the services demanded, but the private rather than the public sector is mainly responsible for services.

Asset distribution and access. Agricultural growth can occur in the context of insecure and inequitable access to land, but *sustained, broad-based* agricultural development requires access to human, material, and technological capital.

3. *Investments have been most successful when they have removed a bottleneck or when existing conditions have favored progressive change.* For example, agricultural research is more likely to have a high payoff in countries that have reached at least a minimum threshold of infrastructure development. Similarly, infrastructure investments are more likely to reap rewards in the presence of supportive economic policies and the availability of improved agricultural technology.

Policy reform and planning. Supportive policies and institutions are a necessary condition for favorable rates of return on virtually any of the investments examined in this chapter. However, economic rates of return are generally not used to evaluate success of investing in policy and institutional reform. Even the World Bank, which as a rule estimates rates of return for its projects, notes that these measures are not applicable to policy reform and planning operations.

Agricultural technology development and diffusion. Technology development and diffusion investments have typically generated high economic rates of return.

The social benefits from the investments justify the costs in a wide variety of countries, for a wide variety of commodities, and under a wide variety of conditions. However, agricultural research can contribute to increased productivity only if farmers adopt the new technologies. This requires a permissive, if not supportive, economic policy environment, one that provides an opportunity for farmers to make a profit.

Rural infrastructure. Resources tend to be allocated to infrastructure development only when pressure for services is felt within the political system. When this occurs, decisions on how much to allocate to infrastructure relative to other activities are typically a matter of judgment. The cost of infrastructure development varies greatly across regions. However, estimates of the cost of road construction and maintenance per kilometer are less for Africa than for Asia and Latin America, partly because of less difficult terrain in Africa. But if the cost of road construction were calculated per unit of agricultural production (per ton of maize, for example, rather than per kilometer), it may be higher in Africa than in the other regions. That is because agricultural production is comparatively low per square kilometer in Africa.

Agricultural services. Grades, standards, market information, and business codes and enforcement are important public services needed by the private sector. Very few studies measure the economic rate of return to investments in agricultural services. Conditions necessary to achieve a high rate of return to investments in agricultural services include favorable natural resources, appropriate macroeconomic policies, well-developed physical infrastructure, capacity to develop or adapt technology, human capital, prior or parallel development of complementary industries, and a dominant role of the private sector in providing services. The private sector can and does invest generously in services if these conditions are satisfied.

Asset distribution and access. Here again, benefit-cost analyses have not been undertaken for investments to achieve a more equitable distribution of, or secure access to, land and other agricultural assets. The literature does, however, identify at least two costs of *not* investing in this area. First are economic costs associated with maintaining an agrarian structure characterized by high efficiency losses, low profitability, and few incentives to invest in physical and human capital in the agriculture sector. Second are social costs resulting from peasant uprisings, civil war, and protracted and violent struggles.

Despite the costs, governments typically do not invest in more equitable land distribution. The reasons are twofold. For one thing, the cost of land reform is so high as to make it infeasible in many cases. Small farmers often cannot pay for the land they receive, and elites tend to resist paying for the reform either through taxes or through receipt of devalued bonds as compensation for expropriated land. Other mechanisms to improve tenure security and access to land (such as titling, land registration, land markets, and land taxation) have also been difficult to implement. The second, more important, reason is that governments lack the political support to carry out change. Their constituencies are often deeply divided on issues of land reform and asset redistribution.

Who Should Do It?

4. *Government should become involved in a particular investment only if it raises real national income more than otherwise would be the case. Similarly, the public sector should become involved when doing so improves the performance of the private sector rather than displaces the private sector.*

The role of the public sector is to provide public goods, correct externalities, and provide a safety net. Thus, it is logical that the public sector invest in such areas as development of agricultural technology, rural infrastructure, and schooling. These investments normally have the characteristics of public goods, whereby it is difficult for a private firm to recover the investment costs. The private sector will not provide them unless paid by the public sector to do so. However, *some* kinds of agricultural research (for example, the development of hybrid seeds) can and should be carried out by the private sector because there are profits to be derived. In like manner, it is logical that the public sector has received most donor assistance designed to support policy reform and planning as well as to improve asset distribution and access, because it is government's responsibility to make decisions in these areas as well as determine the level of a safety net. In contrast, the private sector can be expected to invest in agricultural services when it is profitable to do so.

Policy reform and planning. Nonproject assistance provided by virtually all donors to support policy reform and planning has been directed to central governments alone. Project aid also has gone primarily to support government ministries. In a sense, this is proper because these activities are conducted by the public sector. However, policy analysis need not be conducted in a narrowly defined policy analysis unit of a ministry. Private or autonomous institutions (consulting firms, research institutes, university departments) can perform it, as can teams of analysts drawn from public and private institutions. The evaluation literature consistently shows that policy analysis and capacity building are most effective when they are demand driven; that is, when they respond to current needs identified in a ministry or in the economy. Too often, these kinds of activities are supply driven, and the services of host country government staff and project advisors are utilized as free goods.

Agricultural technology development and diffusion. Governments need to invest in public goods, which include most agricultural research, because it is difficult for a private firm to provide these services and recover its costs by charging users for the benefits they receive. Indeed, the rationale for public sector involvement in agricultural research is that incentives for private sector involvement are not adequate to induce an optimum level of investment; that is, the social rate of return exceeds the private rate of return because a large share of the gains from research are captured by other firms and consumers rather than by the innovating firm. Endowed foundations, which lie somewhere on the continuum between public and private research organizations, may be an alternative.

Rural infrastructure. Most rural infrastructure, like most agricultural research, is a public good provided by the public sector (or by private entities subject to public control) in practically all countries. Because of externalities, the private sector is likely to underinvest in rural infrastructure. However, the private sector can do the actual building and maintaining of roads or irrigation canals, with proper support from the public sector. Note, however, that the cost of using the services (water and electricity, for example) made possible by the rural infrastructure—as distinct from the infrastructure itself—should be paid by the users of those services, not by the government or by donors. Unfortunately, many poor countries subsidize infrastructure, even operating costs.

Agricultural services. Generally, the private sector is best equipped to provide agricultural inputs and services as long as they can be sold for a profit. Farmers will pay the cost of these inputs (such as fertilizer and hybrid seeds) and services (such as credit and marketing) if they find it profitable to do so. The weak performance of government banks and parastatal marketing boards suggests that governments often do a poor job of delivering agricultural services. The proper role of government is to ensure an enabling environment conducive to provision of agricultural services by the private sector.

Asset distribution and access. The evaluation literature does not compare the relative merits of public sector and private sector institutions in dealing with land issues, nor does it compare market mechanisms with nonmarket mechanisms in achieving a more equitable distribution of, and secure access to, land. However, interventions designed to influence the distribution of agricultural assets, and to change the agrarian structure, are invariably taken by public sector institutions. The lack of political will on the part of most governments has been the principal factor limiting land reforms and related interventions. As a country develops, human capital dwarfs land as a source of wealth; in addition, human capital can be distributed by the public sector more broadly than land. Land titling, when devolved to local governments, can be more convenient as well as better undergird property taxes to fund schools, roads, and related rural infrastructure.

5. *For the most part, the evaluation literature is silent on the question of which agencies are best suited to implement which agricultural activities.* The following discussion is, therefore, largely impressionistic.

Policy reform and planning. Nonproject assistance to support policy reform has been implemented strictly by donors working in conjunction with central governments. In contrast, some USAID capacity-building projects have been implemented by universities, NGOs, and private firms, among others. These various implementing agencies have both strengths and weaknesses. University contractors have been particularly well suited for implementing overseas analytical training for host country nationals because they could offer a broad pool of in-house technical staff that was involved with the project on a continuing basis. Yet university contractors have sometimes had the disadvantage of weak management structures, which may cause some concern because the literature on project implementation indicates that good management is the most important factor in successful projects. In contrast, private firms were strongest in their ability to manage projects efficiently, though they may be less appropriate than universities for implementing long-term training programs.

Agricultural technology development and diffusion. Some have asserted that U.S. land-grant universities are well positioned to implement agricultural technology development and diffusion activities, but the evaluation literature provides no empirical evidence to substantiate or refute this assertion. That is, if evaluations have been carried out to test the assertion, they were not among those reviewed for this study.

Rural infrastructure. Conventional wisdom suggests that private contractors are best suited to implement infrastructure activities, but there is no empirical evidence to support this one way or the other. It may be appropriate for user organizations (managed, perhaps, by NGOs) to maintain rural infrastructure, but again, the evaluation literature reviewed for this study provided no substantiating evidence. However, the evaluation literature on local institutions (which was not reviewed for this chapter) does emphasize the importance of water user organizations, for example, in maintaining irrigation canals.

Agricultural services. Commercial banks have a better record of providing sustainable financial services than specialized agricultural development banks in most countries. In some cases, cooperatives and credit unions have also been successful. In contrast, most NGO credit programs have been highly subsidized in the past, and their long-term viability without continuous subsidies has been questionable. Private firms also have a better track record than government agencies of providing efficient and timely agricultural inputs and marketing services.

Asset distribution and access. Donor agencies may be well suited to advise governments on how best to go about setting up cadasters, titling and registration programs, and land taxation systems, but governments are best suited to implement programs designed to improve asset distribution and access.

6. *Similarly, the evaluation literature provides little insight into the comparative advantage of the United States in providing agricultural assistance in the five subsectors.*

Policy reform and planning. The literature suggests that the United States has an advantage over other *bilateral* donors in providing assistance in the area of agricultural policy reform and planning. The advantage holds for both program and project activities. On the program side, resident missions give USAID the ability to conduct and monitor operations in a more direct style than can other donors. The U.S. comparative advantage is also strong in training activities that draw on the resources of the American higher education system. In agriculture, this system is unmatched elsewhere in the world.

Agricultural technology development and diffusion. U.S. agriculture is among the most productive in the world, due mainly to yield-increasing technology developed as a result of investments in agricultural research. Because it is the world leader in basic and applied agricultural research, the United States would appear to enjoy a comparative advantage in providing assistance in this area. But there is little empirical evidence in this study to substantiate or refute this assertion.

Rural infrastructure. Development of rural infrastructure often requires a major capital investment. In view of this, donors with a relatively large supply of resources, including the multilateral development banks, would seem to be in the best position to finance big-ticket capital projects.

Agricultural services. The United States has a large pool of analytical talent to study problems concerning delivery of financial and other agricultural services, but the private sector in the recipient country is ordinarily best equipped to deliver such services. This is particularly the case if the overall policy environment provides a "level playing field."

Asset distribution and access. Absent special historical circumstances (such as the U.S. military occupation of Japan), international donors have very little influence on whether programs are introduced to alter the agrarian structure. Such programs are initiated because of their political nature and require an internal political commitment. One lesson of the Alliance for Progress was that financial assistance and political pressure from the outside are not enough to persuade an unsupportive government to implement meaningful reform. Moreover, by law the United States cannot support land acquisition and transfer costs unless such support is in the national interest. In any event, since the most obvious failures of land reform are those that have left the new owners without ancillary services after the old support system was withdrawn, donors should emphasize the provision of these ancillary services. Also, broad-based human capital investment in the long run overshadows physical asset redistribution as a source of wealth and food security.

RECOMMENDATIONS

A sound policy environment is the keystone of overall economic progress. *In countries where agriculture cannot be profitable because of an adverse economic policy environment, donors should invest reluctantly, if at all, in agricultural development.* Traditional agriculture cannot feed a large, poor, and growing population without massive environmental degradation. Although many individual microprojects may provide worthy benefits, economic development on a broad scale requires following the lessons outlined in this chapter and adhering to the *standard model* outlined in Chapter 9. Following these lessons leads to economic development and other benefits. It (1) raises agricultural productivity, thereby lowering food costs and saving resources such as land, which can be used for forests, grazing, recreation, species preservation, and conservation rather than for crops; (2) leads to reduced population growth as people with higher incomes reduce birth rates in part because they have the information to do so and in part because they no longer need as many children to provide social security; (3) pays for human resource investments, infrastructure, research, institutions, and environmental protection essential for a healthy society; and (4) provides the means for a food safety net and sustainable food security.

Analyses by the International Food Policy Research Institute show that most developing countries that grew rapidly during the 1980s experienced rapid agricultural growth in the preceding years (von Braun et al. 1993). For example, China's remarkable annual growth rate of 9.5 percent in the 1980s was stimulated by agricultural policy reform and support of the farm sector in the late 1970s and early 1980s. Indonesia's annual agricultural growth of 4.3 percent during 1965–1980 facilitated annual GDP growth of 5.5 percent during 1980–1990. Thailand's agricultural growth of 4.6 percent a year during 1965–1980 contributed to annual GDP growth of 7.6 percent in 1980–1990.

There is a 75 percent correlation between agricultural growth and overall economic growth in the least developed countries, and a 21 percent correlation between these growth rates in the less developed and middle-income countries over the period 1965–1989 (von Braun 1991). The high correlation in the least developed countries is not surprising, given the large share of the agriculture sector in these economies: Agriculture contributes about one-third of GDP in these countries and employs more than half the labor force. Neglecting agriculture adversely affects the rest of the economy. In short, it is difficult, if not impossible, to stimulate sustained economic growth in the least developed countries without first moving the largest sector, agriculture.

Bottlenecks to agricultural growth in developing countries are likely to be most binding in policy reform, technology development, and rural infrastructure. They are generally less of an impediment in agricultural services and asset distribution. *Because there is a preferred sequencing of investments in agriculture, donors should concentrate investments on priority areas to alleviate the most binding constraints, not all constraints, to agricultural growth.*

When a donor has decided it makes sense to invest in agricultural development, the following recommendations merit consideration.

1. *Policy reform and planning.* Nonproject assistance can help governments of low-income developing countries create an economic policy environment designed to help agricultural markets work. Such investments are *most* successful when they are used to facilitate ongoing economic policy reforms. They are *less* successful when they are used to initiate new policy reforms or to "buy" reforms to which the government is not committed. Accordingly, *donors should provide nonproject assistance to support economic policy reform only in countries where it will be used to facilitate reforms already initiated.*

2. *Technology development and diffusion.* If high economic rates of return were the only criterion donors used in deciding how to invest in agriculture, development of new agricultural technology would probably top the list. An even

more compelling reason to invest in the development of high-yielding or cost-reducing technologies is that most countries have not achieved sustained economic growth without transforming their agriculture. The agricultural transformation typically requires technical change—that is, improved biological and mechanical technology. Therefore, *donors should invest in the development of new agricultural technologies.* In this context, they should emphasize adaptive, rather than basic, research. They should promote technology transfer from neighboring countries and from international agricultural research centers. They should also support agricultural research necessary simply to sustain existing yield levels. Provision of training in science and technology in the donor or host country is inseparable from investment in technology development and transfer.

3. *Rural infrastructure.* Donors are understandably reluctant to invest in rural infrastructure. Such investments are costly, and existing infrastructure is often not maintained by the public sector. However, it is unlikely that agricultural growth will occur in the absence of investments in rural infrastructure. Therefore, *donors should consider investing in new rural infrastructure and, if justified by economic analysis, in the maintenance of existing infrastructure.* Private banks and multilateral lenders such as the World Bank may be appropriate sources of funding.

4. *Agricultural services.* The *private* sector is best equipped to provide agricultural inputs and services that can be sold for a profit. The *public* sector has an important role in helping markets work better (as distinct from displacing markets) through, for example, policy reform and infrastructure development. Although donors may be in a position to *advise* developing countries and train personnel on how best to establish input distribution systems, strengthen financial services, support marketing and storage activities, and develop market information systems, *actual investments in agricultural services are best left to the private sector.*

5. *Asset distribution and access.* Programs designed to improve access to land and other agricultural assets are motivated by political objectives, not by agricultural development objectives. Donors may be in a position to *advise* governments on how best to implement titling schemes, cadastral surveys, land reforms, and other activities designed to improve access to agricultural assets. But *most investments in this area are best left to the indigenous public sector.*

The foregoing recommendations are reasonable generalizations consistent with conventional wisdom, but there is no substitute for careful analysis. *Donors should analyze each country's specific situation before investing in agricultural development.*

NOTES

1. Human resource development, addressed in Chapter 7, is not treated separately in this chapter. Instead, it is integrated with the discussion of the aforementioned five subsectors. Similarly, investing in natural resources and the environment, needed for *sustainable* agricultural development, is not covered here but rather in Chapter 8.

2. During the longer period from 1960 through 1993, USAID funded 169 planning and policy analysis projects with total expenditures of $664.2 million.

REFERENCES

Agency for International Development. 1975. "Implementation of 'New Directions' in Development Assistance." Report to the Committee on International Relations on Implementation of Legislative Reforms in the Foreign Assistance Act of 1973. Washington, D.C.: U.S. Government Printing Office.

―――. 1991, 1992, 1993. *Congressional Presentation*. Washington, D.C.: USAID.

Ahmed, Raisuddin, and M. Hossain. 1990. "Developmental Impact of Rural Infrastructure in Bangladesh." IFPRI Research Report 83. Washington, D.C.: International Food Policy Research Institute.

Ahmed, Raisuddin, and Cynthia Donovan. 1992. *Issues of Infrastructural Development: A Synthesis of the Literature*. Washington, D.C.: International Food Policy Research Institute.

Berg, Elliot J. 1991. "Comments on the Design and Implementation of Conditionality." In *Restructuring Economies in Distress: Policy Reform and the World Bank*, ed. Vinod Thomas, Ajay Chhibber, Mansoor Dailami, and Jaime de Melo. Oxford: Oxford University Press.

Binswanger, H., M. C. Yang, A. Bowers, and Y. Mundlak. 1987. "On the Determinants of Cross-Country Aggregate Agricultural Supply." *Journal of Econometrics* 36 (1).

Cleaver, K. 1988. "Agricultural Policy Reform and Structural Adjustment in Sub-Saharan Africa: Results to Date." Washington, D.C.: World Bank.

Cummings, Ralph W. Jr. 1989. "External Assistance in Agricultural Extension: The USAID Experience." Paper prepared for the Global Consultation on Agricultural Extension, December 4–8. Rome: Food and Agriculture Organization.

Food and Agriculture Organization of the United Nations. 1989. "The Design of Agricultural Investment Projects." Investment Centre Technical Paper 6. Rome: FAO.

―――. 1991, 1961. *Production Yearbook*. Vols. 45, 15. Rome: FAO.

Hansen, Gary E. 1989. "The Impact of Investments in Agricultural Higher Education." USAID Evaluation Highlights No. 5. Washington, D.C.: USAID.

Heller, Jack, and Miguel Wionczek. 1988. "The Assumptions of the Alliance." In *The Alliance for Progress: A Retrospective*, ed. Ronald Scheman. New York: Praeger.

Islam, Nural. 1991. "Comments on Agricultural Policy." In *Restructuring Economies in Distress: Policy Reform and the World Bank*, ed. Vinod Thomas, Ajay Chhibber, Mansoor Dailami, and Jaime de Melo. Oxford: Oxford University Press.

Knudsen, Odin, and John Nash. 1991. "Agricultural Policy." In *Restructuring Economies in Distress: Policy Reform and the World Bank*, ed. Vinod Thomas, Ajay Chhibber, Mansoor Dailami, and Jaime de Melo. Oxford: Oxford University Press.

Lele, Uma. 1991. "Aid to African Agriculture: Lessons from Two Decades of Donors' Experience." Managing Agricultural Development in Africa Discussion Paper. Baltimore, Md.: Johns Hopkins University Press.

Lewis, John P. "Policy-Based Assistance: A Historical Perspective on A.I.D.'s Experience and Operations in India/Asia in a Bilateral and Multilateral Context." Washington, D.C.: USAID.

McCleary, William. 1991. "The Design and Implementation of Conditionality." In *Restructuring Economies in Distress: Policy Reform and the World Bank*, ed. Vinod

Thomas, Ajay Chhibber, Mansoor Dailami, and Jaime de Melo. Oxford: Oxford University Press.

McClelland, Donald G. 1996. *Investments in Agriculture: A Synthesis of the Evaluation Literature.* USAID Program and Operations Assessment Report No. 15. Center for Development Information and Evaluation. Washington, D.C.: USAID.

Pardey, Philip G., and Johannes Roseboom. 1989. "ISNAR Agricultural Research Indicator Series: A Global Data Base on National Agricultural Research Systems." New York, N.Y.: Cambridge University Press for the International Service for National Agricultural Research Agricultural Research Indicators.

Tilney, John S., and Steven Block. 1988. "Agricultural Policy Analysis and Planning: A Summary of Two Recent Analyses of A.I.D.-supported Projects Worldwide." USAID Evaluation Special Study No. 55. Washington, D.C.: USAID.

———. 1991. "USAID Efforts to Promote Agricultural Policy Reform and Institutional Development in Developing Countries: Lessons for Design and Implementation." APAP II Collaborative Research Report No. 317. Cambridge, Mass.: Abt Associates.

U.S. House of Representatives and Senate. 1994. *Legislation on Foreign Relations Through 1993.* Committee on Foreign Affairs and Committee on Foreign Relations. Vol. I-A. Washington, D.C.: U.S. Government Printing Office.

von Braun, Joachim. 1991. "The Links Between Agricultural Growth, Environmental Degradation, and Nutrition and Health." In *Agricultural Sustainability, Growth, and Poverty Alleviation: Issues and Policies*, ed. S. A. Vosti, T. Reardon, and W. von Urff. Feldafing, Germany: Deutsche Stiftung fur Internationale Entwicklung.

von Braun, Joachim, Raymond F. Hopkins, Detlev Puetz, and Rajul Pandya-Lorch. 1993. *Aid to Agriculture: Reversing the Decline.* Washington. D.C.: International Food Policy Research Institute.

Weintraub, Sidney. 1989. *Policy-Based Assistance: A Historical Perspective.* Washington, D.C.: USAID.

Wolgin, Jerome. 1990. "Fresh Start in Africa: A.I.D. and Structural Adjustment in Africa." Washington, D.C.: USAID.

World Bank. 1991, 1993, 1994. *Annual Report 1991, 1993, and 1994.* Washington, D. C.: World Bank.

2

Agricultural Policy Reform and Planning

Scott Simons and Lawrence Kent

INTRODUCTION

This chapter examines the results of donors' investments in agricultural policy reform and planning based on a review of evaluation literature on the topic. The examination looks separately at the two principal types of donor investments in this area: program assistance for adjustment, and project assistance for capacity building, policy analysis and planning. After describing briefly the two types of investments, the chapter reviews the successfulness of such investments, and factors contributing to success. We find that both types of investments are much more successful if implemented in a host country environment receptive to policy change. Successful investments also tend to be those that put a premium on proper design and implementation, including staffing. However, even well designed investments are unlikely to succeed in non-receptive environments. The final section of this chapter examines investments in agricultural policy reform from a different perspective, using a set of standardized evaluation questions. Our findings in this section reinforce the importance of the policy environment, of investment design and of implementation for success with agricultural investment projects.

TYPES OF ASSISTANCE AND MEASURING RESULTS

Two Types of Assistance

Since the early 1960s, donors have been providing assistance to developing countries' governments in agricultural policy reform and planning. USAID and the World Bank have been two of the most prominent agencies in this field, but many other bilateral and multilateral donors, such as the Food and Agricultural

Organization, have also been active. Donor investments in agricultural policy and planning fall into two broad categories: (1) program assistance for adjustment and (2) project assistance for capacity building and analysis.

Program assistance for adjustment consists of providing balance of payments support (loans, cash, or commodity transfers) to a recipient government to encourage and facilitate policy reform. Some adjustment operations focus on macroeconomic reforms that indirectly affect agriculture, such as devaluation; others focus directly on agricultural policy issues, such as agricultural pricing and trade liberalization. The primary objective of adjustment assistance is to achieve precisely defined policy reforms through policy dialogue and financial incentives, a process some have dubbed "trading cash for policy reform" (Tilney and Block 1991, 18). The International Monetary Fund and the World Bank are the major providers of adjustment assistance in macroeconomic affairs, while the World Bank and to a lesser extent USAID are the major providers of adjustment assistance specific to agriculture.

Project assistance for capacity building and analysis typically consists of support for special government units for agricultural policy analysis, planning, or statistics. These types of projects usually involve expatriate technical assistance to conduct policy and/or planning studies and to develop local capacity to conduct such studies. They also usually provide training for government officials in these subjects. The basic objective of project assistance is two-fold: to build local capacity and to induce policy reform. USAID is the major donor in this area. Most of the evaluation literature on the results of project assistance in agricultural policy and planning consists of evaluations of USAID's experience in this domain.

Measuring Results

Investments in agricultural policy analysis and planning must be evaluated according to their objectives. Objectives differ slightly between the two types of assistance:

1. *The objective of program assistance for adjustment is to induce countries to make policy changes that will improve their agricultural performance.* To evaluate these programs one must ask: Did the donor investment induce the government to make the policy changes? And if so, did the changed policies result in improved agricultural performance?
2. *The objective of project assistance is more complicated because it is two-fold. Like program assistance it seeks to induce countries to make policy changes, but it also aims to build local capacity to conduct policy analysis and planning*—capacity that will sustain policy changes in the longer run. Thus, to evaluate project assistance one must ask: Did the project help convince the government to make policy or planning changes? And did the project build sustainable local capacity to conduct policy analysis and planning in the future?

We turned to the literature to find answers to these questions and quickly learned that measuring results is fraught with difficulties. These difficulties are underscored by several analysts:

The central problem in impact assessment is to establish a link between specific actions and specific measurable outcomes. Establishing this link is particularly difficult in the case of policy reforms because the final impact of interest may be the result of a complex series of intermediate causes and effects. (Peterson 1989, 4)

Evaluations of the outcomes of policy-based lending are inherently complicated. They permit assessment of the results of actions taken, but no comparison, other than by simulation, of other measures that might have been chosen. This point is made repeatedly in the evaluations cited in the bibliography. (Weintraub 1989, 19)

Many reports have been written on adjustment operations, capacity building projects, policy changes, and policy impacts, but only a few reports have been written that effectively trace the linkages between these steps. These difficulties complicate our task.

PROGRAM INVESTMENTS IN ADJUSTMENT OPERATIONS

Background

"Adjustment operations," "conditionality," "policy dialogue," and "program assistance for reform" are four terms used to describe donor attempts to induce economic policy changes in developing countries by offering balance of payments support, such as loans, cash, or commodity transfers. Reforms sought by donors usually consist of measures to achieve macroeconomic stability and/or to promote market-oriented development on the sectoral level. These measures frequently involve agricultural policy reform.

USAID and the World Bank first became involved in leveraging policy reform with aid in the mid-1960s in India and Latin America. During the 1970s, however, USAID "focussed on the project mode of development assistance, de-emphasizing policy dialogue in the process" (Herman 1985, 1). According to the FAO (1989, 33), most donor projects during this decade "were conventionally designed to work within rather than to change the domestic policy environment . . . [and] adjustments to the policy environment lay largely beyond the field of vision of project designers."

The project mode, however, revealed its limitations by the end of the decade. Uma Lele (1991, 591) writes that "in the 1970s donors failed to grasp the complex repercussions of the adverse policy environment in countries such as Tanzania . . . and their projects performed poorly." Herman states (1985, 23) "the limited success of many projects has been due partially to the neglect of fundamental policy problems which undercut or precluded project impact." According to Cassen (1986, 96), "it [became] clear that, in sub-Saharan Africa, reliance upon project aid had brought donors and recipients to an impasse by the late 1970s: projects provided no framework for policy dialogue, and were low-yielding (or complete failures) often because of broad failures in the policy and institutional environment."

Donors began to reach a consensus by 1980 that the policy environment was so negative in so many developing countries that it was necessary to engage again in policy dialogue to promote reform and adjustment. Policy dialogue and conditionality have been in the limelight over the past dozen years or so, with much attention focussed on the structural adjustment programs promoted by the World Bank, the IMF, and, to a lesser extent, USAID. Other bilateral donors tended to channel their support through the World Bank. The World Bank invested over $5 billion in agricultural adjustment operations over the past decade or so, consisting of Agricultural Sector Adjustment Loans (SECALs) and Agricultural Sector Loans that stress policy conditionality. In addition, the Bank has invested over $15 billion in Structural Adjustment Loans (SALs) since 1980; sixty percent of these SALs contain conditionality that relates to agricultural pricing (Knudsen and Nash 1991). During the same period, USAID has invested approximately $2 billion on programs employing conditionality. We examine the results of these programs below, after a brief discussion of the relationship between macroeconomic and agricultural policy.

Direct and Indirect Effects of Policy Reform on Agriculture

Policy reform can affect agricultural development either directly (through, for example, lifting price controls or ending government purchasing monopolies), or indirectly (by, for example, devaluing the local currency to shift the terms of trade in favor of agriculture). An influential comparative study of agricultural price interventions in 18 developing countries led by Anne Krueger (1992, 200) during the 1980s concludes that the bulk of policy discrimination in LDCs against agriculture comes from indirect price interventions, mainly caused by currency overvaluation.

The World Bank concluded in the 1980s that macroeconomic reform is essential for agricultural development. A 1990 World Bank document (1990, 110) explains the linkage:

It is clear that these [macroeconomic] policies, which among others, determine the level of the real exchange rate, play a major role in determining the profitability of farming relative to nonagricultural activities. . . . Adjustment aims to depreciate the real exchange rate through reducing import restrictions, nominal devaluation, and reducing inflation. Adjustment is, therefore, a necessary condition for the reversal of the process of agricultural decline. . . , as long as an adequate share of price gains related to devaluation is passed on to farmers.

Because of the relationship between the macroeconomic environment and agricultural development, donor attempts to leverage macroeconomic policy reform are as important to agriculture as are their attempts to influence agricultural policy directly.

Results of USAID Investments in Adjustment Operations

USAID's involvement in "program assistance" for policy reform spread in the 1980s throughout the developing world, although it certainly never came close to the levels provided by the World Bank. Frequently, cash or commodity incentives for reform were combined with technical assistance for building policy analysis capacity within government ministries, such as agriculture. A comprehensive review of USAID's involvement in non-project assistance and policy dialogue is not available—neither for general economic reform nor for agricultural policy reform. But a number of documents were identified that review more than one case at a time and attempt to draw general conclusions.

The first document is a 1985 study conducted by the Government Accounting Office at the request of the Chairman of the House Foreign Affairs Committee. "Conditionality in the Agency for International Development's Economic Assistance Programs in Six Countries" looks at a number of USAID projects and programs that involved conditionality in Costa Rica, Honduras, Egypt, Bangladesh, the Philippines, and Sudan. The study shows that in Costa Rica agricultural conditions were limited to PL 480 food aid. Most of these conditions were respected. In Honduras, agricultural conditions also appeared only in PL 480 food aid. The conditions were adhered to by the government in most cases, but compliance was often partial or late.

In Egypt, USAID frequently discusses policy changes with Egyptian officials and, when it is able, places policy-related conditions on its assistance programs. However, the need to obligate funds already earmarked for political purposes to the Egypt program often frustrates policy reform efforts. PL 480 is the only assistance vehicle to which agriculture-related conditionalities have been attached. Compliance has been mixed.

In Bangladesh, a large USAID fertilizer distribution project contained a single condition requiring the government to allow private traders to buy and sell fertilizer at "satisfactory" prices. The government had not met this condition at the time of the GAO evaluation. PL 480 food aid conditions required the government to take steps to encourage market forces in agricultural production and marketing. These conditions were respected in most cases. In Sudan, the GAO (p. 85) reports:

The Government of Sudan has taken some positive steps, as part of its PL 480 program, to reform its economic policies, including (a) eliminating export taxes on most agricultural commodities, (b) eliminating subsidies on wheat products.

Other than checking compliance with conditionalities in the sample countries, the GAO study provides virtually no analysis or discussion of impact. The study's rather weak conclusions are: (1) PL 480 can serve as an effective vehicle for policy discussions; (2) Development Assistance (projects) can also serve as a vehicle for conditionalities, although leverage is limited by relatively small size; and (3) USAID's ability to attach conditions to Economic Support Fund assistance can be constrained because of overriding political and security interests in a country.

The second document reviewing multiple USAID experiences with policy conditionality is the 1991 study by Tilney and Block titled "USAID Efforts to Promote Agricultural Policy Reform and Institutional Development in Developing Countries: Lessons for Design and Implementation." This study examines a geographically diverse sample of 19 USAID-financed initiatives in agricultural policy and planning that were implemented in the 1980s, focusing on capacity building, policy reform, or both ("hybrids"). Those concentrating on capacity building are funded by project assistance, while those concentrating on policy reform tend to be funded by "non-project" or program assistance.

According to Tilney and Block, two of the more successful policy reform programs were in Bangladesh and Niger. The report provides, however, only meager information on their impacts. The report finds that 39 percent of the study sample (projects, programs, and hybrids) succeeded in producing policy reform. If one looks only at programs and hybrids, 50 percent of the sample activities were successful in inducing reforms.

The report concludes that there may be a trade-off between sustainable policy reform and institutional development. Programs (for example, sector grants) are more likely than projects to produce policy reforms in the short run. "Yet, there is a serious, and as yet unanswered, question as to whether policy reforms bought through program aid are sustainable. . . . Programs which essentially trade cash for policy reform have tended to underemphasize institutional development" (Tilney and Block 1991, 18).

A third document reviewing multiple USAID experiences with policy dialogue is a 1991 USAID report "A.I.D. Economic Policy Reform Programs in Africa: A Synthesis of Findings from Six Evaluations" by Lieberson. It looks at a sample of experiences under USAID's African Economic Policy Reform Program (AEPRP)—a program established in 1985 to help African governments restructure their economies. From FY 1985 through FY 1990, USAID committed $308.8 million to 19 countries under the AEPRP which usually combined technical assistance with balance of payments support to promote policy reforms.

The Lieberson report reviews evaluations of USAID economic reform programs in Senegal, Mali, Malawi, Uganda, Cameroon, and The Gambia, and concludes that the programs were "generally successful, though in most cases the reforms took longer than expected and many objectives were not fully achieved at the time of the evaluations." The report provides only limited empirical information on the impact of the USAID programs. Nonetheless, Lieberson provides some useful qualitative information on results.

In The Gambia, donors supported an overall economic reform program launched by the government in 1985. USAID supported the portion of the reforms covering financial and agricultural markets by providing balance of payments support under a conditionality requiring the Gambia Produce Marketing Board, a parastatal, to pay the same prices to both public and private traders who sold groundnuts to the Board. The reform was designed to improve efficiency by encouraging fair competition between public and private traders. Lieberson reports that the government met the conditionality, but the intended results were not achieved—farmers continued to sell to public, not private, trading companies, because they feared losing access to publicly-supplied fertilizer if they did otherwise.

In Cameroon, as part of a multi-donor effort, USAID supported reforms in the agricultural sector by targeting the parastatal that distributed subsidized fertilizer. The USAID-supported reforms ended the government's complete control of fertilizer by establishing a private market for the import, distribution, and financing of fertilizer. The reforms were phased in sequentially, with a new incentive system and new institutional arrangements to replace the public monopoly. According to the evaluation, the overall impact of liberalization was highly beneficial and positive. Although the reforms initiated a major change in the fertilizer distribution system, disruptions were minimal: the system continued to distribute roughly the same amount of fertilizer as in the pre-reform period; corruption decreased as the government's fertilizer monopoly ended; significant budgetary savings accrued to the government; and farmers were shielded from undue price increases by efficiency gains made in the import and distribution system.

In Malawi, USAID piggybacked onto a World Bank Structural Adjustment Loan with an economic policy reform program focusing on fertilizer reforms. It encouraged the government to reduce fertilizer subsidies and import a more concentrated mix of fertilizer to reduce costs. USAID negotiated with agriculturalists at the technical level and with policy makers at the higher levels of government. Fertilizer subsidies were reduced as required by the program, but only temporarily, rebounding to earlier levels two years later. The program was more successful in modifying the concentration mix of imported fertilizers. From 1985 to 1990 fertilizer nutrient sales went up 100 percent, but the tonnage increased by only 55 percent. The shift produced $18 million in savings in transportation and fertilizer costs.

In Uganda, the AEPRP used a Commodity Import Program (CIP), a PL 480 agreement, and technical assistance to promote a more liberal trade regime which was to facilitate exports, particularly agricultural exports. Conditionalities associated with the CIP required the government to streamline the export/import license application and approval process, among other things. The PL 480 conditions required the government to reduce restrictions on private air cargo to

encourage the export of high value horticultural crops.   The government
respected its engagements, and the results were positive: the reforms provided
incentives to exporters to commence or accelerate purchases of nontraditional
export commodities, leading to a doubling in the value exported between 1988
and 1990.

One interesting conclusion drawn by Lieberson (1991, 21) in his report is
that choice of vehicle for inducing reform—CIP, cash transfers, or PL 480—
makes little difference in determining the program's outcome:

USAID assistance could have been provided in the form of a loan or a grant, cash
disbursement, CIP, or even project assistance. . . .   Well-conceived and well-
implemented policies are critical to success; the type or form of policy-based assistance
is not the critical factor.[1]

A fourth document that examines USAID's experience with agricultural
policy dialogue is "Fresh Start in Africa: AID and Structural Adjustment in
Africa," by Wolgin (1990). Like the Lieberson piece, this document looks only
at Africa. USAID funded 42 separate policy reform programs in 22 different
African countries between 1984 and 1989, totaling over $760 million. Of the 42
programs, 17 were non-project assistance programs supporting agricultural
policy reform. In addition, USAID used PL 480 to support policy reforms in
agriculture in seven countries.

The report offers useful observations on USAID's policy reform programs:

1. By and large, these programs are limited to sectoral adjustment programs.
2. The hallmark of USAID policy reform programs is the way in which they integrate
    resources—dollars, food assistance, local currencies, studies, training, and technical
    assistance.
3. Many, if not most, of these programs are associated either directly or indirectly with
    World Bank adjustment programs.
4. World Bank programs typically require governments to undertake certain actions
    which the Bank periodically monitors; USAID helps governments implement their
    reforms by providing technical advice and studies to weigh options, and by targeting
    part of its assistance to address some of the costs of adjustment. (Wolgin 1990, 25-
    26)

Overall, Wolgin (1990, 27) is positive about the impact of USAID's
programs: "While there are a number of failures, by and large, the record of
these programs is much better than we hoped when we started out, particularly
given the nature of the problems." The report reviews the impacts of four
categories of programs, two of which are relevant to our study: (1) agricultural
market liberalization, and (2) fertilizer market liberalization.

According to Wolgin, liberalization of agricultural markets is the most
important policy area in terms of number of programs in which USAID has been
involved. Based on his review of the results of a sample of these programs in
Mali, The Gambia, Madagascar, Zambia, Togo, and Mozambique, Wolgin

concludes that successful programs in agricultural market liberalization outnumber the failures by a factor of about three to one. He writes: "The biggest impact from market liberalization is the reduction in marketing costs that results in the increase of incomes of both producers and consumers" (Wolgin 1990, 34). Of the six programs, the Zambia program was largely unsuccessful due to poor implementation and the Togo program had minimal impact due to a seriously flawed design.

The report also examines USAID programs to liberalize fertilizer markets, a necessary process to reduce government outlays on subsidies and to increase fertilizer availability. Wolgin reviews a sample of these programs, including the Malawi and Cameroon programs discussed in the Lieberson study and programs in Kenya and Guinea. In Kenya, USAID made good progress encouraging the government to decontrol fertilizer prices and reduce its role in distribution, although the government did not agree to withdraw totally from the system. In Guinea, USAID's program tried to promote the privatization of two parastatals involved in distribution of fertilizer and other agricultural inputs. The program failed.

Wolgin (1990, 43) concludes:

Somewhere between two-thirds and three-quarters of these programs are clear successes. They have resulted in two main accomplishments. First, they have reduced waste . . . [and] second [they] have opened up opportunity. Access to foreign exchange, and hopefully to medical care and to credit, will no longer be limited to the rich and powerful, but be available to everyone.

Overall, most of the literature on USAID's investments in conditionality for agricultural policy reform indicates that results have been fairly good, particularly in Africa where the experience is best documented. In those countries where design has been based on sound analysis and the government has genuinely committed itself to reforms, USAID support has facilitated and accelerated the process of liberalization in the agricultural sector. While it is too early to judge whether the liberalization measures have had a long-term positive impact on agricultural development, preliminary indicators are positive in many cases, especially in easily measurable areas such as budget deficit reduction and trade expansion.

Results of World Bank Adjustment Operations

Prior to its first Structural Adjustment Loan (SAL) in 1980, the World Bank frequently attempted to piggyback policy conditions onto projects by incorporating "covenants" into the loan agreements. Covenants required the borrowing government to increase producer prices, liberalize markets, and take other measures to favor agriculture.

A review of agricultural projects conducted by the World Bank's Operations Evaluation Department (OED) in 1988 examined 54 agricultural investment projects that contained covenants requiring pricing reforms. It found that only two reported compliance, eight reported non-compliance, and the remaining 44 had no reference to compliance (World Bank 1988, vi). Monitoring appears to have been weak, and threats to cancel projects for non-compliance to covenants were non-credible. The OED report (World Bank 1988, vii) questions the suitability of project lending for promoting policy reform, describing agricultural policy reform measures in project covenants as *ad hoc*, narrowly conceived, and likely to result in short-term benefits, if any. The report suggests that agricultural policy reforms are better pursued through SALs and SECALs, not projects, a sentiment shared by other observers (Lewis, 1–3).

In 1980, the World Bank became involved in Structural Adjustment Loans, linking balance of payments support directly with macroeconomic conditionality. Although not aimed only at agricultural policies, the early SALs contained conditions that were intended to correct the policy bias against agriculture. Sectoral Adjustment Loans (SECALs), developed after 1983, focussed more specifically on agriculture and other sectors. By the mid-1980s, adjustment operations amounted to 25 percent of total Bank lending. Between 1980 and 1991 the Bank financed 258 adjustment operations in 75 countries for a total of $41 billion.

There is only a limited literature on the results of the Bank's experience with adjustment operations in agriculture. One of the better pieces on the topic is an article by Knudsen and Nash entitled "Agricultural Policy" appearing in the Bank publication, *Restructuring Economies in Distress: Policy Reform and the World Bank* (Thomas et al. 1991). Knudsen and Nash's study reviews a large sample of adjustment operations (approximately 80) and shows that agricultural pricing conditions have been incorporated into most SALs (about 60 percent) and virtually all SECALs, usually requiring increases in producer prices. Implementation of these conditions has been successful in about 68 percent of the cases. Conditions related to institutional reform appear in 71 percent of the reviewed operations, usually relating to privatization and deregulation of markets. While recognizing that full data are not available for many cases, Knudsen and Nash state that implementation of these conditions was generally found to be successful.

Knudson and Nash's (1991, 136) view is that "the World Bank's experience in promoting agricultural reform has been too short to permit firm conclusions about what does and does not work." They believe that the effectiveness of adjustment loans should be judged according to the implementation of policy reforms rather than an immediate improvement in agricultural growth and trade balances. According to their implementation criterion, Knudsen and Nash imply that the operations have been moderately successful. Further, superficial evidence is available that agricultural growth increased more in countries receiving adjustment loans than in comparable non-recipient countries; however, conclusions at this point are premature, according to the authors.

The degree to which World Bank adjustment loans achieve their policy change targets is the topic of another study, conducted by William McCleary (1991). According to his measurements, about 60 percent of the policy changes agreed to as conditions of SALs and SECALs were fully implemented. The most successful reforms included agricultural pricing and exchange rate management, which, as noted above, is critical to improving agricultural terms of trade. McCleary, an optimist, considers the cup to be half-full rather than half-empty when looking at the fulfillment of reform conditions. Berg (in Thomas et al. 1991), who offers comments on McCleary's work, expresses skepticism about the degree to which conditionalities are actually implemented on the ground, suggesting that McCleary's figure of 60 percent may be over-estimated.

A World Bank report by Humphreys and Jaeger (1989) compares the agricultural performance of African countries that have undertaken donor-assisted structural adjustments with those countries that have not. Their research shows that agricultural price policy has become more favorable to farmers in the reforming countries, where devaluation and other measures increased real producer prices for export crops by nearly 50 percent between 1980 and 1986, while in non-reforming countries the increases were small. Agricultural taxation has fallen since 1980–84 for both groups of countries, but the reduction has been about twice as great in reforming countries. The growth of agricultural production more than doubled between 1980–84 and 1985–87 in countries that adopted important reforms. Countries without such reforms have seen their agricultural growth rates stagnate at the low levels that prevailed for both groups of countries in the early 1980s.

Work by Cleaver (1988) comes to similar conclusions: aggregate agricultural production in adjusting countries performs significantly better than in non-adjusting countries. Cleaver (1993, 49), in an update of the results of his earlier research, finds that on the whole the evidence indicates that "where policy is good or improving, performance of agriculture is also good or improving."

The Bank's internal evaluation unit reviewed the performance of seven completed agricultural SECALs in 1992, three of which were in Africa, two in Latin America, and one each in Asia and the Middle East. The results of this review, published in the OED's annual report *Evaluation Results for 1991* (World Bank 1993, 26) are decidedly less positive than results reported for SALs:

Bank commitments totaled $988 million [to the seven SECALs], of which $52 million was eventually canceled. Fewer than half of these operations were satisfactory and of these, just two were deemed sustainable. None was judged to have attained its institutional objectives in a substantial way.

The review concludes that sector operations whose effectiveness is subject to macroeconomic policy reforms should not be expected to produce results unless these reforms are carried out simultaneously.

Overall, most of the literature on World Bank investments in adjustment operations in agriculture indicates that results have been fair to good. Knudsen and Nash's work, which is perhaps the most complete, shows that 68 percent of agricultural pricing conditionalities have been met, and Cleaver's work indicates that on average reforms pay dividends. An optimist might interpret this as success—crucial constraints to agricultural development have been overcome most times the Bank has made a genuine effort, and initial results are promising. A pessimist, on the other hand, might interpret Knudsen and Nash's work to indicate that the Bank has failed to induce change in 32 percent of its attempts, and even where it has been successful, ultimate impacts are unclear.

PROJECT ASSISTANCE FOR CAPACITY BUILDING AND ANALYSIS

Background

Though program assistance for adjustment has received most of the attention in recent years, project assistance for capacity building represents the great majority of donor investments undertaken in agricultural policy reform and planning. In the 1970s, most of these projects had a planning orientation and often focused on building capacity for collecting and analyzing agricultural statistics and for conducting sector analyses. In the 1980s, project orientations shifted to include more of a policy focus and capacity building often entailed support to policy analysis units in governments. In both cases, training of host-country personnel comprised a large part of agricultural investment projects. Since a large proportion of bilateral policy-oriented capacity building projects have been USAID funded, this section focuses mostly on reviews of USAID projects.[2]

This section reviews results of capacity building projects from two perspectives: (1) results with respect to actual institutional capacity developed, and (2) the impact on policy reform of analysis and planning conducted through project apparatus. Results in building institutional capacity can be in the form of training staff, developing procedures, and establishing access to policy-makers. Results of analysis and planning refer to direct results in reforming host country policies arising from project activities.

Results in Building Institutional Capacity

In a general sense, most policy and planning projects can be judged to have had positive institution building impacts. In one of the most comprehensive reviews undertaken, 58 out of 61 USAID projects evaluated were found to have made positive contributions with respect to project objectives (Tilney and Block 1988a). However, a more detailed study of 15 capacity building projects which assesses the quality of impacts found only seven projects had a high degree of success. The more successful projects were in Pakistan, The Gambia, Zambia, Egypt, Sri Lanka, Peru, and Morocco. The less successful projects were in Indonesia, Togo, Ecuador, Kenya, Niger, Sudan, Dominican Republic, and Zaire (Tilney and Block 1991, 9). Steedman, too, in another review of the institution building experience is quite negative. He writes, "It is evident that the high expectations of the 1960s and early 1970s, namely that a concentrated effort at training and technical assistance over a few years would yield strong, self-sufficient, and stable institutions, have not materialized" (Steedman 1987, 46). Similarly, Coutu found success in this area to be rare, citing "the almost complete failure to institutionalize public agricultural policy analysis units in over 30 countries" (Coutu 1991, 9).

Factors Contributing to Successful Institutional Capacity Building

Based on the evaluation literature reviewed on agricultural policy and planning projects, there appear to be five factors that contribute to effective institution building. They are: the quality of project staff, incentives for host country staff, effective training of host country staff, appropriate agenda setting for the analysis to be conducted, and dissemination of analytical outputs.

Project staff—both expatriate and host country—is perhaps the most critical element of success for policy and planning project activities. Effective staff must have a combination of technical expertise, collegial work habits, diplomacy, teaching ability, and management ability. Not only is such a combination difficult to find, but recruiting for staff rarely gives sufficient emphasis to the mix of skills needed. On the expatriate side, selection of expatriate staff overly emphasizes technical skills around which the project is focused and which can be most easily evaluated from curriculum vitae. Non-technical skills are often neglected. On the host country side, staff are often selected on political rather than professional grounds (Coutu 1991, 5).

Good management skills, in particular, were found to be critical in contributing to institutional development. "The quality of project management is by far the most important variable in explaining successful institutional development efforts. Good management requires the creative use of project resources to maximize the involvement of host agency staff in activities at all levels. It includes maintaining close ties with influential host-country officials and strong counterpart relationships" (Tilney and Block 1991, 19).

Many examples are cited in the literature of the positive and negative roles key individuals have played in projects. Tilney and Block (1988b, 11) give particular attention to the case of Sri Lanka where highly qualified individuals contributed on both the Sri Lankan side and donor side at both the management and technical levels. Coutu mentions projects in Ecuador, Pakistan, Peru, and Honduras as examples where the most appropriately skilled host country personnel were diverted elsewhere.

Incentives to keep qualified host country staff working on project activities must be built into the projects; otherwise qualified people will leave. In most policy and planning units, incentives are insufficient to retain trained staff. After training, staff often move quickly to better jobs elsewhere in government or in the private sector. This has been a major cause of what Steedman (1987, 18) sees as the failure to institutionalize policy analysis.

Coutu (1991, 6) also states that

the major personnel issue concerns the attraction and retention of qualified analysts and researchers. Salary schedules and reward systems must be competitive with other public entities such as the Central Bank, the Ministry of Finance, and other responsible public research units. In many cases, public entities are unable to compete with private sector opportunities for qualified professionals.

There are few opportunities for projects to influence civil service pay scales. However, both salaries and advancement schedules may be worked into project conditionality. Also, projects have developed non-monetary rewards that make remaining with analysis units attractive to civil servants. Training opportunities, both short-term and long-term, are the most commonly used inducements.

Another approach is to rely less on civil servant personnel by drawing universities, private firms, and individuals into the network of analysts a project utilizes. Universities, for example, tend to have lower staff turnover, and opportunities for consulting can make the total salary package attractive to skilled analysts (USAID Evaluation Special Study, 30). For longer-term research activities, government analysts can participate as individual consultants if they are able to get unpaid leave from their public service positions.

Training of host country analysts in technical skills is a component of every policy and planning project. Training is either formal or on-the-job, and the formal training can be either long-term overseas or short-term local, regional, or overseas. In many projects, particularly in the 1970s, training was the centerpiece of project design (Tilney and Block 1991, 4).

Each of the case studies examined by Tilney and Block had a substantial training component. Of the long-term overseas training activities, the evaluations show that training generally had positive results. The most successful training resulted from sufficient time and attention given to careful selection of students. These selections were based on qualifications (not influence), work experience in the discipline, previous service in the host agency, and language skills. The host agency must then commit to making optimal use of the trainees' new skills. The record indicates that short-term training was also an effective means of motivating host agency staff and improving capabilities in specific areas (Tilney and Block 1988b, 18-19, 21).

On-the-job training both of returning long-term trainees and of existing analytical staff may be more important than formal training. A USAID (AID Evaluation Special Study, 30) study points to "greater success with advisers who train counterparts than with expatriates who advise decision-makers. . . . The most critical factor is a qualified project team that works closely with host country personnel." Unfortunately, on-the-job training receives insufficient attention in project design, recruiting of advisors, project workplans, implementation, and evaluations.

There were few examples of successful on-the-job training cited in the literature reviewed. Among the case studies examined by Tilney and Block (1988b, 22):

On the job training through daily counterpart relations often fell short of expectations. In Cameroon and Niger there was a lack of stability in counterpart relations; in Zambia, the problem was a lack of qualified Zambians to pair with expatriate counterparts. Successful on-the-job training requires that technical assistants make it a priority to impart technical skills and to include host country staff in their technical work. The Peru project was more successful in this regard.

On the other hand, a Botswana project implemented in the late 1970s was relatively successful in on-the-job training (USAID Evaluation Special Study, 30).

Without adequate on-the-job training, "donors run very serious risks of institutionalizing dependence upon technical assistance; programs must be created, therefore, which create local policy analysis capacity at the same time as they phase out technical assistance" (Steedman 1987, 46). Johnston provides an example of such dependence in USAID's technical assistance support to the Kenyan Ministry of Agriculture. Though the advisors made important contributions in conducting analyses, there was little in-service training, with the result that their roles became, in effect, those of line Ministry of Agriculture (MOA) employees (Johnston et al. 1988, 141).

Agenda Setting. For policy units to become institutionalized into the process of policy analysis, they must address a country's analytical needs—both the current policy issues and the longer-term research needs of policy makers. To achieve this, agendas for study topics cannot be drawn up by analysts in isolation, and cannot be selected by expatriate advisors alone. Instead, agendas should be the collaborative product of host country policy makers and analysts with input from non-governmental sources as well. Setting agendas for analysis is a key part of the policy process. And, as Steedman (1987, 48-51) notes, foreign technical advisors should focus on enhancing this policy process, not making policy.

Coutu notes that agricultural policy units often focus too narrowly on sectoral policy issues and avoid seeking input from other ministries and non-governmental analysts. As a result, they fail to address key macroeconomic and inter-sectoral issues for which the policy maker needs analysis. Failure to institutionalize policy analysis units is also due in part to the "types of policy thrusts that challenged prevailing governmental policies. When such efforts led to or helped expose limitations of existing policies, it is quite likely that many governmental leaders were not supportive of such policy units" (Coutu 1991, 7-8).

Dissemination. In addition to soliciting input from outside the policy unit to set agendas, policy units should disseminate output widely to both government and non-government audiences. Dissemination, which can take many forms, is key to stimulating demand for the policy unit's analyses (Steedman 1987, 48-51). The Peru project was cited for its focus on publications, but dissemination can also include press reports, workshops, newsletters, and other activities. The Sri Lanka project successfully incorporated workshops and task forces as ways to increase communication and interaction among analysts, decision-makers, other government agencies, and the private sector (Tilney and Block 1988b, 11). Unfortunately, due to an overly narrow focus of many policy units, there has tended to be little dissemination of analyses, and, as a result, "limited opportunities for the general public to discuss policy changes. This lack of dissemination and discussion has severely limited the demand by the general public for positive and substantive policy studies" (Coutu 1991, 5).

Results of Analytical and Planning Activities

In terms of impacts of analytical and planning activities on policy reform, projects have been somewhat less successful than they have been in building institutional capacity. In their review of USAID projects, Tilney and Block report only 24 of 61 projects had impacts on decision-makers in government. They (Tilney and Block 1988a, 8-10) cited projects in Kenya and Bangladesh as examples of successful policy analysis projects. Projects tended to be more successful in Asia, Latin America, and the Caribbean, than in Africa and the Near East.

More detailed case study reviews also found mixed results with respect to policy reform. Projects in the Gambia, Sri Lanka, Zambia, Peru, and the Dominican Republic successfully influenced decision-makers while others in Ecuador, Togo, Niger, Indonesia, Cameroon and Egypt appear to have had little impact. In Peru for example, a policy analysis unit provided significant input to nine legislative studies, and the results of several studies provided support for ministerial decisions. In the Dominican Republic, studies by a policy unit had a direct policy and program impact in raising the producer price of milk, extending credit risk coverage to local banks, and decontrolling pork prices. In Zambia, studies' recommendations resulted in price increases for groundnuts and reductions in tractor rental subsidies. Projects in Cameroon and Egypt, on the other hand, had "little or no impact on policies and programs." In Cameroon the impact was undermined by limited institutional capacity in the policy unit; and in Egypt, government officials steered analysis of sensitive topics away from the project supported activities (Tilney and Block 1988a, 56-7).

The absence of actual policy change does not necessarily mean that analysis and planning activities failed. Even the highest quality analysis and the best decision-maker access may not lead to policy change. Policy change depends on a variety of factors which projects may be unable to address. Thus, while only one-third of the projects evaluated by Tilney and Block in 1988 produced concrete policy change, most of the remaining two-thirds may still have been successful in producing high quality analysis, providing useful input to decision-makers, or meeting other project goals (Tilney and Block 1988a, 11).

Factors Contributing to Successful Policy Reform

Based on the evaluation literature reviewed, there appear to be five factors that contribute to the success of projects in actually inducing policy reform. They are: host country support for policy change; appropriate types of analysis conducted; selection of topics for analysis; the location of analysis activities; and technical assistance advisors.

Host country support for policy change is the most important factor in achieving the change. This is as true for policy analysis activities as it is for program support for adjustment discussed above. Policy analysis has led to rapid policy change most often where the analysis from the project unit is part of a larger reform agenda of the government. In contrast, analysis challenging prevailing governmental policies is unlikely to produce short-term results. This is not to say that such analysis is not needed, but that analysis alone is generally insufficient to overcome government resistance. When efforts help to expose limitations of existing policies, they can be resisted strongly by governmental leaders, even within the policy unit (Coutu 1991, 3). With the Egypt project, for example, host country officials blocked analysis of controversial policy issues conducted either by project-supported expatriates or by Egyptian government staff.

Donor interests often call for re-examining current host country policies, and the need for such analysis is strong in many cases. Policy units in government ministries can respond by combining analyses of controversial topics with analyses more directly addressing existing policy agendas. Another approach is for projects to rely less on governmental units and instead use capabilities outside of government to conduct analyses. For example, USAID/Tanzania addressed sensitive issues concerning harmful government agricultural policies in the early 1980s by commissioning studies by independent consultants and by supporting work of Tanzanian scholars and university research bureaus (Johnston et al. 1988, 140).

Type of analysis. Policy analyses have had the greatest likelihood for impact on host country policies when they have addressed the specific analytical needs of policy makers. For example, a focus on the country's current, high priority policy issues was an important factor in the success of Peru's policy analysis unit. USAID's policy project in Sri Lanka is another example of successful policy analysis resulting from the practical and implementable output of the analyses performed. The policy studies were highly pragmatic and results were product-oriented; they produced a list of specific policy changes along with steps for successful implementation (Tilney and Block 1988b, 10-11).

There are also numerous examples of analyses failing to meet the tests of practicality and relevancy. In reviewing many projects, Tilney and Block found that, "the least effective studies were highly abstract and quantitative analyses developed independently by foreign advisors. . . . It is essential that technical studies and their methodologies be comprehensible to the host country officials who ultimately are responsible for acting on the technical analysis and recommendations." Analyses involving modeling exercises particularly tended to be overly complex and quantitative for policy formulation. The Zambia project was cited as successful in influencing policies with its non-modeling analyses (Tilney and Block 1988b, 14, 21).

Selection of topics for analysis. In the most successful projects among those reviewed in the literature, topics for analysis were selected collaboratively by host country officials and expatriate project and donor staff. Collaboration leads both to greater "ownership" of the analytical agenda and to better identifying and serving government needs for policy analysis. Steedman notes that successful project activities were those that responded to real demands from decision-makers. But many projects suffered from a lack of contact with policy makers and tended to operate in a vacuum. "Demand for policy analysis is often low, in part because policy is often perceived exclusively as part of a political process. . . . Donors need to involve policy makers by consulting and briefing politicians and permanent secretaries on the uses of policy analysis" (Steedman 1987, 18, 47).

To be demand-responsive also requires that projects be flexible in setting agendas. "Policy analysis requires the ability to respond flexibly to the changing needs and concerns of decision-makers." This flexibility to respond to changes in the economic, political, and institutional environments must be designed into policy projects (USAID Evaluation Special Study, 32-33). Experience from USAID's policy project in Egypt demonstrates that simply increasing the supply of analyses is not sufficient to drive the policy reform process. A great number of analyses were conducted under the auspices of the project with little impact on agricultural policies (Tilney and Block 1988b, 7).

Location of analysis activities. Projects having most favorable policy reform impacts had policy analysis activities located institutionally close to senior decision-makers. This was noted by Tilney and Block in their extensive review of USAID projects (Tilney and Block 1988b, 16) as well as by Steedman in his evaluation (Steedman 1987, 18). For agricultural policies, this generally means proximity to senior Ministry of Agriculture decision-makers.

However, some projects have been more successful working outside agricultural ministries. A key aspect of success in Sri Lanka was the coordinating role played by the Ministry of Finance and Planning (MFP). Even though the project dealt principally with agricultural issues, MFP influence was necessary for the project to have the impact it had. Coutu argues that donor support for agricultural policy analysis should "focus on what public entity has the prime authority in setting agricultural policies." This may be a monetary board or central bank for critical intersectoral policies (Coutu 1991, 9).

With location so important in determining policy impact, units based at more subordinate levels of government will never have significant policy effects. Steedman observes that assistance in such non-influential units and in statistical units, for example, will not result in contact with key policy makers (Steedman 1987, 18). Note though that projects with access to individual policy makers have been vulnerable to changes in policy-making personnel. Such changes happen more regularly at the senior level than lower down in the hierarchy (Tilney and Block 1988b, 16). Thus, there may be a trade-off between access to top policy makers and sustainability of access.

Technical assistance advisors. Successful policy reform stimulated by policy projects will depend to a great extent on the technical assistance advisors provided under the project. Advisors must be able to perform high quality analyses, present results in a way that the intended audience will understand, and have credibility with and access to policy makers. The quality of advisors varies greatly across projects, with generally highly competent advisors characterizing most projects. The Kenya project particularly was noted for the quality of advisors supplied and analyses performed. Advisors grew to be relied on as staff analysts of the Ministry of Agriculture (Johnston et al. 1988).

For analysis to gain sufficient exposure, advisors often had to establish their credibility with host agencies and policy makers. This required time and continuity of staffing in the projects examined (Tilney and Block 1988b, 20). It also frequently required performing tasks that fell outside project and individual terms of reference such as "fire-fighting" analyses and speech-writing for senior government officials. Though these activities may be tangential to the project, in the long-run they contribute to attaining project objectives.

CONCLUSIONS

In order to evaluate different types of agricultural investments along common criteria, each chapter in this book examines its type of investment in terms of six standardized questions. These questions are addressed with respect to policy and planning investments and presented as conclusions to this chapter.

When are investments in policy reform and planning most appropriate?

A country's stage of economic development, in terms of per capita income, does not appear to be greatly important for the success of agricultural policy and planning projects. However, the stage of reform in a sequence of policy reforms does have an important effect. The literature on agricultural policy and planning activities indicates that getting the macroeconomic environment right is extremely important to the success of reforming agricultural sector policies. Similarly, getting the policy environment right within the agricultural sector is a very important first step for successful agricultural investments.

The World Bank's annual review of evaluation results examined links between the level of development and project success over a number of years but failed to find any consistent relationship. Both positive and negative correlations were found between levels of development and project performance in various years. For example, the 1990 *Annual Review of Evaluation Results* showed projects in lower income countries performed less well than those in middle income countries, and poorest countries had the lowest percentage of satisfactory projects. In contrast, the 1991 *Annual Review of Evaluation Results* showed exactly the reverse. For all projects in the Annual Review data base, the evaluation reports a weak positive relation between income level and performance (World Bank 1993, xvi).

The same reviews of evaluations found that macroeconomic conditions were important for the performance of agricultural projects. Indicators of a sound macroeconomy were positively correlated with overall performance ratings for projects undertaken. Performance was evaluated in terms of project returns, institutional achievements, and sustainability in these reviews (World Bank 1993, xvi).

Several other studies that examined macroeconomic and agricultural policies came to a similar conclusion. Knudsen, in conducting a review of structural adjustment lending for the World Bank, questioned whether sectoral adjustment lending can proceed before macroeconomic stabilization has been achieved. He (Knudsen and Nash 1991, 148) write, "Although progress on agricultural reform may be possible in an unstable macroeconomic situation, it is rare, especially in the case of pricing and trade policy." Cleaver (1993) also observes in an evaluation focusing on Africa that, "In African countries with relatively "good" economic and agricultural policy in the late 1970s and early 1980s, 63 percent of Bank agricultural projects audited by the World Bank's Operations Evaluation Department were evaluated as successful in the 1991 review of Project Performance Audit Reports. Only 30 percent of agricultural projects in African countries having relatively "bad" economic and agricultural policy were successful."

Though getting the policy environment right is important for all sectors, it is especially important for agriculture given the history of agricultural distortions in most developing countries. Knudsen and Nash (1991, 131) found that projects implemented in a distorted, anti-agriculture, policy environment even further discouraged agricultural growth by perpetuating overvaluation through provision of foreign exchange and by indirectly sanctioning the continuation of the anti-agriculture policies.

Can agricultural development be successful without investing in policy reform and planning?

Little in the literature directly addresses the counterfactual question of development in the absence of investments. What does emerge is that the most successful policy reform activities evaluated were those in support of an incremental policy change in a country, as opposed to efforts to introduce major new policies. Similarly with project-type assistance, success in having an impact on host country policies occurred most frequently in those countries on the path of reform. Policy analyses have had the greatest impact on reform in countries such as Sri Lanka and Zambia where reforms were already underway and were strongly supported by the country's leadership. Countries that were resisting reform had little use for analyses that projects may produce. Conducting project-assisted policy analyses for reforming countries is more than "preaching to the converted." Policy makers in reforming countries need detailed analysis on options, implementation, and effects of various policy changes.

Project efforts at analytical capacity building also are most effective when they receive active host country support for institutionalization. In a review of numerous project evaluations, Tilney and Block found that, "the most frequently cited constraint to successful project performance was lack of host country support in the form of money, access to policy makers, commitment to the project, or providing counterpart staff. Lack of host country support was mentioned more frequently in Africa than in other regions." (Tilney and Block 1988a, 12; USAID Evaluation Special Study, 61)

What is the rate of return to investments in policy reform and planning?

The literature that we reviewed measures success in terms of meeting program and project objectives in policy and planning rather than calculating rates of return. Rates of return, in fact, are generally inappropriate measures for these types of activities. World Bank evaluations, for example, which as a rule estimate economic rates of return for their projects, note that these measures are not applicable to program and policy operations (World Bank 1993, 75).

On the whole, donor investments in agricultural policy reform and planning have had mixed results. A number of activities have been quite successful. Other activities only partially achieved their objectives or had negligible impact. Knudsen and Nash conducted a review of approximately 80 World Bank adjustment operations and found that 68 percent of those dealing with agricultural price policies successfully fulfilled policy conditionalities. Projects were similarly successful in meeting institutional conditionalities—generally dealing with privatization and market deregulation. Another study by McCleary found about 60 percent of policy changes contained in World Bank conditionalities were fully implemented.

The effect of successful program implementation toward attaining agricultural development goals was not addressed directly by most reviewers. Superficial evidence indicates that growth was greater in countries receiving adjustment loans than in comparable non-recipient countries. However, most reviewers state that conclusions at this point are premature and that more time is needed to make definitive assessments of impact.

USAID project assistance for capacity building and policy analysis typically has multiple objectives by which to assess success. The literature we reviewed focused on institution building, impacts on decision-makers, and policy change. Though assessments differ among reviewers, many of the projects examined were successful to some degree in attaining institution building objectives. Fifty-eight of 61 projects reviewed had significant success in creating policy or planning units and in staff development according to the most extensive review (Tilney and Block 1988a). Other reviewers noted, however, that much of the institution building that has occurred is superficial and not sustainable long beyond project termination.

Fewer projects were successful in terms of their effects on decision-makers. Tilney and Block report that 39 percent (24 out of 61 projects) had decision-maker impacts such as increased demand for analysis or a greater understanding of the agricultural sector and its relationships with other sectors of the economy.

Even fewer projects were successful in achieving concrete changes in policy as a result of analytical and planning activities. One-third of the projects, 20 out of 61, contributed to actual changes in policies. However, analytic and planning activities can be successful even without discrete policy change. Most of the remaining 41 projects succeeded in producing high quality analysis, providing useful input for decision-makers, or meeting other project goals.

Is the private sector or the public sector best suited to invest in policy reform and planning?

Virtually all donor assistance in policy reform and planning has gone to public sector institutions. Project aid has gone principally to ministries of agriculture, with some support going to ministries of finance or planning for conducting agricultural policy and planning activities. Program aid has been directed to central governments alone. This is generally proper since policy and planning activities are conducted by the public sector.

However, the private sector can play a much larger role in policy and planning—as advocates and as analysts. Policy analysis need not be conducted in a narrowly defined government policy analysis unit but can include individuals and participants from universities and private firms. The analyses can be performed by mixed teams of public and private analysts or be contracted out entirely to the private sector. Advocacy in support for or opposition against given policies is also a role for the private sector, but one that is often neglected in policy and planning projects.

Which U.S. Government agencies are best suited to implement policy reform and planning activities?

Within the U.S. Government, program assistance has been implemented strictly by USAID in the past as it probably should be in the future. USAID's continued involvement is important given that program assistance requires a considerable degree of analytical staff input. This is true both in preparation of the program and during program implementation when constant monitoring and adjustment may be necessary (Lieberson 1991, viii-ix). There is a clear correlation between poor performance and inadequate processing, including identification, preparation, and supervision (World Bank 1993, xvii). Project assistance also requires considerable expertise in preparation, implementation, and monitoring with respect to technical subjects and experiences in other countries. The technical expertise may be found in other U.S. government agencies, the Department of Agriculture, particularly, but knowledge of individual countries and of development history is found mostly in USAID. However, input should be obtained from various sources including other U.S. government agencies, universities, private firms, and individuals.

In terms of project implementation, the literature indicates that good management is the single most important factor for successful projects. The Tilney and Block review of evaluations of policy and planning projects assessed the strengths and weaknesses of various types of implementation contractors. They found that university contractors are particularly well suited to implementing overseas training for host country nationals. "Yet university contractors. . . had the disadvantage of weak management structures and limited experience in implementing large-scale overseas projects. . . . Private firms, in contrast, were strongest in their ability to manage projects efficiently, though private firms may be less appropriate than universities for implementing long-term training programs" (Tilney and Block 1988b, 17).

Does the United States have a comparative advantage in investing in policy reform and planning?

A key resource giving the United States a strong advantage over the World Bank and other donors is the number of field missions and field personnel administering agricultural activities. The advantage holds for both program and project activities. On the program side, resident missions give USAID an ability to conduct and monitor operations in a more direct style than the World Bank. USAID staff are able to dialogue regularly and develop collegial relationships with government officials (Wolgin 1990, 24; Vondal 1989, 3-6). USAID missions and personnel also enable the United States to give particular attention to implementation—more than by many donors. Through close monitoring of the economic and political environment and of program and project activities, USAID is able to address implementation issues and, if necessary, recast activities in mid-stream. USAID also has an advantage over multilaterals in promoting development of local human and institutional capacity, which requires fewer financial resources but much more intensive nurturing over a long period (Lele and Jain, 608).

The extensive network of U.S. institutions, including universities, private consulting firms, agribusinesses, and NGOs, also provide a valuable resource for program and project implementation. The U.S. comparative advantage is particularly strong in training activities that draw on the American higher education system. In agriculture, this system is unmatched elsewhere in the world.

NOTES

1. This point is reinforced by a review of PL 480 programs conducted by Herman (1989, p. 10) who found that the conditions associated with PL 480 have been highly effective in stimulating important reforms in the Philippines, Bangladesh, and Pakistan.

2. The FAO has also played an important role in this field, particularly in the 1970s, and a new institution—the African Capacity Building Foundation—has recently begun to fund projects to develop economic skills in Africa.

REFERENCES

Berg, Elliot J. 1991. "Comments on the Design and Implementation of Conditionality." In Vinod, Thomas, Ajay Chhibber, Mansoor Dailami, and Jaime de Melo, eds., *Restructuring Economies in Distress: Policy Reform and the World Bank.* Oxford: Oxford University Press for the World Bank.

Cassen, Robert. 1986. *Does Aid Work? Report to an Intergovernmental Task Force.* Oxford: Clarendon Press.

Cleaver, K. August 1988. "Agricultural Policy Reform and Structural Adjustment in Sub-Saharan Africa: Results to Date." Washington, DC: World Bank.

Cleaver, K. 1993. "A Strategy to Develop Agriculture in Sub-Saharan Africa and a Focus for the World Bank." Technical Paper No. 203. Washington, D.C.: World Bank.

Coutu, A. J. July 1991. "The Failure to Institutionalize Public Agricultural Policy Analysis Units." APAP II Collaborative Research Report No. 318. Cambridge, MA: Abt Associates, Inc.

Food and Agriculture Organization of the United Nations. 1989. "The Design of Agricultural Investment Projects." Investment Centre Technical Paper 6. Rome: United Nations.

General Accounting Office. February 1985. "Conditionality in the Agency for International Development's Economic Assistance Programs in Six Countries." Washington, DC: GAO.

Herman, Chris. 1985. "Implementing Policy and Institutional Change via Performance Disbursement: Examples From the Philippines, Bangladesh, and Niger." A.I.D. Evaluation Occasional Paper No. 1. Washington, DC: USAID.

Herman, Chris. January 1989. "A Review of the ANE Bureau's PL-480 Title I and III Programs: A Summary of Key Findings and Issues." Washington, DC: USAID.

Humphreys, Charles and William Jaeger, et al. 1989. *Africa's Adjustment and Growth in the 1980s*. Washington, DC: A joint World Bank-UNDP publication.

Johnston, Bruce F., et al. April 1988. "An Assessment of A.I.D. Activities to Promote Agricultural and Rural Development in Sub-Saharan Africa." A.I.D. Evaluation Special Study No. 54. Washington, DC: USAID.

Knudsen, Odin and John Nash. 1991. "Agricultural Policy." In Vinod, Thomas, Ajay Chhibber, Mansoor Dailami, and Jaime de Melo, eds., *Restructuring Economies in Distress: Policy Reform and the World Bank*. Oxford: Oxford University Press for the World Bank.

Krueger, Anne O. 1992. "A Synthesis of the Political Economy in Developing Countries." *The Political Economy of Agricultural Pricing Policy*. Vol. 5. Baltimore: Johns Hopkins University Press.

Lele, Uma. 1991. "Aid to African Agriculture: Lessons from Two Decades of Donors' Experience." MADIA Discussion Paper. Baltimore: Johns Hopkins University Press.

Lele, Uma and Rahul Jain. 1991. "Aid to African Agriculture: Lessons from Two Decades of Donors' Experience." In Lele, Uma, ed., *Aid to African Agriculture: Lessons from Two Decades of Donors' Experience*. Baltimore: Johns Hopkins University Press.

Lewis, John. 1989. "Policy Based Assistance: An Historical Perspective on A.I.D.'s Experience and Operations in India/Asia in a Bilateral and Multilateral Context." Washington, DC: USAID.

Lieberson, Joseph M. December 1991. "A.I.D. Economic Policy Reform Programs in Africa: A Synthesis of Findings from Six Evaluations." A.I.D. Program and Operations Assessment Report No. 1. Washington, DC: USAID.

McCleary, William. 1991. "The Design and Implementation of Conditionality." In Vinod, Thomas, Ajay Chhibber, Mansoor Dailami, and Jaime de Melo, eds., *Restructuring Economies in Distress: Policy Reform and the World Bank*. Oxford: Oxford University Press for the World Bank.

Peterson, Wesley. November 1989. "Niger: Monitoring the Effect of Policy Reform." APAP II Report No. 105. Washington, DC: USAID.

Steedman, David W. April 1987. *Capacity Building for Policy Analysis in Sub-Saharan Africa: A Review of the Experience of Selected Donors*. Ottawa, Canada: ARA Consultants.

Thomas, Vinod, Ajay Chhibber, Mansoor Dailami, and Jaime de Melo, eds. 1991. *Restructuring Economies in Distress: Policy Reform and the World Bank*. Oxford: Oxford University Press for the World Bank.

Tilney, John S. and Steven Block. August 1988a. "An Evaluation of A.I.D.-Sponsored Agricultural Policy Analysis and Planning Projects." APAP Main Document No. 6. Cambridge, MA: Abt Associates.

———. August 1988b. "Building Institutional Capacity for Agricultural Policy Analysis and Planning: A Comparative Evaluation of USAID'S Experience." APAP Staff Paper No. 27. Cambridge, MA: Abt Associates.

————. July 1991. "USAID Efforts to Promote Agricultural Policy Reform and
    Institutional Development in Developing Countries: Lessons for Design and
    Implementation." APAP II Collaborative Research Report No. 317. Cambridge,
    MA: Abt Associates.

USAID. February 1989. "Agricultural Policy Analysis: A Manual for AID Agriculture
    and Rural Development Officers." AID Evaluation Special Study No. 61.
    Washington, D.C.: CDIE.

USAID. May 1993. "Managing the Policy Reform Process, Evaluation Design."
    Washington, DC: CDIE.

Vondal, Patricia. October 1989. "Operational Issues in Developing A.I.D. Policy
    Reform Programs." A.I.D. Program Evaluation Discussion Paper No. 28.
    Washington, DC: CDIE.

Weintraub, Sidney. 1989. *Policy-Based Assistance: A Historical Perspective.*
    Washington, DC: USAID.

Wolgin, Jerome. August 1990. *Fresh Start in Africa: A.I.D. and Structural Adjustment
    in Africa.* Washington, DC: USAID.

World Bank. 1990. *Making Adjustment Work for the Poor: A Framework for Policy
    Reform in Africa.* Washington, DC: World Bank.

World Bank, Operations Evaluation Department. 1988. *Conditionality in World Bank
    Lending: Its Relation to Agricultural Pricing Policies.* Washington, DC: World
    Bank.

————. 1991. *Annual Review of Evaluation Results 1990.* Washington, DC: World
    Bank.

————. 1993. *Annual Review of Evaluation Results 1991.* Washington, DC: World
    Bank.

Agricultural Technology Development and Diffusion: A Synthesis of the Literature

James F. Oehmke

INTRODUCTION

The substantial commitment of donor and host country resources to agricultural technology development and diffusion (TDD) begs the question: Have these investments been worthwhile, and, if so, should they be continued? This chapter reviews evidence relevant to these questions with a focus on three specific objectives:

1. Determining if previous investments have been successful or have failed,
2. Identifying those factors that contributed to success or helped cause failure, and
3. Informing strategic thinking on investment in agricultural TDD.

This chapter addresses these objectives by reviewing evaluation syntheses of literature on TDD investments in developing countries made by USAID, other donors, and host countries. It proceeds by defining TDD, reviewing empirical assessments of returns to investments in TDD, and addressing critical issues of resource allocation to TDD. The final section summarizes the chapter.

WHAT ARE TECHNOLOGY DEVELOPMENT AND DIFFUSION?

An agricultural technique is a production or processing practice used in agriculture. *Currently available technology* refers to the set of techniques that is known and available to practitioners. Technology development and diffusion (TDD) expands the set of currently known and available techniques. It usually begins with basic research that increases fundamental biophysical or socio-economic knowledge, and proceeds with the generation of knowledge about potential applications, followed by testing (for example, through experiment-station or on-farm trials). Diffusion occurs when farmers utilize the newly available techniques.

TDD is comprised of three components: research, extension, and education. Research consists of those activities that broaden conceptual or empirical knowledge through scientific investigation. Agriculturalists use the term *research* in the same way industrialists use the term *research and development*. Extension is the process of transferring the new knowledge to farmers or other producers. This transfer often includes contact by public extension agents, but in practice much of the knowledge is embodied in inputs: for example, knowledge about plant genetics is embodied in high-yielding-variety seeds. The iterative nature of extension, farmer feedback, and refinement of techniques through further research complicates the distinction between research and extension. For example, the World Bank proceeds from the premise that research and extension are related functions, concluding that disaggregation is inappropriate (World Bank 1983, iii).

Two types of education affect TDD: (1) the education of farmers and others in the agricultural sector, which affects the adoption of improved techniques; and (2) higher education to train scientists, researchers, and extension agents to promote the capacity to undertake TDD. USAID investments focus on the latter. Consequently, this chapter focuses on developing country universities and other institutions of higher education and their impact on host country research and extension capacity, and omits discussion of the literature on public and private rates of return to primary and, to some extent, secondary education in agriculture, in developing countries (see Psacharopoulos 1985).

Successful TDD contributes to agricultural growth and improves social welfare. TDD contributes to growth when profitable techniques are adopted and increase the value of goods and services produced in the agricultural sector, usually by increasing quantities produced. TDD also often lowers the price of agricultural products. The benefits from lower prices (or improved quality at constant prices) are neglected in the usual measures of sectoral growth. Yet these benefits may be very important to society, particularly in developing countries, where poor consumers and small-holding farmers may spend large portions of their incomes on food. Theoretical and empirical evidence shows that the majority of the benefits from agricultural TDD accrue to consumers (Hayami and Herdt 1977; Norton and Davis 1981).

Expenditures on agricultural TDD in developing countries are small relative to the size of the agricultural sectors (Pardey and Roseboom 1989). Asia and the Near East lead the developing country regions, spending $1.8 billion from 1971 to 1975, $2.5 billion from 1976 to 1980, and $3.3 billion from 1981 to 1985 (constant 1990 U.S. dollars). In Latin America and the Caribbean, expenditures increased from $486 million from 1971 to 1975 to $680 million from 1976 to 1980, with a smaller increase to $709 million from 1981 to 1985. Expenditures in Africa have climbed from $277 million, to $360 million, to $372 million over comparable time periods.

EMPIRICAL STUDIES ON THE IMPACT OF TDD

Rates of Return to Investments in TDD

A single lesson from the rate of return literature overwhelms all others: investments in agricultural TDD have generated social benefits that justify the investments in a wide range of countries, commodities, and conditions. The results of the ex post studies, which quantify returns to currently developed and adopted techniques, are discussed in this section and summarized in the annex to this chapter. Studies that calculate ex ante returns based on projected future benefits of TDD are neglected (see Echeverria 1990).

Following Schultz's (1953) seminal study on returns to investments in U.S. agricultural research, application to developing countries began with the Ph.D. dissertations by Tang (1963) and Barletta (1970) at the University of Chicago and Ayer (1970) at Purdue University (see also Ayer and Schuh 1972). Tang's results include the finding of a 35 percent rate of return (RoR) to aggregate investment in Japanese agricultural TDD from 1800 to 1938. Over the period 1943–1963, Barletta finds rates of return of 90 percent and 35 percent for Mexican wheat and maize research, respectively. Ayer and Schuh find a 77 percent rate of return for Brazilian cotton research over the period 1924–1967. Over the past three decades, there has been rapid growth in the literature estimating RoRs to investments in Latin American and Asian agricultural research, with almost universal findings of RoRs sufficient to justify actual or expanded investments.

For Africa, the number of studies is substantially smaller. Although they also seem to indicate that the impacts justify the investments, a few exceptions make generalizations more difficult. Some studies show relatively low or negative RoRs (for example the 3 percent RoR to investments in cowpea research in Cameroon, which is consistent with descriptive analyses of African agricultural TDD). Negative returns in Uganda are attributed to the fifteen years of civil unrest, disastrous policies, and destruction of research facilities in the 1970s and early 1980s. No release of important new varieties has occurred in Niger, leading to the negative estimated RoR there. The estimate of a 4 to 7 percent return to Malawian maize research is perhaps conservative and reflects in part sporadic investment in a fledgling program. Overall, nine of thirteen studies for Africa show RoRs in excess of the opportunity cost of capital, including Evenson's (1987) regional analysis, which includes costs of failed as well as successful projects.

There is an obvious paucity of rate of return studies in countries or periods subject to civil unrest. Anecdotal evidence from countries such as Laos, Cambodia, and Uganda confirms the intuition that dramatic instability can destroy previously successful research results. The political instability of the 1970s and early 1980s in Uganda halted TDD and destroyed much that had been accomplished, explaining the negative RoR found there.

High returns found across countries, commodities, and policy regimes have led most reviewers to conclude that investment in agricultural TDD is worthwhile (Echeverria 1990; Evenson et al. 1979; Norton and Davis 1981; Ruttan 1982), the African exceptions notwithstanding (Oehmke and Crawford 1996). Two implications emerge: (1) Agricultural TDD has had an impact; and (2) there has been underinvestment in agricultural TDD. The robustness of these results merits more detailed discussion.

Methodological Issues

Schultz's (1953) seminal assessment of the impact of investments in research was intended primarily to complement a solid descriptive argument about the impacts of U.S. agricultural research without a detailed quantification of costs and benefits. Griliches (1958), Evenson (1967), and others improved the quantification methods in further applications. Nonetheless, many critics rejected the rate of return numbers as the result of bias in the methodology.

Early criticisms focused on selection only of success stories (e.g. hybrid maize in the United States), neglected price effects, failure to distinguish research impacts from those of extension or other complementary investments, and calculated average rather than marginal RoRs. In response to the first criticism, subsequent researchers consistently make efforts to include all relevant costs, including those of failed projects. Particularly telling is the evidence in the aggregate studies, which include all benefits and all costs of TDD across commodities, thereby removing any bias toward selecting only successful ventures, and which still show high rates of returns: for example, 40 to 100 percent for India, 64 percent for Pakistan, and 50 percent for Columbia. The criticism about ignoring prices is addressed by Akino and Hayami (1975), who present a simple formula for including benefits to consumers from lower prices, and by Hayami and Herdt (1977), who demonstrate that the benefits to consumers typically exceed any reduction in farmer benefits due to the lower prices. Distinguishing the effect of research from other related investments has been accomplished in one of four ways: (1) by calculating shadow prices for the inputs impacted by the complementary investments (e.g., the shadow price of land that is irrigated); (2) by using statistical methods to attribute portions of impacts to various investments (e.g., Huffman and Evenson 1993); (3) by direct attribution using detailed descriptive analysis; and (4) by calculating returns to the set of investments (e.g., Schwartz et al. 1993). The (accurate) criticism about average RoRs is the argument that even if research has on average been a good investment, one cannot make the claim on this basis that there is underinvestment at the margin. Most studies now use a production function approach to calculate the marginal return to investment, providing a better guide for additional allocations to a particular project or equivalent activities. Estimated RoRs remain high after addressing all of these criticisms.

A current issue is that consideration of gender is almost totally missing from evaluations of TDD. Jiggins (1986) argues that the failure explicitly to account for gender issues imparts an upward bias to rate of return calculations:

Estimates of the income and welfare gains to households associated with modern varieties probably overstate the benefits by undercounting any costs incurred via the reallocation of female labor between crops, between farm and nonfarm activities, and between domestic and public domain roles. (Jiggins 1986, 5–6)

However, the basis for this conclusion apparently rests on a specious interpretation of opportunity cost:

It is patently unsatisfactory, for example, to value female intrahousehold work at female market wage rates if, when a "female" wage opportunity appears in the market, a woman leaves the household to work, her menfolk take over her intrahousehold tasks, and the opportunity cost of that work is then valued at the (higher) male market wage rate. (Jiggins 1986, 26)

This statement leaves the author precariously close to arguing that time allocated to household chores traditionally undertaken by women should be valued at the (lower) women's wage rate because these chores are "female" work. Jiggins incorrectly applies the opportunity cost concept to a particular task, not to the labor involved in accomplishing that task. Nor does she present any examples of alternatives to opportunity cost accounting or of how the estimated returns would change in response to such alternative accounting. The profession espouses the use of opportunity cost to value labor—gender issues notwithstanding.

Perhaps a more telling issue arises when marker opportunities for male labor or new techniques to improve household agricultural productivity are adopted, increasing the workload for women, but not necessarily increasing their remuneration due to intra-household dynamics (see Dalton and Masters 1997). This distributional issue may be quite important. However, it does not detract from the accuracy of the benefit measure at the household level.

However, past success does not guarantee future performance. Past gains may be unsustainable due to degradation of natural resources. Others argue that past TDD endeavors may have been successful because they focused on the easy accomplishments, and that future research success will become increasingly difficult to achieve. While there are certainly large areas of degraded natural resources, and it is clear that some agricultural practices are unsustainable, evidence on the sustainability of agricultural productivity at the aggregate level is less clear, and the historical record in most parts of the world is one of continued yield increases over long periods of time.

There is little solid theoretical or empirical evidence to support or refute the hypothesis that research gains are becoming more difficult. Evenson and Kislev (1975) present a theoretical model of varietal selection in which progress becomes increasingly more difficult. Echeverria and Oehmke (1990) model how research systems may respond to changing socioeconomic needs in a dynamic environment, incorporating the idea that dynamic systems present new and changing opportunities for research success. Cheng and Dinopoulos (1992) posit that research typically generates a major breakthrough followed by minor innovations of decreasing importance until the next breakthrough renews research opportunities. This model seems consistent with the development of modern hybridization techniques several decades ago and current directions of biotechnology. The literature provides only indirect empirical evidence. For the United States, Davis (1979) finds declines in RoRs between the periods 1949–1959 (66 to 100%) and 1964–1974 (37%). Evenson (1978) finds declines in returns to science-oriented research between the periods 1927–1950 (110%) and 1948–1971 (45%) but does not interpret this as evidence that research potential is being exhausted. On the other hand, Akino and Hayami (1975) found an increase in the rate of return to rice research in Japan between the periods 1915–1950 and 1930–1961. Examination of peak yields is similarly uninformative. For example, peak maize yields in Kenya seem to exhibit a tapering off after yields exceeding 6 tons per hectare were achieved in the 1970s; examination of peak yields in marginal areas—which are currently priority areas—indicates that progress continues. The conclusion is unsatisfying but realistic: We cannot predict what future research will or will not accomplish.

While valid criticisms of any particular study and uncertainty about the future are endemic to the exercise, it is unlikely that a mistake large enough to reverse the findings of the body of RoR evidence has remained hidden for thirty years. Consequently, the agricultural economics profession has concluded that the returns to investments in agricultural TDD have been high and that additional investment is warranted.

AFRICA: PROBLEMS OR PROGRESS?

The relative paucity of African RoR studies, the somewhat lower RoRs found in the extant studies, the lack of a Green Revolution in Africa, and the poor aggregate performance of African agriculture in the 1970s and 1980s suggest the need for a more detailed examination of African agricultural TDD.

African agricultural research as we know it began in the 1890s with private investigations by colonial farmers in East Africa. Prior to independence, most publicly financed research was conducted at the request of colonial farmers or producers. These efforts had important impacts in high-potential areas dominated by white settlers or processors, but they had less impact in the lower potential areas accessible to most Africans. Following independence, much of the agricultural research agenda was redirected toward African smallholders.

The conventional perception of TDD in Africa is that little has been accomplished since independence. Anecdotal evidence in support of this proposition includes examples of the SR52 hybrid maize developed in Southern Rhodesia, which is still a top-yielding variety in southern African, and the Kitale synthetic varieties developed prior to Kenyan independence and used widely in East Africa. This perception, coupled with the difficulty of working under some African agroclimatic conditions and with continuing political instability in a number of countries, contributed to declines in USAID obligations for African agricultural TDD from $55 million in 1986 to $35 million in 1991. As a proportion of all USAID expenditures on African agriculture, this represents a decline of twenty percentage points, from 34 percent to 14 percent (Oehmke and Crawford 1993).

However, there was little hard evidence to support the conclusion that TDD had not had an impact. In 1990 only three ex-post studies on the rate of return to African TDD were available. Although all three indicated positive returns (Oehmke 1994), by and large there were no answers to questions such as what has happened to agricultural productivity, what is the trend in food production per agricultural laborer, and what have been the payoffs. To the contrary, rapid population growth and per capita food production figures masked important advances in productivity.

Since 1990 additional evidence on the success or failure of African TDD has been developed. The most telling pieces of evidence are the RoR studies, which show that returns to TDD have been positive and in excess of the opportunity cost of capital, indicating that the investment was worthwhile. High returns are found in different countries and for different commodities. The highest African rates of return are comparable to the highest found in other regions: Maize in Mali, potato in East Africa, and maize in Ghana each generate an RoR in excess of 90 percent. At the bottom end of the scale, negative returns are unique to Africa. In some cases the low returns are due to factors such as civil unrest outside the realm of TDD (Uganda) or possibly the youth of the TDD system.

Perhaps the youth of African NARS (national agricultural research systems) is their most salient feature. By way of comparison, between 1790 and 1858 nearly 2,000 agricultural patents were awarded in the United States; the current system of U.S. public agricultural research did not begin until 1855, with the creation of the first state agricultural college in anticipation of the Morrill Act; and U.S. agricultural research did not enter its mature phase until the 1930s (Huffman and Evenson 1992). Yet the high estimated RoRs to U.S. agricultural research analyze only the mature phase. Similarly,

The present state of development of research institutions in Asia and Latin America is the result of more than 20 to 25 years of continued support evolution [sic]. Most postcolonial African experiences are much more recent. Second, donor assistance in Asia and Latin America was channeled mostly into institution building programs; in

Africa the predominant trend has been to support individual projects, often directed at solving very specific problems rather than at creating new capacity. (Trigo 1985, 276)

In spite of the limited time and resources to build capacity and institutionalize programs to address the needs of smallholders, results have been impressive. With only a few exceptions, the returns to African TDD are slightly smaller but of the same general magnitude as the returns to U.S. research in its mature phase (for a summary of U. S. results see Echeverria 1990).

Additional studies show that smallholders have adopted new varieties of various crops tailored to particular agroclimatic conditions and farming needs, such as those with drought tolerance, improved grain quality, or short cycle to maturity. In sub-Saharan Africa, 35 to 50 percent of maize area is currently planted to improved varieties (Byerlee 1992). Improved maize varieties have been released and are being adopted in a number of African countries, with adoption rates up to 100 percent in Senegal, albeit on a small area. Byerlee presents evidence that over the 1966–1990 period, the number of varietal releases per maize breeder was higher in Africa than in Asia or Latin America.

While a number of examples are noteworthy, the RoR to maize TDD in Mali is higher than the highest published RoR found to investments in Green Revolution technology in Asia. The Mali Textile Development Company, the cotton parastatal, introduced into the cropping system a maize variety that had been identified prior to independence. This not only provided diversification but also increased the earnings potential of farmers. The parastatal's ability to provide inputs and market output, together with the farmers' previous experience using chemical fertilizers and animal traction to produce cotton, led to rapid adoption of the recommended maize package. The area planted to maize reached 90,000 hectares in 1991, so that it constitutes a niche crop within the cotton-based system. The rate of return to investments in the maize program was 135 percent (Boughton and de Frahan 1992). Recent activities have included almost no basic research, focusing instead on borrowing techniques and recommendations from surrounding NARS. This has proved a low-cost way to achieve impact.

Success is not limited to maize. In East Africa, the creation of a potato gene bank in 1978 facilitated the introduction of improved potato varieties resistant to wilt and blight. Over the past ten years, traditional varieties have been completely replaced (Ewell 1992). Because of improved sorghum varieties, sorghum, as a percent of total agricultural production, increased from 13 to 24 percent over the 1982–1991 period (Sanders 1993). Cotton yields in Cameroon increased by a factor of six over the past thirty years (Plucknett 1993). Cowpea varieties released since 1982 have been adopted on 100 percent of the cowpea area in the Guinean zone of Burkina Faso, 95 percent of the Sahelo-Sudanian zone of Burkina Faso, and 95 percent of north-central Mali (Sanders 1993). Additional examples of successful African agricultural TDD are found in Oehmke et al. (1997).

ISSUES OF RESOURCE ALLOCATION TO TDD

When is it appropriate to invest in agricultural TDD?

TDD is an integral component of economic growth and development, and its importance is not related to the income of a country. Investment in public sector agricultural research is required at all stages of development. Public research must change with development. "As the private sector develops, public research can shift their [sic] focus to poor people's problems and more basic research which supports private sector research" (Pray 1987, iii). Because TDD objectives and methods must be consistent with local agroclimatic and socioeconomic conditions, and because these change over time, the focus of TDD shifts as a country develops. At early stages of development, when market imperfections are larger, TDD has more aspects of a public good. In addition, TDD institutions may be underdeveloped and have little political support. At this stage, donors have a legitimate role in supporting institution building and encouraging local political support for TDD. Institution building per se requires investments in physical and human capital and in contractual arrangements attractive enough to retain trained scientists and support their scientific endeavors. Political support is usually earned through the development and diffusion of one or more improved techniques—and public awareness of the impact of these techniques. Africa currently needs this type of assistance.

As a country develops, the type of TDD and assistance changes. For example, as the food system develops, postharvest activities take on greater importance. This means that consumers become a more frequently targeted client group, and this expands the research agenda. At the same time, agriculture becomes more reliant on inputs developed outside the traditional agricultural sector (e.g., chemical fertilizers and mechanical implements). These two changes mean that the nonfarm private sector will become more involved in research and the use of research results developed by the public sector. The public sector may place greater emphasis on basic research adaptable by the private sector and on building linkages with and political support from private sector firms. Latin America and Asia appear to be at this stage of agricultural modernization, as does large-scale commercial agriculture in sub-Saharan Africa.

Are investments in TDD necessary for successful agricultural development?

Research. Agricultural development is a complex phenomenon, subject to a variety of different stimuli and forces. There is general agreement that agricultural TDD contributes significantly to the process:

Only when the constraints on growth imposed by the primary reliance on indigenous inputs—those produced primarily within the [agricultural] sector—are relieved by new factors whose productivity is augmented by the use of new technology is it possible for agriculture to become an efficient source of growth in a modernizing economy. (Ruttan 1982, 18)

Although there are isolated instances of development based on nonagricultural resources (Botswana, Singapore), countries with a large proportion of their natural resource base comprised of agricultural resources have not developed without transforming their agriculture through intensification and technical change. White (1990, 451) suggests that "agricultural research, in particular, is both critically important and chronically underfunded."

Extension. While no authors argue that extension is unimportant, it receives lower priority than research and education. For example, Umali (1992) does not include extension or transfer activities in her list of factors influencing the costs and returns to agricultural research. The nonnecessity of extension is illustrated in the Philippines by the widespread use of a rice variety developed, but never released, by the International Rice Research Institute (IRRI); there is anecdotal evidence that farmers apparently found a way to transfer this technology without the formal use of the extension system. While "extension will not have a high payoff unless the research effort has been successful" (Birkhaeuser et al. 1991, 611), comparable statements about payoffs to research or education were not found in the literature.

Regarding its extension programs, the World Bank notes that "weaknesses in the mechanisms for communication of research results to farmers were evident in all case studies, even in countries where the Bank supported national extension projects" (World Bank 1983, 33, ix). While some extension projects have had a significant impact in transferring technology and improving the agricultural sector, extension as it is practiced in most countries offers little to argue for its necessity to agricultural growth or rural development.

Extension services may have little to offer because research failed to develop relevant techniques, or because the extension system failed to recognize and transfer useful innovations. To address this possibility, a number of authors argue for institutional linkages between research and extension, including making them part of the same administrative unit (e.g., World Bank 1983). However, when this strategy has been implemented, it has not always been successful. Several sample projects were designed to be self-contained and disseminate their research results without the assistance of a separate extension service. In the Niger Cereals and Yemen Sorghum and Millet Improvement projects, this was identified as a serious project design error (World Bank 1983).

The case of maize in Kenya illustrates that research can be successful in the absence of strong extension and/or strong links with extension. Karanja (1996) estimated the rate of return to maize research in Kenya from 1955 to 1988 at 55 percent. The extension service contributed positively to this estimate. However, in the counterfactual case, when the extension system saw its effectiveness cut in half, Karanja estimated the rate of return to maize research at 47 percent, still relatively high, projecting research success even in the absence of effective extension.

There is significant evidence that extension can and has had positive impacts on adoption, production, and individual welfare in the agricultural sector. However, there is little evidence that extension is a necessary component of successful TDD, and there are scattered indications that TDD can be successful in the absence or in spite of extension. For example, the Birkaheuser et al. (1991) review includes studies indicating that extension has a negative impact on wheat production in North India (Evenson 1990), staple crops in Latin America (Evenson 1987) and rice on farms using chemicals in Thailand (Chou and Lau 1987). The conclusion is that effective extension is in many (but not all) cases a facilitating activity for research and the generation of impact from that research. In contrast, most authors consider research necessary for successful TDD and sustained agricultural growth.

Education. Arguments emphasizing the importance of education stem from the observation that "the capacity to develop and to manage technology in a manner consistent with a nation's physical and cultural endowments is the single most important variable accounting for differences in agricultural productivity among nations" (Ruttan 1982, 17). By implication, nations that want to increase agricultural productivity need the capacity to develop and manage improved technologies. NARS are usually expected to provide this capacity, based on the presumption that "an indigenous capacity to train agricultural scientists is a necessary requirement for satisfactory progress in agricultural development" (Johnston et al. 1987, 127). Similarly, an extraordinary variety of production patterns in constant evolution must be expected and, indeed, encouraged. This puts a high premium on flexible, market-oriented policies and on the development of indigenous innovative capacity (Picciotto 1985, 46).

Despite the premium placed on host country scientists, there is no statement in the literature that this is a necessary condition for technology development per se. Examples such as the success of cotton in West Africa would indicate otherwise. The question is whether technological development is sustainable in the absence of host country capacity.

Thus, research and education are important and seem to be more important than extension. Whether research or education comes first may not be critical. Although scientists play a crucial role in conducting TDD activities, in practice it is not always necessary or desirable to wait for host country institutions to provide a cadre of doctorates.

The Role of the Public Sector

When the private sector provides a less than socially optimal level of agricultural TDD services, the public sector may need to provide information or innovative techniques that benefit primarily consumers. In addition, the public sector often engages in price and market interventions to encourage adoption and use of new techniques.

Provision of information. Private sector, profit-seeking firms will provide information on agricultural techniques if they can get paid. However, "since the private sector provider of the information cannot exclude other potential users from free access to information provided to one user . . . [there is justification for] public sector involvement in information provision" (Birkhaeuser et al. 1991, p. 608). Similarly, when information generated by the research process has public good attributes and if social benefits are greater than private profits, then the profit-maximizing allocation of resources to research by a private firm will not be socially optimal (Echeverria and Thirtle 1991, 5).   Finally, agricultural TDD outputs "cannot often be patented and therefore the agricultural scientist captures only a very small portion of the benefits emerging from his work. This is why agricultural research tends to be a public sector activity." (Picciotto 1985, 47). The traditional remedy for this underinvestment by the private sector has been direct public sector investment in TDD activities and/or policy inducements to adopt improved techniques.

Provision of techniques that benefit primarily consumers. Many improved agricultural techniques reduce the costs of production. If output prices remain reasonably constant, then this reduction in costs will lead to an increase in farm profits. Under these circumstances, private sector, profit-seeking firms can charge farmers for improved techniques, since farmers can pay the fees from their increased farm profits. However, if the reduction in farm costs leads to or is accompanied by reduced output prices of comparable magnitude, the innovating firm will not be able to capture much of the gains from cost-reducing techniques. In this case, consumers will benefit from the price reduction, but farm profits will not increase, and farmers will not be able to pay substantial fees to the innovating firm. Theoretical and empirical evidence suggests that this latter type of price reduction is common (e.g., Hayami and Herdt 1977; Lindner and Jarrett 1978; Rose 1980). In many cases the benefits of the improved technique accrue primarily to consumers and cannot be captured by the innovating private firm:

The primary rationale for the public sector's involvement in agricultural research has been that in many areas incentives for private sector research have not been adequate to induce an optimum level of research investment—that the social rate of return exceeds the private rate of return because a large share of the gains from research are captured by other firms and consumers rather than by the innovating firm. (Ruttan 1982, 182).

Price and market interventions. Smale et al. (1992) contend that the adoption pattern of an improved input actually consists of three distinct decisions:

The first choice—adoption—is the decision to adopt or not to adopt the recommended variety and related practices, and in what combination. The second choice—extent of adoption—is how much land to allocate to the new and old techniques. The third choice—intensity of adoption—is the level per hectare, or rate of application of inputs such as fertilizer. (Smale et al. 1992, 14).

Consequently, a number of policy options are available to the public and/or private sector to affect one or more of these three choices, most notably output price subsidies or taxes, input subsidies, and government regulation of produce movement and marketing.

The evidence is incontrovertible that well-managed price incentives can stimulate the adoption and use of improved techniques and thereby increase output. It is much less clear that governments are able to manage properly the market interventions which they make, or that such interventions are financially sustainable. For example,

the role of many African governments in institutional innovation is entirely at odds with the interventionist scheme outlined above, and tends to give credence to the position of the Chicago School [let markets work]. In many cases, the public is disproportionately large, and little has been left to the market. Rather than attempting to assist in the development of market institutions, government policies have been antagonistic to private [TDD] activity and have stifled what existed. (Echeverria and Thirtle 1991, 11).

Apart from their often negative effect on TDD activities, such policy interventions have often been abandoned because they were not financially sustainable.

However, it is not clear that direct investment by a public sector, subject to political influences, will lead to the optimal level of TDD (Olson 1977). This is because "large gains to consumers as a group are, when divided among individual consumers, too small to induce sustained consumer support for production research" (Ruttan 1982, 258). Due to the nature of political support, this suggests that the public sector will underinvest in TDD. For example, in Africa an important problem with previous public sector research efforts was failure to realize that consumers are an important clientele group (Oehmke 1993b).

Endowed Foundations

The recent emergence of "private sector" foundations sheds further light on the roles of the public and private sector in TDD.

Latin America.   In the 1960s and 1970s, Latin American governments played the largest role in agricultural research.   Public sector research institutions, initially experiment stations oriented toward solving local agricultural problems, evolved into consolidated national systems attempting to achieve modest levels of autonomy.   Public sector funding for agricultural research increased throughout the 1960s and 1970s, although peak levels remained low.   In the 1980s increasing external debt and subsequent structural adjustment programs drastically reduced public funding for TDD.   Throughout this period USAID also reduced support of public sector research and began to place greater emphasis on private sector alternatives.   When United Brands shut down its long-term research station at La Lima, Honduras, USAID created a "private sector" foundation to run the station and conduct agricultural TDD (Sarles 1988).

As of 1988, seven agricultural research foundations were either funded or proposed by USAID in Latin America: Honduras, Jamaica, Peru, Dominican Republic, Ecuador, El Salvador, and Guatemala.   (This does not include the Agricultural College of the Humid Tropical Region, which started in 1985 and admitted its first class in 1990.) These foundations define themselves as private sector organizations, evidently because they usually have boards of directors from the private sector. But this is not necessarily a defining characteristic. For example, the Foundation for the Philippine Environment, one of the few foundations outside of Latin America, is controlled by NGOs (Weatherly and Warnken 1994).   Foundations rely heavily on scientists from public sector institutions who have either been released or incurred dramatically reduced salaries as a consequence of structural adjustment programs of the 1980s. Funding of the foundations is primarily from USAID.   The exception is the Agricultural Development Foundation in the Dominican Republic:

In the Dominican Republic, USAID encouraged members of the National Businessmen's Council to create the foundation and become its founding members. They were then responsible for establishing its bylaws, organizing it, *and* for helping to finance it. USAID, in fact, made the release of its own funding contingent on counterpart funds received from the private sector, and contributions actually came in at a much faster pace than expected.   This was the first, and so far the only, foundation that has actually required the private sector to come up with financing, not for specific services, but as part of the core budget of the organization. (Sarles 1988, 224)

Each of the foundations arose out of a unique opportunity, such as the availability of the United Brands research center, which led to the creation of FHIA (Fundacion Hondurea de Investigacion Agropecuaria) in Honduras, or the appropriation of ITT (International Telephone and Telegraph) assets in Chile, which led to the creation of Fundacion Chile. In each case, political support for continued research was strong. Weatherly and Warnken argue that in Latin America and the Caribbean, no two successful foundations look alike; each is its own unique model. The only apparent common characteristic is that the successful models are those that manifest a clear vision of purpose, and innovation and creativity in fulfilling that purpose. (Weatherly and Warnken 1994, 8)

It appears that these foundations are still attempting to establish a niche in the public to private continuum of research organizations. Their success rests on the answers to three important questions:

1. Can they provide better links to farmers than the traditional public sector organizations?
2. Can they improve collaboration among research, teaching, and extension?
3. Do they have the flexibility to respond to social needs in a timely fashion?

Africa. The current plight of African NARS has created interest in endowments as means of providing financial stability for TDD activities. Currently, USAID has created only two African endowments of any type: an environmental fund in Madagascar and a Tanzanian trust for orphans whose parents have died of AIDS (Weatherly and Warnken 1994). African endowments for agriculture have been proposed in Guinea (Conakry), Uganda, and Cameroon. "In agriculture, the primary issues to be addressed through endowments are the financial and institutional sustainability of the research and market development necessary to a healthy and growing agricultural sector" (Weatherly and Warnken 1994, 3). It is clear that African foundations will need to engage vigorously in fund raising activities. It is not clear if this will increase the overall level of TDD activity in the endowed foundation, or if it will free these foundations from the fluctuations of funding levels associated with a reliance on donors and national governments for annual operating budgets.

The Role of Other Agencies

Except for documents written by or for a particular agency, the literature often treats the amalgam of donors as a single actor. Money from U.S. sources is regarded as about the same as money from other countries, and when multilateral projects are reviewed, attribution to different funding sources is virtually impossible. The contribution of the amalgam of donor agencies is neatly summarized by Trigo (1985, 271–272):

Foreign assistance played a key role in facilitating [improved TDD in Latin America and Asia] in several important ways: first, by helping link the production and productivity problems with research and conceptualizing the need for institutional change; second, by providing foreign scientists and administrators to help identify appropriate institutional forms and adapt them to local needs; finally, by providing support for the implementation of the new structures. USAID, the Ford and Rockefeller Foundations, together with a number of American universities, participated actively in these processes.

A key element of the success of donor support to the Latin American and Asian programs was the explicit concern for local needs. In contrast, support to the African programs has generally been designed around donor needs and expertise with insufficient regard for national objectives. Until recently, USAID has been restricted by law or at least reluctant to work on cash crop production that might compete with U.S. agriculture. In addition, some donors emphasized the wrong crops in the wrong agroclimatic areas. That is, USAID might emphasize maize, or CIDA (Canadian International Development Authority) might emphasize wheat, in areas best suited for horticulture, floriculture, or other use. In Kenya, for example, donor programs encouraged wheat and maize farming on land previously used by the Masai for grazing, land that was probably incapable of sustaining intensive monocropping. The same was true with maize monocropping on low-potential lands in Zambia and Malawi. These programs needed to be more coincident with long-run national goals and objectives.

The smaller impact of foreign assistance in Africa is also attributed to the lack of local demand for research (until recently) and the fact that donor assistance focused on TDD projects to the neglect of TDD institutions (Trigo 1985). Despite this, the literature does not prescribe a particular institutional paradigm. Perhaps the most important lesson for institutional design is responsiveness to the needs of farmers and other participants in the agricultural sector. A wide range of institutional structures have succeeded in Latin America and Asia, supporting the idea that "there is no one best way to organize" (Trigo 1985, 275). In Africa, both agricultural institutions and programs tend to neglect local politics and needs (e.g., see Rukuni 1996).

The Role of the United States

Does the United States have a comparative advantage in TDD, and if so, where? The current enabling legislation for much of USAID's activities is derived from the "New Directions" of the 1973 Foreign Assistance Act, which calls for USAID to focus on "the poor majority (in particular, the rural poor) of developing countries" (Crawford 1982, 26). In agriculture, the poor majority usually means smallholders and often means those smallholders on the most fragile lands farthest from off-farm income-generating opportunities. In attempting to help the poor majority, USAID has a critical role to play.

First, this group is unlikely to be targeted by the private sector in technology development efforts. The poor have little money for purchasing improved inputs; they may not have enough land on which to use improved mechanical techniques profitably (or other techniques for which there are economies of scale); and they probably will not purchase large quantities of any input associated with a technique they do adopt. Under these circumstances, the private sector will have difficulty generating profits from this client group. Consequently, the public sector—especially USAID, with its mandate to assist the poor majority—has an important role to play in improving the welfare of this group of people.

Second, USAID has advantages over many other donor agencies in providing TDD services because of the U.S. land grant system. Four factors "explain success in producing significant and relevant research—support from US land grant universities, political and financial support, organizational incentives, and linkages with extension systems and farming communities" (White 1990, 664). Links between host country and U.S. land grant universities have been extremely important in developing the human capital necessary for successful TDD within developing countries. However, augmenting the institutional capacity for research and extension within the host country may be best achieved, not under the land grant paradigm, but under alternatives for integrating research, extension, and teaching (Hansen 1989).

Links with land grant universities have also given USAID a comparative advantage in the provision of basic research services. The private sector is more likely to engage in applied research, which is more directly linked with profits. NARSs, under pressure to generate impacts quickly, are also likely to focus more on applied research. Consequently, there may be underfunding of basic research. Empirical evidence from the United States suggests that basic research may be the most important contributor to economy-wide productivity increases (Adams 1990), and in agriculture it generates RoRs in excess of those generated by more applied research and extension (Huffman and Evenson, 1992). Basic research is the foundation on which the next generation of applied research depends, and so is a necessary component of any long-run research agenda. USAID is able to contract easily with U.S. universities, where much basic research is carried out, and could support research on those issues most likely to augment growth in developing countries.

The relevance of USAID's advantage in the provision of basic research has unclear implications, as the current call for land grant universities to make their research and other activities more relevant emphasizes private sector relationships, income generated from patents and prototypes, etc. to the neglect of basic research, which is incorrectly characterized as esoteric and interesting only to academicians. The empirical evidence in agriculture and every other sector of the economy unambiguously shows that basic research is fundamental to sustained productivity increases. USAID—which is both a key stakeholder utilizing land grant resources and a key supporter of land grant universities via financial and intellectual support—and other donors should argue vehemently against the current fad of deemphasizing basic research.

USAID has a critical comparative advantage in capacity building. This stems partly from its access to the land grant university system and partly from its ability to provide funding that is stable relative to host country funding. The development and improvement of TDD institutions is crucial to the continued success of research. In Africa, however, assistance is consistently characterized as program oriented, not institution oriented (e.g., Eicher 1988).

Finally, USAID has a comparative advantage in targeting its assistance because of its flexibility in supporting and funding a mix of different types of development organizations. For example, the poor majority are often located far away from central areas, and therefore are difficult to reach. However, "NGOs' flexibility in choosing their subject area, the sources of information on which to draw, the vehicle of communication, and their clientele give them a potentially important and independent role in information exchange" (Farrington and Biggs 1990, 483). To the extent that USAID funds NGOs and similar organizations, it can take advantage of their outreach capabilities and utilize their other unique advantages.

SUMMARY AND CONCLUSIONS

Agricultural TDD is an appropriate investment throughout the development process. Technical progress generated by TDD is an integral contributor to sustainable, broad-based agricultural growth. There are no recorded instances of successful agricultural development in the absence of TDD. While economic development is possible without agricultural development (e.g., Singapore), such a strategy is inappropriate or impossible for those developing countries which employ the bulk of their population in agriculture. Since most of the world's poor are employed in agriculture, the economics of the agricultural sector is of primary importance (Schultz 1980). Improving the welfare of people employed in agriculture requires innovative techniques and improvements in the quality of inputs—and the discovery and adoption of such techniques and inputs requires TDD. Research and education are particularly crucial components of TDD. Extension does not play as important a role in generating sustainable agricultural growth.

The rate of return to investments in agricultural TDD has been remarkably high across continents, countries, and commodities. A plethora of studies confirm these findings for Latin America, Asia, and the Near East. There are only a handful of studies for Africa, and none was found for the Newly Independent States. Although the African studies generally report that the bulk of agricultural research programs have been successful, exhibiting high rates of return, caution should be exercised in generalizing from the small number of studies. A number of methodological challenges have been posed in the three decades spanned by this literature, and the high returns are robust (that is, the general findings of high RoRs do not change meaningfully as new methods, etc. are implemented) to refinements and improvements in methods. This is indicative of *underinvestment* in agricultural TDD throughout most of the developing world.

The evidence is incontrovertible that well-managed price incentives can stimulate the adoption and use of improved techniques and thereby increase the rate of return to TDD. It is much less clear that governments are able to manage properly the market interventions they make, or that such interventions are financially sustainable. Financially unsustainable interventions can reduce the rate of return to TDD investments.

There are important roles for both the private and public sectors in agricultural TDD. Reliance on one sector exclusively will not maximize agricultural growth. The private sector is best suited to provide innovations for which farmers or other participants in the agricultural sector are willing to pay. The public sector is best suited to invest in those activities which are unlikely to generate profits, such as provision of information, investment in TDD institutions, and research leading to innovations that reduce the cost of food and agricultural products to consumers. In addition, there is a larger role for the public sector in the early stages of development, when markets and other institutions serving the private sector are underdeveloped.

Different agencies have advantages in providing different types of TDD services. USAID has an important advantage because of its flexibility to work with and provide funding to diverse development groups, including governments, NGOs, national and regional research institutes, and the private sector. USAID has a comparative advantage in research and education because of its relationship with U.S. land grant universities.

REFERENCES

Adams, James D. 1990. "Fundamental Stocks of Knowledge and Productivity Growth." Journal of Political Economy 98(4): 673–702.

Agency for International Development. "Malawi Agricultural Research and Extension Project Paper." Project No. 612-0215. Washington, D.C.: USAID.

Akino, M., and Y. Hayami. 1975. "Efficiency and Equity in Public Research: Rice Breeding in Japan's Economic Development." *American Journal of Agricultural Economics* 57: 1–10.

Ayer, H. W. 1970. "The Costs, Returns and Effects of Agricultural Research in São Paulo, Brazil." Ph.D. Dissertation, Purdue University.

Ayer, H. W., and G. E. Schuh. 1972. "Social Rates of Return and Other Aspects of Agricultural Research: The Case of Cotton Research in São Paulo Brazil." *American Journal of Agricultural Economics* 54: 557–69.

Barletta, N. Ardito. 1970. "Costs and Social Benefits of Agricultural Research in Mexico." Ph.D. Dissertation, Department of Economics, University of Chicago.

Birkhaeuser, Dean, Robert E. Evenson, and Gershon Feder. 1991. "The Economic Impact of Agricultural Extension: A Review." *Economic Development and Cultural Change* 39: 607–50.

Boughton, Duncan, and Bruno Henry de Frahan. 1992. "Agricultural Research Impact Assessment: The Case of Maize Technology Adoption in Southern Mali." Report for the Agency for International Development, Bureau for Africa. Washington, D.C.: USAID.

Byerlee, Derek. 1992. "Maize Research in Sub-Saharan Africa: An Overview of Past Impacts and Future Prospects." In *The Impact of Technology on Agricultural Transformation in Africa: Symposium Proceedings*, October 14–16, 1992. Washington, D.C, 1992.

Byrnes, Kerry J. 1990. "A Review of A.I.D. experience with Farming Systems Research and Extension Projects." A.I.D. Evaluation Special Study No. 67. Washington, D.C.: Center for Development Information and Evaluation, USAID.

Cheng, Leonard, and Elias Dinopoulos. 1992. "Stochastic Schumpterian Fluctuations." *American Economic Review* 82: 409–14.

Chou, E. C., and L. J. Lau. 1987. "Farmer Ability and Farm Productivity: A Study of Farm Households in the Chiangmai Valley Thailand, 1972–1978." World Bank Discussion Paper, Education and Training Series, Report no. EDT 49. Washington D.C.: World Bank.

Crawford, Paul R. 1982. "A.I.D. Experience in Agricultural Research: A Review of Project Evaluations." AID Program Evaluation Discussion Paper No. 13. Washington, D.C.: Bureau for Program and Policy Coordination, USAID.

Dalton, Timothy J., and William A. Masters. 1997. "Pasture Taxes and Agricultural Intensification in Southern Mali." Paper presented at the XXIII International Conference of Agricultural Economics, August 10–16, Sacramento, CA. West Lafayette, IN: Mimeo, Purdue University.

Davis, J. S. 1979. "Stability of the research production coefficient for U.S. agriculture." Ph.D. Dissertation, University of Minnesota.

Echeverria, Ruben G. 1990. "Assessing the Impact of Agricultural Research." Vols. 1 and 2. The Hague, the Netherlands: International Service for National Agricultural Research.

Echeverria, Ruben, and Colin Thirtle. 1991. "Potential Roles of Public and Private Sector Agricultural Research in Sub-Saharan Africa." The Hague, the Netherlands: International Service for National Agricultural Research.

Echeverria, Ruben G., and James F. Oehmke. 1990. "Sequential Evaluation of Agricultural Research." Staff Notes No. 90-83. The Hague, the Netherlands: International Service for National Agricultural Research.

Eicher, Carl K. 1988. "Sustainable Institutions for African Agricultural Development." The Hague, the Netherlands: International Service for National Agricultural Research.

Eicher, Carl K., and John A. Staatz, eds. 1984. *Agricultural Development in the Third World*. Baltimore, Md.: Johns Hopkins University Press.

Evenson, Robert E. 1967. "The Contribution of Agricultural Research to Production." *Journal of Farm Economics*, 49: 1415–25.

———. 1978. "A Century of Productivity Change in U.S. Agriculture: An Analysis of the Role of Invention, Research, and Extension." Economic Growth Center, Discussion Paper 296. New Haven, Conn.: Yale University.

———. 1984. "Developing Appropriate Agricultural Technology." In *Agricultural Development in the Third World*, ed. Carl K. Eicher and John A. Staatz. Baltimore, Md.: Johns Hopkins University Press.

———. 1987. "The International Agricultural Research Centers: Their Impact on Spending for National Agricultural Research and Extension." Study Paper No. 22. Washington, D.C.: Consultative Group on International Agricultural Research.

————. 1990. "Research, HYVs, Output Supply and Variable Factor Productivity in North Indian Agriculture." In *Research, Productivity, and Incomes in Asian Agriculture*, ed. R. E. Evenson and C. Pray. Ithaca, N.Y.: Cornell University Press.

Evenson, Robert E., and D. Jha. 1973. "The Contribution of Agricultural Research Systems to Agricultural Production in India." *Indian Journal of Agricultural Economics* 28: 212–30.

Evenson, Robert E., P. E. Waggoner, and Vernon W. Ruttan. 1979. "Economic Benefits From Research: An Example from Agriculture." *Science* 205: 1101–1107.

Evenson, Robert E., and Yoav Kislev. 1975. *Agricultural Research and Productivity*. New Haven, Conn.: Yale University Press.

Ewell, Peter. 1992. *The PRAPACE Network: CIP-NARS Collaboration for Sustainable Agricultural Production in Africa*. Nairobi: International Potato Center.

Farrington, John and Stephen D. Biggs. 1990. "NGOs, Agricultural Technology, and the Rural Poor." *Food Policy*, 15 (6): 479–91.

Gittinger, J. Price. 1984. *Economic Analysis of Agricultural Projects*. Baltimore, Md.: Johns Hopkins University Press for the Economic Development Institute of the World Bank.

Griliches, Zvi. 1958. "Research Costs and Social Returns: Hybrid Corn and Related Innovations." *Journal of Political Economy* 66: 419–431.

Hansen, Gary E. 1989. "The Impact of Investments in Agricultural Higher Education." A.I.D. Evaluation Highlights No. 5. Washington, D.C.: Center for Development Information and Evaluation, USAID.

Hayami, Yujiro, and Robert W. Herdt. 1977. "Market Price Effects of Technological Change on Income Distribution in Semisubsistence Agriculture." *American Journal of Agricultural Economics* 59: 245–56.

Howard, Julie A., George M. Chitalu, and Sylvester M. Kalonge. 1994. "The Impact of Investments in Maize Research and Dissemination in Zambia: Part I: Main Report." International Development Working Paper 39(1). East Lansing, MI: Department of Agricultural Economics, Michigan State University.

Huffman, Wallace, and Robert Evenson. 1993. *Science for Agriculture*. Ames, IA: Iowa State University Press.

International Service for National Agricultural Research. 1992. "Management of Scientific Information for Agricultural Research in Small Countries." ISNAR Study Paper #8. The Hague: International Service for National Agricultural Research.

Jiggins, Janice. 1986. "Gender-Related Impacts and the Work of the International Agricultural Research Centers." CGIAR Study Paper No. 17. Washington, D.C.: World Bank.

Johnston, Bruce F., Allan Hoben, Dirk Dijkerman, and William K Jaeger. 1987. "An Assessment of A.I.D. Activities To Promote Agricultural and Rural Development in Sub-Saharan Africa." A.I.D. Evaluation Special Study No. 54. Washington, D.C.: Center for Development Information and Evaluation, USAID.

Karanja, Daniel D. 1996. "An Economic and Institutional Analysis of Maize Research in Kenya." International Development Working Paper No. 57. East Lansing, MI: Michigan State University, Department of Agricultural Economics and Department of Economics.

Kydd, J. 1989. "Maize Research in Malawi: Lessons from Failure." *Journal of International Development* 1: 112–44.

Laker-Ojok, Rita. 1994. Forthcoming in "The Rate of Return to Agricultural Research in Uganda: The Case of Oilseeds and Maize." International Development Working Paper 42. East Lansing, MI: Department of Agricultural Economics, Michigan State University.

Lindner, Robert K., and F. G. Jarrett. 1978. "Supply Shifts and the Size of Research Benefits." *American Journal of Agricultural Economics* 60: 48–56.

Makanda, David W., and James F. Oehmke. 1993. "Promise and Problem in the Development of Kenya's Wheat Agriculture." Staff Paper No. 93-33. East Lansing, MI: Department of Agricultural Economics, Michigan State University.

Masters, William A., Touba Bedingar, and James F. Oehmke. 1997. "The Impact of Agricultural Research in Africa: Aggregate and Case Study Evidence." Paper prepared for the 1997 meetings of the International Agricultural Economics Association. West Lafayette, IN: Mimeo, Purdue University.

Mazzucato, Valentina, and Samba Ly. 1994. "An Economic Analysis of Research and Technology Transfer of Millet, Sorghum and Cowpeas in Niger." East Lansing, MI: Michigan State University, Department of Agricultural Economics and Department of Economics, International Development Working Paper No. 40.

McDowell, George R., and David C. Wilcock. "Lessons from Institution Building Efforts in Africa: U.S. University Experiences Building Colleges of Agriculture." Washington, D.C.: Development Alternatives.

Mellor, John W. 1976. *The New Economics of Growth: A Strategy for India and the Developing World.* Ithaca, N.Y.: Cornell University Press.

Norton, George, and Geoff Davis. 1981. "Evaluating Returns to Agricultural Research: A Review." *American Journal of Agricultural Economics* 63: 685–699.

Oehmke, James F. 1993a. "Assessing the Impacts of Malawian Maize Research." International Development Working Paper. East Lansing, MI: Department of Agricultural Economics, Michigan State University.

———. 1993b. "Strategic Planning for African Agricultural Research." Presentation to the United States Agency for International Development, Bureau for Africa, September 30.

———. 1995. "Can Agricultural Technology Stimulate African Economic Growth?" Staff Paper 95-50. East Lansing, MI: Department of Agricultural Economics, Michigan State University.

———. 1994. "Achievements of African Agricultural Technology Development and Transfer." Staff Paper 94-33. East Lansing, MI: Department of Agricultural Economics, Michigan State University.

Oehmke, James F., P. Anandajayasekeram, and William A. Masters. 1997. "Agricultural Technology Development and Transfer in Africa: Impacts Achieved and Lessons Learned." Technical Paper. Productive Sector Growth and Environment Division/Office of Sustainable Development/Bureau for Africa/U.S. Agency for International Development.

Oehmke, James F., and Eric W. Crawford. 1993. "The Impact of Agricultural Technology in Sub-Saharan Africa: A Synthesis of Symposium Findings." Technical Paper 3. Washington, D.C.: Bureau for Africa, USAID.

Olson, Mancur. 1977. *The Logic of Collective Action: Public Goods and the Theory of Groups.* Cambridge: Harvard University Press.

Pardey, Phillip G., and Johannes Roseboom. 1989. *ISNAR Agricultural Research Indicators Series: A Global Data Base on National Agricultural Research Systems.* Cambridge, U.K.: Cambridge University Press.

Picciotto, Robert. 1985. "National Agricultural Research." *Finance and Development* 22: 45–48.

Plucknett, Donald L. 1993. "Science and Agricultural Transformation." IFPRI lecture, September 8. Washington, D.C.: International Food Policy Research Institute.

Pray, Carl E. 1987. "Private Sector Agricultural Research and Technology Transfer in LDCs: Report on Phase II." New Brunswick, N.J.: Department of Agricultural Economics, Rutgers University.

Psacharopoulos, G. 1985. "Returns to Education: A Further International Update and Implications." *Journal of Human Resources* 20: 583–604.

Rose, R. N. 1980. "Supply Shifts and Research Benefits: Comment." *American Journal of Agricultural Economics* 62: 834–837.

Rukuni, Mandivamba. 1996. "A Framework for Crafting Demand-Driven National Agricultural Research Institutions in Southern Africa." Staff Paper 96–97. East Lansing, MI: Department of Agricultural Economics, Michigan State University.

Ruttan, Vernon W. 1982. *Agricultural Research Policy*. Minneapolis: University of Minnesota Press.

Sahn, David E. and Jehan Arulpragasam. 1991. "Development through Dualism? Land Tenure, Policy, and Poverty in Malawi." Washington, D. C.: Cornell Food and Nutrition Policy Program.

Sanders, John H. 1993. "Economic Impact of the Commodity Research Networks of SAFGRAD." Unpublished mimeo. West Lafayette, Ind.: Purdue University.

Sarles, Margaret. 1988. "USAID's Experiment with the Private Sector in Agricultural Research in Latin America and the Caribbean." In Methods for Diagnosing Research Systems Constraints and Assessing the Impact of Agricultural Research: Proceedings of the ISNAR/Rutgers Agricultural Technology Management Workshop, July 6-8, 1988, Rutgers University, New Brunswick, New Jersey.

Schultz, Theodore W. 1953. *The Economic Organization of Agriculture*. New York: McGraw Hill.

———. 1980. "Nobel Lecture: The Economics of Being Poor." *Journal of Political Economy* 88: 639–51.

Schwartz, Lisa, James Sterns, and James Oehmke. 1993. "Economic Returns to Cowpea Research, Extension and Input Distribution in Senegal." *Agricultural Economics* 8: 161–171.

Smale, Melinda, and Paul W. Heisey. 1994. "Maize Research in Malawi Revisited: An Emerging Success Story?" *Journal of International Development*, forthcoming.

Smale, Melinda, Z., H. W. Kaunda, M.M.M.K. Mkandawire, M.N.S. Msowoya, D.J.E.K. Mwale, and P. W. Heisey. 1992. *"Chimanga Cha Makolo*, Hybrids and Composites: Farmers' Adoption of Maize Technology in Malawi, 1989–90." CIMMYT Farming Systems Bulletin, Eastern and Southern Africa, No. 11. Lilongwe, Malawi: CIMMYT.

Staatz, John A. 1992. "What Is Agricultural Transformation?" *The Impact of Technology on Agricultural Transformation in Africa: Symposium Proceedings*, October 14–16. Washington, D. C.: Department of Agricultural Economics, Michigan State University.

Sterns, James A., and Richard H. Bernsten. 1994. "Assessing the Impact of Cowpea and Sorghum Research and Extension in Northern Cameroon." International Development Working Paper 43. East Lansing, MI: Department of Agricultural Economics and Department of Economics, Michigan State University.

Sterns, James A., and James F. Oehmke. 1993. "Assessing Returns to Research: Implications for Subsaharan Africa." Staff Paper 92-43. East Lansing, MI: Department of Agricultural Economics, Michigan State University.

Tang, A. 1963. "Research and Education in Japanese Agricultural Development." *Economic Studies Quarterly* 13: 27–41.

Trigo, Eduardo. 1985. "Agricultural Research Organization in the Developing World: Diversity and Evolution. In *Agricultural Research Policy*, Carl E. Pray and Vernon W. Ruttan, eds. Minneapolis, MN: University of Minnesota Press.

Umali, Dina L. 1992. "Public and Private Sector Roles in Agricultural Research." World Bank Discussion Paper No. 176. Washington, D. C.: World Bank.

Weatherly, Paul, and Philip Warnken. 1994. "Programming Agricultural and Environmental Endowments and Foundations in Africa: Lessons from Latin America." Report for the Agency for International Development, Bureau for Africa, January 7. Washington, D. C.: USAID.

White, Louise G. 1990. "Increasing the Relevance of Agricultural Research: Institution Building in Third World Universities." *Journal of Developing Areas* 24: 451–66.

World Bank. 1983. "Strengthening Agricultural Research and Extension: The World Bank Experience." Operations Evaluations Department. Report No. 4684. Washington, D. C.: World Bank.

ANNEX TO CHAPTER 3

Summary of *Ex Post* Rate of Return (RoR) Studies for Agricultural TDD

Author(s) and Date of Study	Commodity, Location and Years Covered	RoR (%)	Comments
Asia and the Near East			
Tang 1963	Japan aggregate, 1880–1938	35	Econometric methods.
Evenson and Jha 1973	India, aggregate 1953–71	40	Includes extension and the interaction between research and extension.
Mohan and Evenson 1975	India, aggregate 1937–42 1947-57 1957-62 1967-72	50 51 49 34	Econometric methods.
Akino and Hayami 1975	Japan, rice, 1915–50 1931–60	25–27 73–75	Economic surplus. Before assigned Exp. Sta. After assigned Exp. Sta. Each analysis considers open and closed economies.
Pee 1977	Malaysia, rubber, 1932-72	24	Economic surplus.
Kahlon et al. 1977	India (four states), aggregate 1960–73 1956–73	63 14–64	Econometric methods. States are A. Pradesh, Bihar, Maharastra, and Punjab.
Evenson and Flores 1978	Asia, rice, 1950–65 (national) 1966–75 (int'l)	32–39 73–78 74–102	Econometric methods.
Flores et al. 1978	Philippines, rice, 1966–75	75	Econometric methods. RoR of 46-71% for the tropics.
Pray 1978	Punjab, aggregate British India, 1906–56 Pakistan, 1948–63	33-44 23-37	Economic surplus. Includes extension. Includes extension.
Pray 1980	Bangladesh, wheat and rice, 1961–77	30–35	Economic surplus.
Nagy 1981	Pakistan, maize, 1967–81	19	Economic surplus. Includes extension.
Nagy 1983	Pakistan, wheat, 1967–81	58	Economic surplus.

Asia and the Near East (cont.)

Pudasaini 1983	Nepal, aggregate, 1979–80	N.A.	Estimate of returns to extension, no significant results.
Salmon 1984	Indonesia, Rice, 1965–77	133	Econometric.
Nagy 1985	Pakistan, aggregate, 1959–79	64	Econometric. Includes extension.
Khan and Akbari 1986	Pakistan, aggregate, 1955–81	36	Econometric. Includes extension.
Unnevehr 1986	S.E. Asia, rice, 1983–84	61	Economic surplus. Examines quality improvement.
Librero and Perez 1987	Philippines, maize, 1956–83	27–48 27–43	Economic surplus, no ext. Includes extension.
Evenson 1987	India, aggregate, 1959–1975	100	Econometric.
Pray and Ahmed 1990	Bangladesh, aggregate, 1948–81	100	Economic surplus.

Latin America

Barletta 1970	Mexico Wheat, 1943–63 Maize, 1943–63	90 35	Economic surplus for wheat, some econometric methods used in the document.
Ayer 1970	Brazil, Cotton 1924–67	77	Economic surplus method.
Elias 1971 (revised by Cordomi 1989)	Argentina, Sugarcane, 1943–63 (EEAT-Tucuman)	33–49	Econometric. Includes extension.
Ayer and Schuh 1972	Brazil, Cotton 1924–85	80–100	
Hines 1972	Peru, Maize, 1954–1967	35–40 50–55	Includes cultivation.
Patrick and Kehrberg 1973	Brazil, eastern, Aggregate, 1968		Econometric methods show non-significant returns to extension.
Monteiro 1975	Brazil Cocoa 1923–74 1958–74 1958–85 1923–85	16–18 60–79 61–79 19–20	Economic surplus method.

Latin America (cont.)

del Rey 1975 (revised by Cordomi 1989)	Argentina, Sugarcane, 1943–64 (EEAT-Tucuman)	35–41	Econometric method, includes extension.
Hertford et al. 1977	Columbia		
	Rice, 1957-72	60–82	
	Soybeans, 1960-71	79–96	
	Wheat, 1953-72	11–12	
	Cotton, 1953-72	0	
Wennergren and Whittaker 1977	Bolivia		
	Sheep, 1966–75	44	
	Wheat, 1966–75	48	
M. Scobie and T. R. Posada 1978	Colombia, Rice, 1957–64	75-96	Economic surplus.
Avila 1981	Brazil, São Paulo		Index number methods.
	Citrus, 1933–85	18–28	Includes ext. costs.
	R.G. Sul		
	Irr. Rice 1959–78	83–114	Includes ext. costs.
	Irr. Rice 1959–78	87–119	
	Irr. Rice 1959–78	107	
	Irr. Rice 1959–78	96	Includes ext. costs.
	Central		
	Irr. Rice 1959–78	87	
	Irr. Rice 1959–78	83	Includes ext. costs.
	N. Coast		
	Irr. Rice 1959–78	107	
	Irr. Rice 1959–78	92	Includes ext. costs.
	S. Coast		
	Irr. Rice 1959–78	115	
	Irr. Rice 1959–78	111	Includes ext. costs.
	Frontier		
	Irr. Rice 1959–78	119	
	Irr. Rice 1959–78	114	Includes ext. costs.
Cruz et al. 1982	Brazil, 1974–81, Physical Capital	53	Economic surplus method.
Evenson 1982	Brazil, 19??–1974, Aggregate	69	Index number method.
Yrarrazaval et al. 1982	Chile		
	Wheat, 1949–77	21–28	Economic surplus
	Maize, 1940–77	32–34	method.
E. R. da Cruz and A.F.D. Avial 1983	Brazil (EMBRAPA), 1977–82	20	Economic surplus evaluation of and EMBRAPA-IBRD project).

Latin America (cont.)

Martinez and Sain 1983	Panama (IDIAP-Caisan), Maize, 1979–82	188–332	Economic surplus method applied to on-farm research.
Ambrosi and Cruz 1984	Brazil, Wheat, 1974–1982		Economic surplus method. Includes investments in physical capital.
	EMBRAPA-CNPT	59	
	EMBRAPA-CNPT	40	
Feijoo 1984 (revised by Cordomi 1989)	Argentina (INTA), Aggregate, 1950–1980	41	Econometric. Includes extension.
Pinazza et al. 1984	Brazil (São Paulo), Sugarcane, 1972–82	35	Economic surplus.
Roessing 1984	Brazil (EMBRAPA-CNPS), Soybeans, 1975–82	45–62	Economic surplus.
Silva 1984	Brazil (São Paulo), Aggregate	60–102	Econometric. Includes extension.
Ayres 1985	Brazil, Soybeans,		Economic surplus method.
	Aggregate, 1955–83	46–49	
	Parana, 1955–83	51	
	R.G. Sul, 1955–83	51–53	
	S. Catarina, 1955–83	29–31	
	São Paulo, 1955–83	23–24	
Echeverria et al. 1988	Uruguay, Rice, 1965–85	52	Economic surplus. Includes extension and private research.
Evenson 1988	Paraguay, Crops, 1988	75–90	Econometric estimate of marginal rate of return to investment in extension.
Romano 1988	Colombia, Aggregate, 1960–82	50	Econometric.
Evenson and da Cruz 1989	South America (PROCISUR), 1979–88,		Measures the impact of a research network among the following countries: Argentina, Bolivia, Brazil, Chile, Paraguay and Uruguay.
	Wheat	110	
	Soybeans	179	
	Maize	191	

Africa

Abidogun 1982	Cocoa, Nigeria	42	
Makau 1984	Kenya, 1922–80, Wheat	33	
Evenson 1987	Africa, Maize and Staple Crops	30–40	Aggregate RoRs by region.

Africa (cont.)

Karanja 1990	Kenya, 1955–88, Maize	40–60	RoR to research via statistical methods of attributing impact.
Mazzucato 1991	Kenya, 1978, Maize	58–60	Using Karanja data, finds minimal effect of fertilizer policy on RoR.
Mazzucato and Ly 1992	Niger, 1975–91, Cowpea, Millet and Sorghum	< 0	
Laker-Ojok 1994	Uganda, 1985–91, Sunflower, Cowpea, Soybean	< 0	Six-year study period used due to civil unrest in previous 15 years.
Boughton and de Frahan 1982	Mali, Maize, 1969–1990	135	Introduction of maize into cotton system by CMDT.
Ewell 1992	East Africa, Potato, 1978–91	91	Regional network/NARS collaboration.
Sterns and Bernsten 1992	Cameroon, Cowpea, 1979–1991 Sorghum, 1979–91	3 <0	RoR to research and extension.
Howard, Chitalu and Kalonge 1993	Zambia, Maize, 1978–91	84–87	RoR to research, extension and seed distribution.
Schwartz, Sterns and Oehmke 1993	Senegal, Cowpea, 1980–85	31–92	RoR to research-based famine relief includes all aspects of TDD.
Sanders 1993	Ghana, Maize, 1982–92	74	Starting date determined by initiation of SAFGRAD program.
Smale and Heisey 1994	Malawi, maize, 1957–92	4–7	Improved research performance since 1985.

Sources: For sources of references, see James F. Oehmke, "Issues of Agricultural Technology Development and Diffusion," a manuscript prepared for USAID, Washington, D.C. and Development Alternatives, Baltimore, Md. (1994) available from the author upon request.

4

Issues of Infrastructural Development

Raisuddin Ahmed and Cynthia Donovan

INTRODUCTION[1]

Economists have long been working to discover why some countries move ahead fast, while others lag behind on the path of economic development. The role of infrastructural factors in economic development either remains to be fully unfolded or has been unraveled with a considerable degree of ambiguity. The objective of this chapter is to scan the literature on infrastructure in order to establish the state of knowledge on the subject. However, this literature review is limited to issues concerning developing countries in general, and rural infrastructure in particular. An excellent review of literature on issues of infrastructural development in developed countries, particularly the United States, has been made by Gramlich (1994).

The review of literature indicates that the state of statistics on infrastructural endowment is very poor and systematic empirical research on the impact of infrastructure is rare. Available literature demonstrates that theoretical articulation of the role of infrastructure in economic development is modest, empirical validation of these theoretical works is very thin, and impact of infrastructure on economic activities is robust. To organize this review, the literature is classified into four groups: (1) definitional issues, (2) identification and measurement of effects, (3) methods of measurement of effects, and (4) public policy for infrastructural development.

WHAT IS INFRASTRUCTURE?

The term *infrastructure* evolved during World War II by military strategists to indicate wide-ranging elements of war logistics. Thereafter, economists introduced the term into the literature of development economics to be used interchangeably with "overhead capital" (Youngson 1967). *Infrastructure* became a popular word, often used loosely. Distinctions such as *social infrastructure, economic infrastructure, hard infrastructure, soft infrastructure, physical infrastructure,* and *institutional infrastructure* were being made in order to emphasize a particular aspect of the many attributes that the word *infrastructure* now represented.

But a common definition is essential for understanding and resolving issues related to research and the public sector role in development of infrastructure. This common thread was sought in the definition of *public goods* because infrastructural development essentially means creation of public capital goods. Such capital goods carry the distinction of producing external economies (technological and pecuniary) and social benefits different from private benefits. That is, the consumption by one individual of services provided by these public goods does not prevent consumption by another individual (Samuelson 1954). Because of this characteristic of joint consumption, individual preferences for such goods are hard to ascertain. On the supply side, production of public goods is not necessarily free or costless. But the marginal cost of having an additional individual consume the good, once produced, is zero. No private firm would produce a public good because charging the marginal cost would result in no revenues; yet charging any other price would not be possible because individuals would always want someone else to pay. Provision of the public good would not occur, and all would be worse off. This is the theoretical basis for public goods being considered the domain of the public sector.

There is a distinction between pure public goods and impure public goods in the sense that some phases or aspects of a public good may not fully meet the tests of the definition posited previously. Because of this question of degree of purity in the attributes of public goods, some scope for judgment and pragmatism persists in decisions on public investments and infrastructure. Youngson (1967) attempted to make the definition of *infrastructure* relatively simple by emphasizing that infrastructure is not a set of things but a set of attributes. Some or all or none of these attributes may reside in a capital asset. To the degree that an asset possesses the attributes, it could be regarded as infrastructure. Two such attributes, both of which accord with the notions enunciated by Rosenstein-Rodan (1943) and Nurske (1953), can be recognized. Capital can be viewed as infrastructure to the extent that (1) it is a source of external economies, and (2) it is provided in large units, ahead of demand.

The 1950s and the 1960s witnessed a surge of attempts in development economics to specify further the contents of infrastructure or overhead capital, as it was termed. Thus, Lewis (1955) includes public utilities, ports, water supplies, and electricity in the specification of infrastructure. Higgins (1959) includes transport, public utilities, schools, and hospitals. Hirschman (1958) lists law and order, education, public health, transportation, communications, power, water supply, irrigation, and drainage. He makes a distinction between a wider concept of social overhead capital, as listed previously, and a "hard core," which he limits to transport and power. Hirschman sets out four conditions for distinguishing "social overhead capital" from "directly productive activities": (1) The services provided by the activity are to facilitate, or in some sense are basic to, the carrying out of a wide variety of economic activities; (2) the services are provided in practically all countries by public agencies or by private agencies subject to public control and are provided free of charge or at rates publicly regulated; (3) the services cannot be imported; and (4) the investment needed to provide the services is characterized by "lumpiness." *Lumpiness* means that large investments, rather than small incremental investments, are needed to provide the service due to technical indivisibilities. With increasing recognition of the role of agriculture in economic development, the literature of the 1960s reflects some added emphasis on agricultural research and extension, rural financial institutions, and irrigation and drainage (De Vries 1960; Ishikawa 1967; Nicholls 1963).

It is apparent from this short review of literature on the definition of *infrastructure* that the meaning of infrastructure is quite flexible. Depending on the degree of emphasis between agriculture and industry in the development strategy of a country, one could emphasize the elements that matter more for either rural or urban development. But whatever may be the emphasis on spatial dimensions, infrastructure creation requires public initiatives and provides the basic environment for the directly productive activities of individuals and groups in a society. Therefore, Hirschman's four conditions, presented earlier, are reasonably precise guidelines for deciding what is and what is not infrastructure.

STATE OF INFRASTRUCTURAL DEVELOPMENT

In spite of the recognized importance of infrastructure in development, information is sparse on the status of transport, energy, and communications infrastructure in developing countries. A brief look at the road statistics of the International Road Federation (1988) indicates the extent of this data problem, which is particularly acute in Africa. Even more of a problem than lack of data is the actual state of infrastructure in many developing countries and the decreasing resources dedicated to infrastructure maintenance and development. For African countries with available data, road densities range from 0.01 to 0.11 kilometers per square kilometer of land area; in Asia, those densities range from 0.35 to 0.41. Similarly, the percentage of roads that are paved is much smaller in Africa (10 percent) than in Asia (35 percent).

In spite of this state of backwardness, investment on infrastructure is declining. Central government expenditure on transport and communications as a percentage of total central government expenditure decreased during the 1978–1988 period in many African and Latin American countries and some countries of Asia. In 1978 spending on transport and communications averaged 11 percent of total government expenditure in the African countries for which data were available, but by 1988 that had decreased to 7 percent. For Latin American, the figures were 9 percent for 1978 and 7 percent for 1988 (IMF 1978; 1988). World Bank lending commitments show a decline in investment for construction over the last twenty years as well (World Bank, various years).

The lack of statistics on infrastructural endowment in developing countries motivated International Food Policy Research Institute (IFPRI) to conduct a short survey in countries where it had some field projects or special connections in Asia and Africa. The survey involved collection of data from public agencies that were responsible for creation, maintenance, or registration of infrastructure or for gathering statistical information as a routine activity. Results for only those countries that appeared amenable to some analysis are presented here. Before presenting the survey results, however, some background information on the selected countries—seven from Africa and five from Asia—relevant to the context of infrastructural development is presented in Table 4.1.

South Korea represents a newly developed country with a per capita income of U.S. $5,200. All other countries represent developing countries with per capita incomes ranging from U.S. $170 to U.S. $720. For the annual average public expenditures for transport and communication development (1985–1988), Table 4.1 shows that, on a per capita basis, this expenditure is similar in Asian and African countries. However, on the basis of cultivated land per hectare, the development expenditure for transport and communications in African countries is about half that in Asian countries. Public expenditures on this infrastructure as a percentage of GNP, however, are similar in the selected countries of the two continents. The low per hectare expenditure on infrastructure in Africa signifies the limited access of the peasant sector to infrastructure. African agriculture is extremely dualistic (with both estate farms and peasant farms), compared with relatively homogeneous systems of farming in Asia. It is well known that the estate sector has a greater chance of attracting public investment on infrastructure than the peasant sector. Therefore, even though the per capita expenditure or the share of GNP spent on infrastructure is the same, the peasant sector of Africa has much more restricted access to infrastructure than does the peasant sector of Asia.

Turning to the survey results, all African countries except Zimbabwe have from 0.15 to 0.44 miles of paved road and rail line infrastructure per 1,000 persons (Table 4.2). With the exception of Bangladesh, the comparable mileage is 0.58 to 1.65 per 1,000 persons in Asia. The exceptions arise from unusually high population density in Bangladesh and the relatively higher status of road and railway development in Zimbabwe. The second indicator—road and railway mileage per 1,000 hectares of cultivated land—again indicates that the extent of transport and communication infrastructure in African countries is about one-third of that in Asian countries. Of course, roads do not matter if there are no vehicles to ply the road: Asian roads have almost four times the vehicle density of African roads. The African transport sector is often plagued by import constraints (arising from scarcity of foreign exchange and import controls) and domestic controls in the transportation industry (Badiane 1992; Gabre-Madhin 1991).

Table 4.1.
Expenditure on Transport and Communications Infrastructure in Selected Asian and African Countries, 1989

Region/ Country	Per Capita Income (U.S. $)	Expenditure (U.S. $ million)	1989 Population (million)	Cultivated Land, 1989 (1,000 hectares)	Expenditure per Capita (U.S. $)	Expenditure per Hectare (U.S. $)	Expenditure as Percent of GNP (percent)
Africa							
Benin	310	14	4.5	2,250	3.1	6.2	1.0
Kenya	350	103	22.5	6,100	4.6	16.9	1.3
Malawi	190	50	8.0	1,450	6.3	34.5	3.3
Senegal	520	27	7.0	5,200	3.9	5.2	0.7
Tanzania	170	110	24.7	40,260	4.5	2.7	2.6
Togo	280	20	3.4	990	5.9	20.2	2.1
Zimbabwe	620	175	9.3	2,460	18.8	71.1	3.0
Asia							
Bangladesh	190	260	110	9,760	2.4	26.6	1.3
India	340	3,600	824	156,100	4.4	23.1	1.3
Pakistan	370	780	106	20,900	7.4	37.3	2.0
Philippines	720	650	60	13,400	10.8	48.5	1.5
South Korea	5,200	800	42	2,140	19.0	373.8	0.4

Note: Per capita income is an average of 1988 and 1989. Expenditure refers to public expenditures on transport and communications, based on the average of 1985 through 1988.

Sources: Compiled from IMF (International Monetary Fund), *Government Statistics Yearbook* (Washington, D.C.: IMF, various years 1978–1988); IMF, *International Financial Statistics* (Washington, D.C.: IMF, 1991); FAO (Food and Agriculture Organization of the United Nations) *Production Yearbook* (Rome: FAO, 1990).

The proportion of villages supplied with electricity is also very small in Africa; only 3 to 5 percent of villages in some countries have any electrification (Table 4.2). In contrast, in Asian countries roughly 50 percent of the villages have electricity. Bangladesh again appears to be an exception, even though the proportion of villages electrified in this poor Asian country is double that of Zimbabwe. In number of telephones per 1,000 persons, Asian countries again appear to be ahead of Africa. What electricity and telephone facilities are available in African countries are mostly limited to urban areas, thus reinforcing the urban-rural dichotomy of countries in that continent. The prevalence of primary schools, measured by the number of schools per 1,000 persons, does not appear to differ as widely between Asia and Africa as other infrastructure.

Table 4.2.
Selected Indicators of Infrastructure in Asia and Africa, 1990

Region/ Country	Total Mileage Road/ Rails	Miles/ 1,000 Persons	Miles/ 1,000 Ha. Cult.	Mech. Vehicles/ Mile Road	Prop. Villages Elec. (%)	Prim. Sch./ 1,000 Persons	Tel./ 1,000 Persons
Africa							
Benin	800	0.17	0.36	9.0	n.a.	0.60	0.38
Kenya	6,622	0.30	1.09	19.2	3	0.38	15.06
Malawi	2,252	0.28	1.55	17.0	n.a.	0.33	5.86
Senegal	3,067	0.44	0.60	12.2	4	0.31	5.01
Tanzania	3,635	0.15	0.09	14.2	n.a.	0.41	5.46
Togo	1,248	0.37	1.26	13.5	3	0.70	5.73
Zimbabwe	10,117	1.09	4.11	35.7	5	0.50	31.55
Asia							
Bangladesh	7,278	0.07	0.75	47.5	17	0.40	2.71
India	559,375	0.68	3.58	49.0	61	0.66	5.75
Pakistan	77,469	0.73	3.71	42.5	62	0.86	8.26
Philippines	98,908	1.65	7.38	51.8	52	0.56	15.43
South Korea	24,425	1.58	11.41	67.2	87	0.65	267.61

Note: n.a. means not available. Survey data were collected for 1990 or most recent year for which data were available.

Source: Estimated from unpublished IFPRI survey data.

These statistics of infrastructural endowment indicate that development of rural infrastructure has been primarily demand driven in most developing countries. Conscious creation of excess capacity that would stimulate economic activity in productive sectors has not been adopted as a strategy of rural development.

THEORETICAL CONCERNS ABOUT THE IMPACT OF INFRASTRUCTURE

On a theoretical plane, economists have used deductive logic to formulate hypotheses on the possible effects of the creation of infrastructure. Development of these hypotheses is based on the premise that creation of infrastructure generates external economies—widespread benefits. Then logic is applied to indicate the extent of this externality and to provide a framework to measure the directions and the net effect. The empirical problem of measurement of externalities is not a concern at this stage of theoretical development. Moreover, for the sake of convenience in theoretical abstraction, multidimensional problems are often reduced to two dimensions. Figure 4.1 shows how traditional theory conceptualizes the effects of infrastructural development on production for a competitive market economy. In a situation of inadequately developed infrastructure, firms or farms are confronted with higher marginal cost (MC1) at every level of production, and given the market price of their output, produce at Q1. With an improvement in infrastructure, the marginal cost curve shifts downward to the right (MC2), resulting in a total cost savings of area abcd for the earlier level of output, Q1, and an increase in output from Q1 to Q2.

This is a simple abstraction with a profound conclusion. An increase in the complexity of this relation, by assuming different demand and cost functions and aggregation problems and other modifications, will not alter the central message of this construct: that infrastructural changes can affect the relationships of the production function.

The construct is indeed an extreme simplification. It does not say anything about how these effects are realized, how adjustments are made, and what time dimension is involved. The cost reduction occurs through the interaction of infrastructure with directly productive inputs of firms and farms. This may, however, come about in a variety of ways, such as reduction in transaction costs, improved diffusion of technology, new combinations of output and inputs, better input prices, increased specialization and commercialization, and improved entrepreneurial capacity, all realized through infrastructural investment.

Moreover, the construct does not say anything about social developments, which may produce effects outside the production activities of a society. For example, effects on consumption patterns, family planning, and health could be equally significant. Negative effects may also occur, as with possible undesirable environmental effects. Additional considerations include the technology involved in construction and maintenance and the effects on wage relationships, incomes,

Figure 4.1.
Infrastructure Provision and the Efficiency of Production

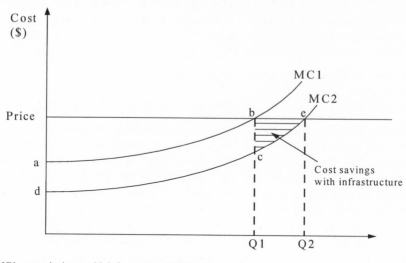

MC1 = marginal cost with infrastructure deficiencies
MC2 = marginal cost with adequate infrastructure
Source: Lakshmanan 1992.

and consumption in the short and long terms. Empirical analysis of infrastructure, therefore, has to proceed with open eyes and perceptive minds.

Due to the complexity of the functions of infrastructure and the indirect nature of its effects, development economists have not been as emphatic about infrastructure as about directly productive activities in agriculture and industries. Most models of development and numerous discrete studies of growth have come up with explanations of growth and development that imply a strategic but often hidden role for infrastructure. This is particularly true for models that give a special role to agriculture. Thus, Von Thünen's attempt to explain geographic variations in the intensity of farming systems and productivity of labor in an industrial country focused on urban-industrial pull and the critical role of transport and communication systems in the strength of that pull (Von Thünen [1842] 1966). The pull of urban and rural growth centers as foci of development on the rest of the economy also depends on physical linkages through transport and communication.

The "frontier model," which explains rapid agricultural growth in North and South America and Australia by the opening up of new land, has transportation and communication infrastructure as its central foundation (Ruttan 1984). Similarly, the "diffusion model," which formulates the process of technological spread in agriculture as a source of dramatic growth in agricultural production, critically depends on physical and institutional infrastructure (Ruttan 1984). Mellor's (1976) outline for the future economic development of India places infrastructural development as one of the top priorities. Mellor indicates that infrastructure plays a strategic role in producing large multiplier effects in the economy with agricultural growth. As agricultural incomes grow, consumption expenditures increase in rural areas, creating increased demand for urban goods—the multiplier effect. Hirschman's (1958) model of growth was specifically on the theme of strategic imbalance between social overhead capital and directly productive capital. The central message of this model will be considered in a later section of this chapter.

EMPIRICAL STUDIES ON THE IMPACT OF INFRASTRUCTURE

Empirical studies on the effects of infrastructural development can be classified into three broad groups: (1) systematic research, based on primary data of specific locations, which attempts to use rigorous methods for measuring impact; (2) appraisal, evaluation, and assessment of infrastructural projects by international multilateral agencies, particularly the World Bank and bilateral donor agencies such as the USAID; and (3) books, articles, and papers based on secondary information, sometimes drawing on information from groups (1) and (2) but often based on deductive logic. Research studies (category 1) are not common, due to the high costs of cross-sectional and time-series data collection and the difficulties entailed in measurement. Appraisal and evaluation reports (category 2) are generally, but not always, the outcome of mission reports completed hurriedly by groups of professionals. Books, articles, and papers (category 3) generally meet their information needs from diverse sources.

Research Studies

Empirical studies on the effects of infrastructure on production have been conducted since the 1950s, first using cross-sectional analyses of secondary data in the estimation of the aggregate agricultural production function and recently using profit functions based on duality theory. Most often, attention is on a specific type of infrastructure, particularly transport and electricity, along with other production inputs.

Aggregate Production Studies

Antle's (1983) cross-sectional study of forty-seven less developed countries is representative of such studies. It finds a strong positive relationship between infrastructure and aggregate agricultural productivity.

Antle specified a Cobb-Douglas production function model, in which the productivity level was a function of physical inputs, education, research, and infrastructure variables. Across the total sample of sixty-six countries, the infrastructure variable had a "large, precisely estimated coefficient. This provides strong support for the hypothesis that the transportation and communication infrastructure contributes to the explanation of aggregate agricultural productivity across a sample of more and less developed countries" (Antle 1983). A similar result was found when only forty-seven developing countries were used in the estimation. Principal components analysis was also used, given the potential problems with collinearity, resulting once again in a positive, significant coefficient for infrastructure. Agricultural research also had a positive, significant coefficient. The study indicated that infrastructural development in the form of investments in transport and communications industries is positively linked to agricultural production in both combined and developing country analyses. However, the infrastructure variable in Antle's analysis did not measure the quality of infrastructure and the distribution of coverage within a country. More important, the use of cross-sectional data limited inference about causation. Thus, this study raised more questions than it answered.

The aggregate agricultural supply and input demand functions estimated by Binswanger et al. (1987) are based on more extensive information than used by Antle. The annual data (1969–1978) of fifty-eight countries were collected, and estimations were reported for cross-country analyses and within-country time-series analysis of the factors that were considered to affect agricultural output supply and the demand for various physical production inputs, as well as public sector investments and endowments. Two variables relate to transport. The first, road density, was measured by the total length of roads divided by the land area in agriculture and forestry; it was similar to Antle's road variable. The second variable, percentage of roads paved, attempted to capture the quality of existing roads. These two variables, along with irrigation and human capital, were the "shifters." The estimated aggregate and crop production functions had significant and positive coefficients for the two road variables in the pooled country analysis as well as in the within-country analysis. The input demand functions for tractors and fertilizers also demonstrated significant positive coefficients for those road variables. More specifically, the density in the pooled sample indicated that a 10 percent increase in road density resulted in a 2.4 percent increase in fertilizer demand. The price variables in those demand functions were found to be much less important than the shifter variables of roads, irrigation, and human capital. The within-country study found that the elasticity of crop production with respect to road density was 0.10; for the pooled analysis, that elasticity was 0.265. Roads were shown to "have contributed directly 7 percent each to the growth of agricultural output and fertilizer use over the 1971 to 1981 period" (Binswanger et al. 1987).

In general, the road density and pavement variables accounted for most of the country effects in the pooled estimates, leaving the analyst to wonder whether such variables are capturing other country attributes as well. The shifter variables, including road density and pavement, were taken as exogenous (determined outside the model) in this and most other studies, and further research is necessary to understand the supply and demand response for such public sector inputs.

Village-level Studies

The two previous studies used country-level data to determine aggregate production functions and input supply functions. In contrast, the study by Barnes and Binswanger (1986) analyzes Indian data from 108 villages for the period 1966–1980 to determine the effects of rural electrification and infrastructure on agricultural productivity and input use. Agricultural productivity increases were hypothesized to result from rural electrification through irrigation improvements in processing and technology transfer. As with the Binswanger et al. (1987) study, the use of panel data enhanced analysis of causal relationships, unobservable using cross-sectional data alone.

To understand the relationship between exogenous factors (infrastructure, human capital, and so forth) and the dependent variables (such as pump and well irrigation and multiple cropping), two types of regression techniques were used: ordinary least squares (OLS) and principal components (PC). The regression analyses determined that population was the main deciding factor among village demographic characteristics for the location of infrastructure (banks, schools, agricultural services, transport) and markets. Rural electrification had a direct positive effect on well irrigation and multiple cropping, although the effect on total irrigation was weak. Proximity to transportation was negatively related to irrigation variables, while presence of markets had a positive relation to irrigation.

The results of the study also indicated that the growth of rural grain mills was stimulated by the availability of electricity, both through the use of electricity in mill operation and through the increased agricultural production due to irrigation. Adoption of agricultural innovations seemed to increase with the arrival of electricity and then diminished in the typical S-shaped curve for adoption of innovation. The location of banks, influenced by the presence of infrastructure, in turn had a significant impact on the number of grains mills, but the presence of banks was not directly associated with agricultural innovations and services (Barnes and Binswanger 1986). School variables were positively associated with grain mills and agricultural innovations, indicating a relationship between an educated labor force and improved agricultural production that other researchers have also noticed, as shown in Chapter 7.

In another study of India, Binswanger et al. (1989) sought to understand the response of agricultural investment and output to the actions of farmers, government agencies, and banks. The analysis used district-level, time-series, and cross-section data from eighty-five districts in seventeen states, covering the period 1960–1961 to 1981–1982. Government infrastructure variables were canal irrigation, primary schools, rural electrification, regulated rural markets, and total road length. Measures of selected agroclimatic endowments were developed as the exogenous variables that affect the size and growth of agricultural opportunities in a region. The model used fixed effects methods and exogenous agroclimatic variables to incorporate the simultaneity problems of banks, infrastructure, and private agricultural investment. Interest rates were set by the government and so were assumed to have no simultaneity problem. An index of international commodity prices was used as an instrumental variable for the domestic price index. Thus, commodity prices were considered to be exogenously given because India is a small country in the commodity market, a questionable assumption. For technology, a district-specific technology trend was entered into the model. Common time trends and interaction terms of all agroclimatic variables and time were also included.

The analysis found that agricultural infrastructure cannot be considered an exogenous variable in output supply analysis because the agroclimatic variables were found to explain up to 41 percent of the variation in the infrastructure variables. Different factors among the agroclimatic conditions had different effects on investment in roads, regulated markets, electricity, and canal irrigation, demonstrating the need to include a variety of factors rather than a single agroclimatic variable.

A number of regressions were run. A fixed effects model of fertilizer demand indicated that a 10 percent increase in roads (measured as total road length) resulted in a 2.2 percent increase in fertilizer demand. "Except for irrigation, all other infrastructure variables affect aggregate crop output positively. Quantitatively the effects of primary schools and roads were the largest, with elasticities of 0.34 and 0.20 respectively" (Binswanger, Khandker, and Rosenzweig 1989). Seven percent of the growth in aggregate output and 7 percent in fertilizer use could be directly attributed to road investments, in addition to indirect contributions through the attraction of banks to areas with improved roads. Growth in fixed irrigation investments could be directly attributed to electrification investments, increasing aggregate output by about 2 percent (Binswanger et al. 1989).

Farm-Level Studies

Evenson (1986) provided another approach, developing a model of agricultural production at the farm level. He used a profit function incorporating profit maximization with production efficiency on regional "average farm" data for the Philippines from 1948 to 1984 to estimate the effect of public investments on farm-level output supply and input demand. The explanatory variables included roads, measured in miles per 1,000 arable hectares, and rural electrification, measured as the percentage of rural *barrios* (neighborhoods) with electricity. Roads were found to have a significantly positive effect on aggregate output per farm, as well as a positive effect on input use, especially fertilizer. The output elasticity indicated that a 10 percent increase in roads would result in an increase in output of about 3 percent, holding land quantities constant (Evenson 1986). Much of that output increase would be generated through the increase in fertilizer use, which had an elasticity of 0.44 with respect to roads. The negative output elasticity with respect to rural electrification remained an enigma, which the author attributed to reverse causality with farm productivity levels. In general, this study represented an initial effort to use the duality-based profits function approach. The difficulties inherent in this approach, with its extensive data and computational needs, were demonstrated by this study.

A study in Bangladesh by Ahmed and Hossain (1990) offered new evidence of the importance of rural infrastructure for farm-level production and consumption decisions. The report analyzed the role of various types of rural infrastructure, including means of transport, communication, education, and markets, in the agricultural development of Bangladesh. Microlevel cross-sectional data were used to derive an infrastructure index for villages, which was then used in conjunction with data on target variables, including agricultural production, labor and goods markets, income, and savings. The infrastructure index was defined as a combination of distance and cost of travel to various services, such as banks, secondary schools, post offices, and markets—thus incorporating accessibility to services, not just the existence of the services.

Correlation and regression analyses were conducted on farm production and consumption variables, based on the infrastructure index (Ahmed and Hossain, 1990). Fertilizer prices were 14 percent lower in villages with better access to services. The use of fertilizer was greater in infrastructurally developed villages (150 kilograms per hectare) than in less developed villages (78 kilograms per hectare). Developed villages had 42 percent of land under irrigation and 42 percent under high-yielding varieties compared with 21 percent and 25 percent, respectively, in underdeveloped villages. Gross agricultural production increased from 31 to 42 percent due to infrastructure development, and individual farmers in more developed villages produced greater quantities of paddy for marketing. The average amount of paddy marketed was 36 percent higher per household in infrastructurally developed villages. In such villages prices varied less from one location to another for paddy and milled rice. Paddy prices immediately after harvest averaged 7.7 percent higher in the more infrastructurally developed villages than in the less developed ones.

The effects on employment of infrastructure in the Ahmed and Hossain (1990) study were varied. Rural wages were 12 percent higher in villages with more developed infrastructure than in less-developed villages in Bangladesh. The increase in wage income due to infrastructural improvement was found to be very high. The propensity to consume cereals was lower in developed than in underdeveloped villages at the same income level. This study recognized the interrelationship between different types of infrastructure but sacrificed analyses of individual types of infrastructure to assess the combined effects.

Studies of Electrification

Using two case studies (India and Colombia), Cecelski and Glatt (1982) detailed current methods for evaluating rural electrification projects and their effects on economic development, incorporating both aggregate and individual producer information.   The authors cited difficulties in determining and quantifying the effects of electrification, many of which occur over time and indirectly. In addition, the demand for electricity was a derived demand; hence the benefits depend upon complementary investment decisions and inputs, including credit, transport, schools, and other infrastructure.

In India irrigation was recognized by policymakers to be the most important rural use of electricity. The National Council of Applied Economic Research (cited in Cecelski and Glatt 1982) determined that 54 percent of the total variance in agricultural production in India as a whole is explained by irrigation. In a farm-level study of Uttar Pradesh and Madhya Pradesh, India, the electrification of tubewells resulted in a 173 percent increase in paddy output, due partially to a 63 percent increase in irrigated paddy acreage and partially to increased yields with the irrigation technology. A shift was noted from lower quality grains (*korra*, *jowar*, *bajra*) to higher-value paddy, wheat, and vegetable crops. Either electric or diesel pumps or a combination of the two enabled the shift from rainfed to irrigated cultivation. Small farmers (those with less than 2 hectares) had higher gains in income per hectare after electrification than did larger farmers.

Conclusions from Studies

The aforementioned studies indicate the breadth of research that has been attempted from aggregate to individual farm levels, using a variety of econometric techniques and their respective assumptions. Each study offers information, yet none can demonstrate the full dynamic effects of various types of infrastructure. The majority of the studies are based in Asian countries. This emphasis reflects the relative availability of data in Asian countries, compared with other developing areas, and the considerable data needed to understand the dynamic effects of infrastructure.

Project Evaluations and Appraisal Reports

Project appraisals and evaluations have commonly centered on the direct, easily measured effects or simple proxies for those effects accounted for in benefit-cost analysis. A sample of forty-four project appraisal reports, mostly from the World Bank and USAID, were examined to determine the type of analysis used. The methods of impact assessment and the findings vary dramatically. Integrated rural development projects were analyzed for their transport and power aspects because feeder road development and rural electrification distribution programs often fall within the context of such integrated projects.

Of the specific projects mentioned, twenty-nine were primarily transport projects (of which twenty-six were specifically roads), ten were electrification projects, three were integrated rural development projects, one was an irrigation project, and one was a communications project. Regarding the types of analysis used in the project appraisal or evaluations, the majority (twenty-three projects) used cost-benefit analysis, while three earlier projects showed only financial analysis. Qualitative or some other form of analysis was used for the remaining projects. The projects range from early 1950s World Bank projects to a recent USAID project in the Philippines. For most projects, the major benefits can be found in two basic categories: (1) user cost savings, and (2) producer-consumer surplus generation.

Early Use of User Cost Estimates

The World Bank Mexican roads projects discussed by King (1967) provide an early example of estimation of benefits through user cost savings. User cost savings usually were calculated as the amount of time saved by the use of new facilities (either in transport or communications or in the use of electrical machines) and, for transport projects, the savings in vehicle operating costs through improved road surfaces (for example, Cobb et al. 1980; Hossain and Chowdhury 1984; van der Tak and de Weille 1969). Based on vehicle counts and estimates of time and vehicle maintenance savings, the Mexican roads project had an estimated economic rate of return (ERR) of 11 to 18 percent, depending upon the road section analyzed (King 1967). The project was justified during the appraisal process on the basis of unquantified "other benefits," which, if measured, would raise the ERR above 20 percent. The East African rails project (King, 1967), planned during the same era, was also justified on the basis of the assumed positive externalities involved with defense, trade, and governmental administration, not the low estimated ERR of 11 percent. In contrast to most transport projects, electrification and telecommunication projects were evaluated for financial viability, based upon a comparison of revenues and direct financial costs. Development impacts on industrialization and agriculture were assumed, but the rate of return estimates were based solely on revenues, as was the Pakistan electrification project (Lieftinck et al. 1968). The user cost savings approach was recognized as limited, but it was used to provide some minimal tangible evidence of economic impact.

Producer Surplus Estimates of Benefits

The second category of measured effects, producer surplus, can be found primarily in transport projects associated with agricultural investments. Most project evaluations completed since the mid-1960s include assessments of the production benefits that producers were to obtain with enhanced access to markets for inputs and outputs (see Devres, 1980, for various examples). In El Salvador, a World Bank roads project was estimated to have a benefit-cost ratio of 3:1 on the basis of increases in shrimp marketing and cotton production that were to occur due to the roads. Benefit estimations usually assumed that transport cost savings would be reflected in reduced prices for agricultural inputs and increased incentives for cash crop production. Some projects combined the user cost savings and the producer surplus into a single estimated ERR, as was the case in Tunisia with a World Bank rural roads project (Chanmari and Beenhakker 1984), although the dangers of double counting were acknowledged.

Variations on Benefits Estimation

A brief look at the Devres (1980) report on rural road evaluation by USAID provides a long list of perceived effects on all aspects of human life. Given the mandate of USAID to provide assistance (USAID 1989), in contrast to the World Bank's institutional need to provide loans on a fiscally responsible basis, the evaluations by USAID are not limited to the direct, measurable impacts found in cost-benefit analysis. The evidence, however, is often anecdotal or the result of informal interviews. In the case of the Liberia rural roads project, a transport economist used cost-benefit analysis—both user cost savings and producer surplus estimates—to compare alternative construction and maintenance projections. ERRs were found to range from 7.9 to 23 percent. Vehicle operating costs were reduced by 90 percent (Cobb et al. 1980). However, the other effects found by Cobb et al. were based on interviews and surveys asking questions about "before the road" and "after the road." The report detailed substantial production effects, including more extensive cash crop cultivation, expansion into tree crops, and higher farmgate prices for cash crops. Improved access to health care and education was cited by villagers as an important benefit. Women noted greater income-earning opportunities, with the economy becoming increasingly a cash economy. Solem (1989) found similar results in interviews with Thai villagers in an area where an integrated rural development program operated, including road and communications projects.

In Bangladesh, Hossain and Chowdhury (1984) selected households in twelve villages with varying degrees of accessibility and agricultural development in order to analyze differences in agricultural production, markets, and employment that could be attributed to accessibility. Control areas ("without project" sites) with less access to roads and transport were selected. Areas that had experienced recent investment in roads and that were connected to the road system were selected as the "with project" sites. Surveys were conducted at village and district levels, and extensive traffic counts were recorded. In addition to the traditional user savings in lower transport costs and benefits due to the traffic generated as the result of lower costs, the study found that complementary investments in irrigation, technology, and other production factors enabled farmers to be more price responsive in production. In the area where the road project had occurred, impacts included higher producer prices for outputs and lower inputs prices, greater use of modern inputs and correspondingly higher productivity, greater cultivation intensity, and more frequent contact with extension officials. The use of control and project areas enabled the authors to look at the rural sector as a whole in order to understand the complementarity of inputs, which changes the benefits assessment of projects.

Indirect Benefits

The presence of linkage effects and many indirect benefits from infrastructure has led to the use of income and expenditure multipliers in benefits estimations (Mwase 1989). In the case of Tanzania, Mwase recommends the use of an income multiplier of 1.5 to capture the indirect development effects that transport investments generate through increased income for rural households. In other words, each $1.00 invested in roads results in income and expenditures benefits of $1.50.

The Organization for Economic Cooperation and Development (OECD) Development Center and the Inter-American Development Bank (IDB) (1989) assessed the direct and indirect effects of projects on low-income groups using low-income coefficients. This measure, called the coefficient of income distribution (CID), is a ratio of net benefits to low-income households to total private net economic benefits. From 1979 to 1982, transport sector loans averaged a CID of 26.6 (over twenty projects); in 1983–1986, the CID averaged over twenty-six projects was 27.7. For comparison, forty-five agriculture projects during the 1979–1982 period averaged a CID of 74.1, while the CID for forty-two projects from 1983 to 1986 averaged 48.3. During the 1979–1986 period, 92 percent of transport projects and 74 percent of the energy projects of the IDB were analyzed using cost-benefit analyses, compared with only 55 percent of agricultural projects. Thus, the projects with the lowest average CIDs are also the projects with the greatest percentage of loans analyzed with cost-benefit methods. As the report states,

Certainly, identifying low-income benefits in infrastructure projects is more difficult, because a greater proportion of gross benefits often accrue to intermediate rather than final users. These projects also tend to exhibit one of the conditions for presence of indirect substitution effects, which is that price changes in output are possible, because project scale relative to the market served tends to be large. (OECD and IDB 1989)

Relevant Books and Articles

Although professionals and policymakers often stress the need for increasing nonfarm employment, particularly in rural areas, they lack the knowledge to do it effectively. Increasing production in agriculture and industry is, of course, the objective. But critical to employment generation is the strategy—the way to bring about production increases. That infrastructure is a critical element in that strategy is demonstrated in an International Labor Organization study comparing Taiwan, South Korea, Japan, and China (Saith 1986). This study found that Korea and Taiwan share identical growth paths and historical backgrounds but achieved quite a different degree of success in rural, nonfarm income and employment. In Taiwan about 80 percent of rural income was received from nonfarm sources, compared with less than 48 percent in Korea. Seventy percent of farm households in Taiwan had access to electricity even in 1960, compared with only 13 percent in Korea. Density of paved roads in Taiwan was 76 kilometers per 1,000 square kilometers in 1962 and 215 kilometers in 1972, whereas road density in Korea was less than 10 kilometers per 1,000 square kilometers in 1966 and still below 50 in 1975 (Saith 1986).

In a comparison of Asian and African countries, Ahmed and Rustagi (1987) examined agricultural goods prices in order to identify the causal effect of market efficiency and inefficiency. Marketing margins were estimated to be much higher in Africa than in Asia, indicating possible efficiency problems in Africa compared to Asia. Decomposition analysis of marketing margins for agricultural crops determined that transport and associated marketing costs explained 39 percent of the difference in marketing margins between African and Asian countries. Thinness of markets (few buyers and/or sellers) and lack of transport infrastructure were linked to high marketing costs.

Mittendorf and Hertag (1982), in evaluating marketing margins for major products in various countries, found wide margins for some products, including rice in Pakistan (the marketing margin was more than 50 percent of the consumer price) and maize flour in Kenya (more than 40 percent of the consumer price). Transport costs were a major part of the high margins in Pakistan. Further research by Hine and Rizet (1991) indicated that transport costs for road freight were up to five times higher in three African countries (Mali, Cameroon, and Côte d'Ivoire) than in Pakistan, even though Pakistan itself had relatively high costs. A combination of import regulations on vehicles, high-quality vehicles, high speeds, and inefficient (low total volume) use of trucks contributed to these high costs, which restrict the flow of goods. Meissner (1989) points to marketing as the area for the "second generation of green revolution" problems, so that increased production will be hindered by difficulties in the marketing channels in moving, processing, and trading commodities. As noted earlier, road densities and percentages of paved roads are much smaller for Africa than for most of Asia.

Infrastructure development, particularly for transport, figures as an important factor in Latin American trade and integration policies. The Cartagena Accord of 1972 contains clauses committing the Andean countries to study transport infrastructure. In this view, transport costs are understood to be implicit taxes on exports and imports, diminishing the overall level of trade while affecting the composition of trade. Studies in the region have sought to understand the relationship between value, weight, and transport costs. In comparison with the European Community, the Andean Pact countries have more than twice the land area with only 11 percent the length of roads and a commercial motor fleet only 10 percent as large (Cárdenas 1990). Given that, it is not surprising that the gross tonnage of cargo in the Andean Pact region is only about 2 percent of that carried in the European Community. Further work in the trade area concerning the implicit tax imposed by differential transport costs is necessary, so that the costs are no longer considered exogenous in trade studies.

Saunders et al. (1983) provided a summary of studies and theoretical literature on telecommunications, which is valuable though now outdated. Investment in telecommunications in the early 1980s in developing countries was found to be about 0.3 percent of gross domestic product (GDP), less than half the level of investment in the more developed countries. The lack of investment was not due to lack of demand: The most common problem with telecommunications was the overloading of call-handling capabilities, and most systems had long waiting lists for hook-ups. It was also not due to the drain on government financial resources because revenues covered investment and maintenance in most instances. "Were the economic efficiency aspects of development the sole goal, such evidence of market forces would in economic terms be sufficient to justify a rapid expansion of the sector" (Saunders et al. 1983, 14.) Yet, as the authors stated, "the review of selected literature on telecommunications investment and economic development, which is summarized in the main body of this book, suggests a paucity of sound analytical material and relevant empirical data on which to base policy decisions about investment in telecommunications."

A relatively recent addition to the literature related to infrastructure development is found in the urban-rural linkages documents of Cour (1990), Evans (1990), and others, based on the earlier work of Rodinelli and Ruddle (1978). Rural-urban linkages are defined by Evans (1990, 17) to be "trade, exchange, and the flow of resources between one spatial component of the national economic system and another." Economic development in a region occurs through the growth in linkages between urban and rural markets, fostering effective demand for products and labor and resulting in increased trade and greater mobility of populations. A key role in promoting rural growth is assigned to growth in urban effective demand. Transport and communications form the physical links necessary to facilitate the market links. Linkage of markets has been postulated by economists for years as a basic factor in development (see Mellor 1976). Current work by Evans, Cour, and others attempts to contribute empirical studies and methodologies for assessing such linkages.

ISSUES OF RESOURCE ALLOCATION TO INFRASTRUCTURE

In measuring the impact of infrastructural investment, the methodological issues surface in full force in the process of benefit-cost analysis of infrastructural projects. The literature on benefit-cost analysis is rich. The publications by Little and Mirrlees (1974) and Dasgupta et al. (1972) are classics. Most of the literature shows enormous preoccupation with the mechanics of valuation (for example, price, interest rate, and exchange rate estimation) but does not shed much light on the methods for identifying and measuring the direct and indirect benefits of infrastructure. Moreover, benefit-cost analysis is an extremely project-oriented approach focusing on a particular element of infrastructure (transport or electricity or telecommunications); hence it often misses the effects of interaction among these elements.

In the benefit-cost analysis of such projects, the benefits attributable to a project have generally been measured through (1) consumer-producer surplus models, (2) user cost savings models, (3) production functions analysis, or (4) qualitative assessment by users.   Most of these approaches are geared to measurement of direct effects, while infrastructural projects primarily have indirect effects or externalities.   For example, defining consumers' surplus as the difference between what the consumers are willing to pay and what they actually pay, and assuming a downward-sloping demand curve with an arbitrary demand elasticity, Saunders et al. (1983) show measures of consumers' surplus as the benefit of a telecommunication project.   But as Jussawalla and Ogden (1989, 45) point out,

It is difficult to measure demand for a service that is not supplied, and it is equally difficult to justify supplying a service where there is no measurable expressed demand. The situation is further complicated in that typically demand for infrastructure is a derived demand, namely, a desire for a good as an input for another final good. Telecommunications is desired not simply for a telephone in the living room, but for information which can be used for production or social purposes.

Mishan (1982) notes similar problems of measuring benefits.

Identification and measurement of indirect effects of infrastructure have therefore remained the most challenging empirical tasks. Identification of benefits is complicated because there is no neat theory to tell us the direction and extent of the impact.   Economists working at project levels designed the concept of "benchmark surveys" to compare the before-project status with the results after the effects are full blown (see, for example, early studies cited in Howe and Richards, 1984). The difference between benchmark statistics and the after-project statistics is interpreted as the contribution of the project, assuming that without a project production and consumption would have remained static. Very soon the concept of "with" and "without" project consequences was thought to be more accurate than the "before" and "after" comparison of project effects (Adler 1987). However, the scenario without the project remains a counterfactual situation. The assessment of the appropriate counterfactual position is critical for correct estimation of benefits. How to do it is a question that has received little attention from professionals.

The concept of "project" and "control" situations is the practical approach employed by Ahmed and Hossain (1990) in their study on rural infrastructure in Bangladesh, discussed earlier.   Even such a conceptual model requires supplemental econometric models to isolate the effects of variables that are not related to infrastructure but that undergo changes over time. In essence, many of the econometric models cited earlier for measuring the effects of infrastructure can be classified similarly.

A number of extraordinary precautions are necessary in using the "control" and the "project" approach of measurement of benefits. The agroecological factors should be carefully incorporated into the study design so that these effects do not confuse the effects of infrastructure. Time is an important healer of many ills. Therefore, length of life of much infrastructure has to be carefully noted. Similarly, data from households may lack comparability. For example, if you ask a farmer in a less-developed village what price he received for paddy, he may quote the same figure quoted by a farmer in an infrastructurally developed village. But the farmer in the less-developed village carried the paddy on headload or horseback to a distant market—the same developed village where the other farmer lived and sold his paddy. In the former case, there is a high transportation cost (nonmonetary) borne by the farmer, which is not included in the price, while in the latter case, there is little or no transportation cost reflected in the price (Ahmed and Hossain 1990). There are numerous other traps that the researcher needs to recognize and avoid.

Benefits, Sequencing, and Interaction between Infrastructures

As mentioned earlier, studies on infrastructure generally focus on a particular element, either roads or electricity or telecommunications or markets. The sum of the individual effects of these elements would generally be different from the total effect realized in a similar situation because of their interactions. The timing or sequencing of investments has important policy implications in such cases (for example, with feeder roads and main highways). Few methodologies in infrastructure studies appear to be geared to the task of constructing an infrastructure package and measuring the effects of the package as a whole. Moreover, effects of infrastructure are often dependent on a country's trade and regulatory policies. A road may not serve its full potential if the import of vehicles is restricted and regulatory measures stifle the growth of transportation services (Badiane and Delgado 1992; Roberts et al. 1982). The interaction of such policies and infrastructural investment always requires a careful examination.

Any systematic study of the impact of infrastructure is not only methodologically complex but also very expensive in terms of time and money. On the other hand, conventional approaches are considered inadequate. This dilemma has pushed many donor agencies, policymakers, and researchers to make qualitative assessments by asking questions of the people in a locality where an infrastructural investment has take place (Solem 1989). Sometimes these qualitative assessments have been helpful in restoring confidence in infrastructural investment but, more often than not, this approach has failed to provide systematic guidance to policymakers.

Making Decisions on Infrastructure Investment

In public decision making on infrastructure investment, decision makers confront five typical questions: (1) What level of resources must be allocated to infrastructure or social overhead capital (SOC)? (2) What is the least-cost means of constructing an infrastructure facility? (3) What is the most efficient sequence for locating and creating various elements of infrastructure? (4) How should the maintenance problem be handled once infrastructure is created? and (5) What political and institutional developments (such as development of local government institutions) are critical for the construction and maintenance of infrastructure, particularly rural infrastructure? The first question is a macroeconomic one, whereas the rest are microeconomic.

Directly Productive Activities (DPAs) versus SOCs

The aforementioned macroeconomic question has been addressed theoretically by economists, but empirical case studies on the optimal combination of SOC and DPA are so rare that none could be found. An exposition of the theoretical approach is presented by Hirschman in his formulation for his imbalanced growth theory (Hirschman 1958).

Hirschman characterizes development as a gigantic jigsaw puzzle. The choice of the efficient sequence for fitting that puzzle together depends on the pressure an individual piece in place exerts upon other pieces, so that they, too, fall in place. Trial and error will soon lead to some simple rules of thumb: The time needed to fit each piece into place depends inversely on the number of contacts with pieces already in place; the larger the number of neighboring pieces already in place, the easier it is to fit in the missing pieces (Hirschman 1958). The principle of technical complementarity governs the choice of efficient development sequences. Activities should be initiated in such a manner that increasing the production of A would lead to pressure for increasing the supply of B. This happens when B is the beneficiary of external economies (technical and pecuniary) emanating from A. Investment in infrastructure has the necessary attributes for inducing growth in the directly productive sector in the economy.

Hirschman concludes that in a country plagued by deficiency of demand and high cost of production, a development-oriented government may do well to initiate the inducement mechanism by creating a surplus of SOC over that required for current output. This investment increases the demand for final output and decreases the costs of producing it. Increased profitability leads production from one level to the next higher level, and the challenge-response sequence continues to drive production levels to the frontier.

Empirical Work for Allocation Decisions

As indicated earlier, empirical attestation of the foregoing theoretical formulation has not been found in the literature. This is believed to be a reflection of a serious gap in research on infrastructure and its relation to production activities. Therefore, decisions on how much to allocate for infrastructural development have remained a matter of judgment bordering on the act of shooting in the dark. One recent effort by McMillan and Amoako-Tuffour (1991) attempted to determine the demand for local public services, including roads, education, recreation, and health facilities based on public expenditure data from rural and urban areas of Victoria, Australia. The approach shows some promise for more developed areas, where land taxation and spending are linked and demand is effective for services. However, in many developing countries this methodology would provide little guidance to policymakers. In the African context, Gaviria et al. (1989) have used road densities for needs assessment. Using this methodology, they compare road densities in areas of India during different periods of development and estimate the needs for Nigeria based on those India road densities. This assumes that infrastructure needs in African development parallel Indian needs, with the given emphasis on road transport, an assumption that needs to be evaluated. Nevertheless, the methodology does represent an improvement over the use of assessment tools from developed countries that rely on existing traffic and effective demand rather than potential or latent demand. Some professionals, drawing lessons from Hirschman's writings, have argued for overinvestment in infrastructure in the context of contemporary developing countries. The practice, however, of allocating resources only when bottlenecks and pressure for services are felt within the political system remains overwhelmingly widespread (Rietveld 1989).

The micro questions of appropriate technology, sequence, location, maintenance, and institutional development have received attention from those who are involved in project formulation and implementation. Therefore, the literature on these issues is mostly limited to evaluation and appraisal reports, as well as special publications of multilateral donor agencies (Cook et al. 1985). Four conclusions from such reports can be summarized here.

1. Maintenance of infrastructure is a serious problem in many developing countries. In some African countries, usable road mileage has shrunk dramatically due to poor maintenance (Addus 1989). The lack of appropriate priorities in the allocation of public resources and institutional deficiencies in maintenance systems, particularly at rural levels, have been responsible for this malaise.

2. Benefit-cost analysis is not very helpful in guiding resource allocation among sectors of an economy. But benefit-cost analyses have played a constructive role in making intrasectoral choices among various types of projects, technical alternatives, and priorities.

3. Political development, particularly democratic practices and decentralization of political power, will continue to be a necessary condition for development of rural areas and rural infrastructure. The role of this necessary condition is often forgotten even though it lies at the heart of the problem of creation of public assets and the maintenance of those assets.

4. The cost of construction varies tremendously across geographic regions. However, estimates indicate that road construction and maintenance in Africa is less costly than similar activities in Asia and Latin America. This is true whether comparing labor-intensive road construction projects in different regions or conventional, capital-intensive projects. Part of the higher cost is due to differences in terrain, with more rivers and watersheds in Asia requiring more bridges and costly earthworks.

CONCLUSIONS

Given the importance and wide range of effects of infrastructure in economic and social development, this review of the literature cannot be viewed as all inclusive. It serves to give an idea of the main issues concerning the ways economists and others have attempted to quantify or otherwise evaluate how transport, communications, and electrification affect agricultural production, access to education and health services, market structure, and land use in development.

Aggregate production studies all indicate that infrastructure variables, when included in the analysis, play an important part in production technology choices and output increases. One study found that a 7 percent increase in agricultural production during a ten year period could be attributed solely to roads (Binswanger et al. 1987).

Farm-level studies in Bangladesh showed that farms in villages with relatively developed infrastructure use relatively greater amounts of fertilizer, market a higher percentage of their agricultural production, and have higher rural wages and wage income (Ahmed and Hossain 1990). Evenson (1986), in a study based on farms in the Philippines, also found a strong relationship between roads and increased agricultural production. He concluded that a 10 percent increase in roads would lead to a 3 percent increase in production, given no changes in land cultivated. Electrification has been found to be important in raising farm incomes in India, particularly for the smaller farmers (NCAER 1977). Rural services tend to be used much more by households when they have easier access to them (Wanmali 1985).

Project appraisals and evaluations often contain a number of positive (but occasionally negative) effects with high potential rates of return. Project analyses are found to include user cost savings and producer surplus estimates. Often analyses are qualified with a statement concerning underestimation due to the inability to quantify some benefits (King 1967). Cost-benefit analyses are found to be limited in their ability to inform decisions. Deficiencies in methodology for measuring effects is part of the problem. The concept of "control" versus "project" effects, combined with some econometric analyses measuring the effects of autonomous factors, has begun to shed new light.

Road building introduces issues of the value of spread (or linkage) effects of construction and maintenance income for local populations when labor-intensive technology is used. Public works projects have the potential to assist in food security directly as well as indirectly through the usual effects of roads (von Braun, Teklu, and Webb 1991), although trade-offs may exist between the food security objectives and the asset creation objectives of such projects. Mwase (1989) estimates income multiples for transport investments that are as high as 1.5, indicating that an investment of $1.00 in transport would yield as much as $1.50 in increased income, based on Tanzanian data.

In attempting to evaluate projects regarding their effects on income distribution, the OECD and the Inter-American Development Bank found that infrastructure projects rate very well. However, the project evaluation tools focus on cost-benefit analysis, much to the disadvantage of infrastructure projects, in which the indirect benefits are rarely included.

Historical studies of more developed countries attempt to disentangle the relationship between transport and development. In a comparison study of Taiwan and South Korea, differences in rural nonfarm income levels and employment are striking. Saith (1986) attributes the difference to electrification and roads.

Recent work on trade issues and market integration points to limitations in transport and communications that inhibit expansion of markets. High marketing costs reduce the potential for regional trade, and policy constraints on vehicle and parts imports exacerbate the difficulties (Badiane and Delgado 1992; Cárdenas Busto 1990). Additional work on urban-rural linkages (Evans 1990, for example) indicates that the physical links, through transport and communications, are critical to growth linkages between urban and rural areas.

Important policy issues have not adequately addressed resource allocation to infrastructure. Difficulties with the measurement of indirect effects of infrastructure are further complicated by interactions among different type of infrastructure. Policymakers need to evaluate not only what types of infrastructure to build, but also when and what to build to facilitate joint use. The sequencing of investments becomes critical, given the resource constraints faced by developing nations. Empirical work on the allocation of resources to infrastructure is lagging behind this demand, however. Survey results indicate that policymakers in developing countries must base their decisions on a paucity of information. When combined with a lack of adequate analytical methods, allocation of resources to infrastructure projects becomes a lottery game where chance plays too large a role. Because of these difficulties, the pragmatic suggestion of Albert Hirschman in his 1958 book, *Strategy of Economic Development*, that a development-oriented government should create overcapacity in infrastructure, seems to be sensible in the context of many developing countries of contemporary Asia, Africa, and Latin America. Nevertheless, the need to develop practical tools for resource allocation based on objective criteria cannot be overrated.

Systematic research on issues related to development and management of infrastructure, particularly rural infrastructure, is quite thin, as this survey reveals, in comparison with such research in many other branches of development economics. The contemporary thinking on development that is reflected in open-economy policies and macroeconomic reforms is often interpreted mistakenly as inconsistent with the thrust on infrastructural development. This confusion arises mainly from the fact that control of public expenditure is a central element in macroeconomic reforms, but increased priority to infrastructure generally calls for larger public expenditures. Research related to allocation of public resources assumes added importance with the market-oriented strategy of development. The degree of infrastructural development is in reality the critical factor determining the success of market-oriented sectoral and macroeconomic policies in the developing world.

NOTE

1. Modified and reprinted with permission of the International Food Policy Research Institute, Washington, D.C.

REFERENCES

Addus, A. A. 1989. "Road Transportation in Africa." *Transportation Quarterly* 43 (July): 421–433.

Adler, H. A. *Economic Appraisal of Transport Projects: A Manual with Case Studies.* Baltimore, Md.: Johns Hopkins University Press.

Ahmed, R., and M. Hossain. 1990. *Developmental Impact of Rural Infrastructure in Bangladesh.* IFPRI Research Report 83. Washington, D.C.: International Food Policy Research Institute.

Ahmed, R., and N. Rustagi. 1987. "Marketing and Price Incentives in African and Asian Countries: A Comparison." In *Agricultural Marketing Strategy and Pricing Policy*, ed. Dieter Elz. Washington, D.C.: World Bank.

Anderson, G. W., C. G. Vandervoort, C. M. Suggs, and C. Clapp-Wincek. 1982. *Rural Roads Evaluation, Summary Report.* A.I.D. Program Evaluation Report 5. Washington, D.C.: U.S. Agency for International Development.

Andersson, A. E., D. Batten, B. Johansson, and P. Nijkamp. 1989. *Advances in Spatial Theory and Dynamics.* Amsterdam: Elsevier.

Antle, J. M. 1983. "Infrastructure and Aggregate Agricultural Productivity: International Evidence." *Economic Development and Cultural Change* 31 (April): 609–619.

Badiane, O. 1992. "National Policies for Integrated Regional Markets in West Africa." Mimeo. Washington, D.C.: International Food Policy Research Institute.

Badiane, O., and C. Delgado. 1992. "Relative Roles of Macroeconomic Strategies and Sectoral Marketing Policies in the Integration of Agricultural Markets in West Africa." Paper presented at a seminar on L'integration Economique par les Produits Vegetaux et Animaux en Afrique de l'Ouest, sponsored by the Centre International de Recherche Economique and Sociale (CIRES) and Laval Centre, June 15–18.

Barnes, D., and H. P. Binswanger. 1986. "Impact of Rural Electrification and Infrastructure on Agricultural Changes, 1966–1980." *Economic and Political Weekly* 21 (1): 26-34.

Binswanger, H., S. Khandker, and M. Rosenzweig. 1989. *How Infrastructure and Financial Institutions Affect Agricultural Output and Investment in India.* Working Paper Series 163. Washington, D.C.: World Bank.

Binswanger, H., M. C. Yang, A. Bowers, and Y. Mundlak. 1987. "On the Determinants of Cross-Country Aggregate Agricultural Supply." *Journal of Econometrics* 36 (1): 111–131.

Cárdenas, Busto J. 1990. "Transporte e Integracin en el Gruppo Andino." *Integracin Latinoamericana* 14 (143): 11-28.

Cecelski, E., and S. Glatt. 1982. *The Role of Rural Electrification in Development.* Washington, D.C.: Resources for the Future.

Chanmari, A., and H. L. Beenhakker. 1984. *Projets desl Pistes Rurales.* Service de Documentation du Ministre de l'Equipment, République Tunisienne (Government of Tunisia).

Cobb, R., R. Hunt, C. Vandervoort, C. Bledsoe, and R. McClusky. 1980. *Impact of Rural Roads in Liberia.* AID Project Impact Evaluation Report 6. Washington, D.C.: U.S. Agency for International Development.

Cook, C., H. Beenhakker, and R. Hartwig. 1985. *Institutional Considerations in Rural Road Projects.* Staff Working Paper 758. Washington, D.C.: World Bank.

Cour, J. M. 1990. *Urban-Rural Linkages: Macroeconomic and Regional Implications.* Washington, D.C.: World Bank.

Dasgupta, P., S. Margulin, and A. Sen. 1972. *Guidelines for Project Evaluation.* New York: United Nations.

Devres, Inc. 1980. *Socioeconomic and Environmental Impacts of Low Volume Rural Roads: A Review of the Literature.* A.I.D. Program Evaluation Discussion Paper 7. Washington, D.C.: U.S. Agency for International Development.

De Vries, E. 1960. "Finance for Development." In *Proceedings of the International Conference of Agricultural Economists.* London: Oxford University Press.

Evans, Hugh E. 1990. *Rural-Urban Linkages and Structural Transformation.* World Bank Sector Policy and Research Discussion Paper, Report No. INF-71. Washington, D.C.: Infrastructure and Urban Development Department, World Bank.

Evenson, R. E. 1986. "Infrastructure, Output Supply, and Input Demand in Philippine Agriculture: Provisional Estimates." *Journal of Philippine Development* 13 (23): 62-76.

Food and Agriculture Organization of the United Nations. 1990. *Production Yearbook.* Rome: FAO.

Gabre-Madhin, E. Z. 1991. "Transfer Costs of Cereals Marketing in Mali." M. A. thesis. East Lansing: Michigan State University.

Gaviria, J., V. Bindlish, and U. Lele. 1989. *The Rural Road Question and Nigeria's Agricultural Development.* Managing Agricultural Development in Africa (MADIA). Discussion Paper 10. Washington, D.C.: World Bank.

Gramlich, Edward M. 1994. "Infrastructure Investment: A Review of Literature Essay." *Journal of Economic Literature* 32 (3): 1176–1196.

Higgins, B. 1959. *Economic Development.* New York: Norton.

Hine, J., and C. Rizet. 1991. "Halving Africa's Freight Transport Costs: Could It Be Done?" Paper presented at the International Symposium on Transport and Communications in Africa, sponsored by the Royal Academy of Overseas Sciences and the United Nations, Brussels, November 27–29.

Hirschman, A. O. 1958. *Strategy of Economic Development.* New Haven, Conn.: Yale University Press.

Hossain, M., and O. H. Chowdhury. 1984. *Socioeconomic Impact of Roads in Rural Areas.* Dhaka: Center for Development Science.

Howe, John and Peter Richards. 1984. *Rural Roads and Poverty Alleviation.* A study prepared for the International Labour office within the framework of the World Employment Programme. London: Intermediate Technology Publications.

International Food Policy Research Institute. 1991. "Infrastructure survey, selected countries." Computer printout. Washington, D.C.: IFPRI.

International Monetary Fund. 1991. *International Financial Statistics*. Washington, D.C.: IMF.

———. Various years, 1978–88. *Government Finance Statistics Yearbook*. Washington, D.C.: IMF.

International Road Federation. 1988. *World Road Statistics 1983–1987*. Washington, DC.

Ishikawa, S. 1967. *Economic Development in Asian Perspective*. Tokyo: Kinokuniya Bookstore.

Jussawalla, M., and M. R. Ogden. 1989. "The Pacific Islands: Policy Options for Telecommunications Development." *Telecommunications Policy* 13 (1): 40–50.

King, J. A. 1967. *Economic Development Projects and their Appraisal: Cases and Principles from the Experience of the World Bank*. Baltimore, Md.: Johns Hopkins University Press for the World Bank.

Lakshmanan, T. R. 1992. "Infrastructure and Economic Transformation." In *Advances in Spatial Theory and Dynamics*, ed. A. E. Andersson et al. Amsterdam: Elsevier.

Lewis, W. A. 1955. *Strategy of Economic Growth*. London: Allen and Unwin.

Lieftinck, P., R. Sadove, and T. Creyke. 1968. *Water and Power Resources of West Pakistan: A Study in Sector Planning*. 3 vols. Baltimore, Md.: Johns Hopkins University Press.

Little, I.M.D., and J. A. Mirrlees. 1974. *Project Appraisal and Planning for Developing Countries*. New York: Basic Books.

McMillan, M., and J. Amoako-Tuffour. 1991. "Demands for Local Public Sector Outputs in Rural and Urban Municipalities." *American Journal of Agricultural Economics* 73 (2): 312–325.

Meissner, F. 1989. "Effective Food Marketing: A Tool of Socioeconomic Development in the Third World." *Food Policy* 14 (2): 90–96.

Mellor, J. W. 1976. *The New Economics of Growth*. Ithaca, NY: Cornell University Press.

Mishan, E. J. 1982. *Cost-Benefit Analysis*. 3rd ed. London: Allen and Unwin.

Mittendorf, H. J., and O. Hertag. 1982. "Marketing Costs and Margins for Major Food Items in Developing Countries." *Food and Nutrition* 8(1): 26–31.

Mwase, N. R. 1989. "Role of Transport in Rural Development in Africa." *Transport Review* 9 (3): 235–253.

National Council of Applied Economic Research. 1977. *Cost-Benefit Study of Selected Rural Electrification Schemes in Madhya Pradesh and Uttar Pradesh*. New Delhi: NCAER. Cited in E. Cecelski and S. Glatt, *The Role of Rural Electrification in Development*. Washington, DC: Resources for the Future, 1982.

Nicholls, W. H. 1963. "An 'Agricultural Surplus' as a Factor in Economic Development." *Journal of Political Economy* 71 (February): 1–29.

Nurske, R. 1953. *Problems of Capital Formation in Underdeveloped Countries*. New York: Oxford University Press.

OECD Development Center and InterAmerican Development Bank. 1989. *The Impact of Development Projects on Poverty*. Paris: Organization for Economic Cooperation and Development.

Rietveld, P. 1989. "Infrastructure and Regional Development: A Survey of Multiregional Economic Models." *Annals of Regional Sciences* 23 (2): 255–274.

Roberts, J. E., C. Clapp-Wincek, C. Vandervoort, and D. Brokensha. 1982. *Kenya Rural Roads: Vihiga Special Rural Development Program*. Project Impact Evaluation Report 26. Washington, D.C.: U.S. Agency for International Development.

Rodinelli, D. A., and K. Ruddle. 1978. *Urbanization and Rural Development: A Spatial Policy for Equitable Growth*. New York: Praeger.

Rosenstein-Rodan, P. N. 1943. "Problems of Industrialization of Eastern and Southeastern Europe." *The Economic Journal* 53 (June): 202–211.

Ruttan, V. 1984. "Models of Agricultural Development." In *Agricultural Development in the Third World*, ed. C. Eicher and J. Staatz, 38–45. Baltimore, Md.: Johns Hopkins University Press.

Saith, A. 1986. *Contrasting Experiences in Rural Industry: Are the East Asian Experiences Transferable?* New Delhi: International Labor Organization.

Samuelson, P. 1954. "The Pure Theory of Public Expenditure." *Review of Economics and Statistics* 36 (4): 387–89.

Saunders, R. J., J. Warford, and B. Wellenius. 1983. *Telecommunications and Economic Development*. Baltimore, Md.: Johns Hopkins University Press for the World Bank.

Solem, R. R. 1989. "Small Farmer Perspective on Development: Village Survey in Northeast Thailand: Synthesis Report." Mimeo. Washington, D.C.: U.S. Agency for International Development.

U.S. Agency for International Development. 1989. *Congressional Presentation, Fiscal Year 1989*. Washington, D.C.: USAID.

van der Tak, H., and J. de Weille. 1969. *Reappraisal of a Road Project in Iran*. World Bank Staff Occasional Paper 7. Washington, D.C.: World Bank.

von Braun, J., T. Teklu, and P. Webb. 1991. *Labor Intensive Public*. Works for Food Security: Experience in Africa. Working Papers on Food Security 6. Washington, D. C.: International Food Policy Research Institute.

Von Thünen, J. H. [1842] 1966. *Der Isolierte Staat*. Translated and with an introduction and notes by C. M. Wartenburg and P. Hall. London: Pergamon Press.

Wanmali, Sudhir. 1985. *Rural Households Use of Services: A Study of Miryalguda Taluka, India*. Research Report 48. Washington, D. C.: International Food Policy Research Institute.

World Bank. Various years. *Annual Report*. Washington, D.C.: World Bank.

Youngson, A. J. 1967. *Overhead Capital: A Study in Development Economics*. Edinburgh: Edinburgh University Press.

5

Issues in Providing Agricultural Services in Developing Countries

Richard L. Meyer and Donald W. Larson

INTRODUCTION[1]

This chapter addresses issues in providing agricultural credit and marketing services, including both inputs and outputs, in developing countries. Agricultural services are defined as those related to production agriculture. We do not cover some special types of services, such as credit and marketing services for microenterprises or export credit. Credit services include both loans and deposits. Marketing is defined as the system of markets and related institutions which organize the economic activity of the food and fiber sector. This system involves information flows, institutional arrangements, infrastructure, organizations, and entrepreneurial or risk-taking activity. Documents from several major inter-national donor organizations; the academic literature found in books, journal articles, and working papers; and the past experience of the authors were the major information sources used in this chapter.

The next section addresses major issues in the provision of agricultural services. This is followed by an evaluation of rural financial services, agricultural output marketing services, and agricultural input marketing services, respectively. The last section discusses the conclusions and implications for future investments in agricultural services.

ISSUES IN PROVIDING AGRICULTURAL SERVICES

Evolution in Views about Rural Financial Services

The Traditional View about Credit Needs

Agricultural credit has been considered essential for expanded food production, adoption of new farming technology, and improvements in rural income distribution. The traditional view of agricultural credit was linked to early views about technological change and the way that liquidity constraints affect farm household resource allocation (David and Meyer 1980). Many developing countries and donor agencies were preoccupied during the 1960s, 1970s, and 1980s with expanding agricultural production. The Green Revolution offered hope for breaking production constraints, but the new technologies usually required greater cash outlays to purchase inputs, including seeds, chemical fertilizers, and pesticides. Credit for purchasing the new inputs was considered key, especially for small producers. Neither informal lenders nor formal financial institutions were considered able or willing to provide reasonably priced credit, so governments and donors concluded that this credit market failure could be corrected by selective policies and projects. This "credit needs" rationale led to special credit programs, often at subsidized interest rates.

Two types of agricultural credit projects were implemented. The first was a "credit-component" project in which credit was viewed as a production input along with seed, fertilizer, and chemicals. The implicit assumption was that either the farmer had no savings or was unwilling to commit them to the new, risky technology. The second "credit-only" project targeted specific classes of borrowers for loans but left to lenders the actual allocation of funds. Loans were provided through special credit lines or institutions, often supervised to ensure their proper use. Similar arguments were used to rationalize medium and long-term loans to purchase capital inputs. Input and interest rate subsidies were believed necessary to temporarily increase profitability when farmers were just beginning to experiment with the new technology. Later, interest subsidies were rationalized as a way to compensate farmers for the urban bias of food and wage policies. It was also argued that targeted credit, such as loans for small farmers or the rural poor, would improve income distribution and reduce poverty (Adams and Graham 1981).

The research summarized in this chapter reveals that these early projects suffered serious limitations. They failed to recognize that credit is fungible, so borrowers will allocate it to the highest expected return, which may not be the new technology. Moreover, loans may substitute for the borrowers' own funds or informal finance, so the additional use of new inputs may be much less than expected. Evidence from some areas of rapid adoption of Green Revolution technology showed that farmers used their own savings when the new technology was profitable. Furthermore, many projects paid little attention to the impact on the financial institutions that supplied loans, so projects often collapsed when donor funds disappeared. This experience spawned a new view which stressed the profitability of innovations, the secure supply of inexpensive inputs, and the viability of financial institutions serving agriculture.

New View of Rural Financial Markets

The traditional market-failure view of agricultural credit came under criticism as early as the 1973 AID Spring Review of Small Farmer Credit (Donald 1976).

The early studies suggested that special small farmer credit projects did not have the expected impact, and there was evidence of unexpected negative consequences, such as loan concentration and a weakening of financial institutions. The systematic presentation of the "new view" occurred in the Colloquium on Rural Finance cosponsored by AID and the World Bank in 1981 (Adams et al. 1984). Papers and books by Adams (1988), Adams and Graham (1981), Adams and Vogel (1986), Von Pischke et al. (1983), and Schmidt and Kropp (1987) made important contributions to refining the new view.

The new view argued for fundamental changes in the way that governments and donors use finance to support agricultural development and how credit projects should be evaluated. The changes included less loan targeting, more flexible interest rates for loans and deposits, more emphasis on deposit mobilization, less concessionary lines of rediscounting from central banks, and more effort to reduce borrower transaction costs. It was also argued that projects should spend less effort on the difficult task of measuring impact on borrowers and focus instead on how projects influence the viability of financial institutions and financial market performance.

Evolution in Views About Agricultural Marketing Services

Traditional View of Market Failure and Government Intervention in Input and Output Markets

Prior to the 1980s, market failure was viewed as a primary justification for government intervention in agricultural credit, output, and input markets. The continued poverty, income inequalities, hunger, food shortages, low productivity, and lack of modernization of agriculture as well as other sectors of the economy were considered as evidence that markets had failed to produce the desired economic growth in many countries of Africa, Asia, and Latin America (Reusse 1987). Problems of small farmer access to markets, slow adoption of new technology, and high marketing costs were cited as indicators of market failure (Wolgin 1990; World Bank 1990 and 1991).

The market failure view was especially popular among the socialist oriented governments in power because it complemented much of what the leaders wanted to do to reform the economy. They thought government could outperform the marketplace to achieve faster economic growth. These governments, often assisted by AID and other donors, proceeded to intervene in markets in a wide variety of ways to correct the perceived failures. In many countries the degree of government intervention reached every sector of the economy. Governments nationalized many of the marketing functions in domestic and/or foreign trade, in agriculture, manufacturing, banking, insurance, and housing. This was often done through the creation of parastatal companies that had monopoly control of the entire sector. The governments passed laws and regulations to control prices, interest rates, exchange rates, rental rates, marketing margins, product shipments, and the like. All this government intervention in markets created a rigid, centralized, bureaucratic system that had great difficulty operating its "businesses" efficiently (World Bank 1991).

New View of Government Failure in Input and Output Markets and Creation of Open Competitive Markets

State intervention in agricultural marketing services has generally failed to contribute to sustained economic growth and failed to solve the problems of poverty, food shortages, and low productivity that plague many developing countries. Most of the government-created parastatal "businesses" failed to perform and are now in various stages of bankruptcy and closure. In several cases, such as Nicaragua and Mozambique, the countries have lost fifteen years or more of economic growth and are poorer relative to other countries than in the early 1970s. Other countries, such as Uganda and Ghana, had negative growth rates for several years.

The new view represents the creation of open competitive markets with more distinct roles defined for the private sector and government (Wolgin 1990; World Bank 1991). The private sector should be dominant in production and distribution in order to realize economic efficiencies and stimulate growth. The role of the state (often neglected in the 1970s and 1980s) is to ensure a correct environment for private sector business operation and prosperity. Many developing countries are conducting structural reform programs that transfer ownership of many nationalized assets back to the private sector. Laws and regulations are being changed to eliminate monopolies and encourage competitiveness. Farm land, import and export businesses, processing companies, banks, marketing services, and input services are being privatized. World Bank, IMF, and AID structural adjustment loans are being used to facilitate the reforms. Demand and supply in a competitive market are being used to determine prices that guide the allocation of resources and the returns to resources. Prices, interest rates, exchange rates, movement of goods, imports, and exports are being freed of government control. The private sector is investing in existing businesses and in new opportunities.

In the new view governments realize their comparative advantage and their resource limitations. It is argued that governments need to focus on creating an economic and political environment in which the private sector has a major role in the performance of the economic activities of the country. In the case of input and output markets, this means the government should promote competition in markets and emphasize the provision of facilitating functions such as infrastructure, information, rules and regulations, contract enforcement, grades and standards, and research that have large public good components. This new view places the performance of most economic activity in the private sector.

EVALUATION OF RURAL FINANCIAL SERVICES

Importance of Rural Credit Programs

Credit programs and projects represent a major source of governmental and donor support to agriculture in many developing countries. Huge subsidies have gone to farmers and financial institutions through credit projects. The World Bank has been the largest provider of external funds. A World Bank review (1993d) concluded that of the ten developing countries with the largest populations (excluding Europe), the Bank had an important role in supporting the dominant agricultural lender in every country except Nigeria. Altogether, ninety-four countries received Bank funding for agricultural credit from FY 1948 to FY 1992 totaling $16.5 billion measured in current dollars. This amount represented about 26 percent of the Bank's total agricultural lending during the period. Almost 40 percent of the funds were concentrated in just three countries—India, Mexico, and Brazil.

AID has a long history of supporting agricultural credit. Between 1950 and 1973, AID had channeled more than $700 million into agricultural credit projects (Donald 1976). An important characteristic of these projects was their small-farmer orientation. Between 1973 and 1985, AID allocated an additional $300 million to agricultural credit. These estimates do not include the large amount of technical assistance also provided (Chew 1987). Adams (1990) estimated that for the Latin American region alone credit projects amounted to about $350 million in the 1942–1970 period, and over $1.5 billion in the 1973–1990 period.

A significant portion of the regional development banks' portfolio has also gone into agricultural credit projects. During the 1970–1982 period, over $1.2 billion went into agricultural credit in over sixty Inter-American Development Bank (IDB) loans, and additional projects included credit as a component (IDB 1984). The pipeline for 1983–1986 included thirteen loans in an amount of $640 million in addition to another thirty-five loans for $900 million in agricultural or rural development programs, which usually contain sizable credit components. The Asian Development Bank (ADB) approved seventy-two projects between 1970 and August 1991 for a total of almost $1.4 billion. Just over $1.0 billion went to thirty-six projects providing credit to crop farmers and cooperatives for the acquisition of equipment. Over 60 percent of the credit projects went to thirteen market economy countries in the region (ADB 1993).

Common Characteristics of Credit Projects and Policies

AID projects in the mid-1950s first began with technical assistance; credit was expected to play a secondary role. Cooperatives were often promoted as the credit vehicle (Donald 1976). With the Green Revolution, many projects identified the inputs that farmers should use with the credit that was often supervised. Many credit projects were designed to stimulate lending to specific clientele groups, such as small farmers. Some "institutional-strengthening" projects have been funded in recent years to strengthen financial institutions.

Donor and government involvement in agricultural credit has often been based on perceptions of farmers' "needs." Lieberson et al. (1985, 17) summarized this rationale:

One reason for the emphasis on credit was the assumption that access to credit was a critical constraint to the adoption of improved inputs and modern technologies. Modernizing agriculture requires large infusions of credit to finance the use of purchased inputs such as fertilizer, improved seeds, insecticides, and additional labor. Because savings in traditional agriculture tend to be relatively small at the initial stages of development, increased demand for working and fixed capital must largely come from an increased supply of credit. Small farmers have meager internal resources and, therefore, are most in need of production credit.

The perception of credit needs led policymakers to increase the supply of loans to "lead" agricultural development. Government and donor-funded agricultural credit projects had the following features:

1. They increased the supply of funds for agricultural lending through loan portfolio quotas or targets for lenders, the creation of specialized financial institutions, grants and subsidies for nonfinancial institutions (ministries, departments, institutes, NGOs [Non-Government Organizations], PVOs [Private Voluntary Organizations]), central bank rediscount programs, mandatory placement of bank deposits in specialized lending institutions, and nationalization of banks that failed to make the desired loans.
2. They reduced the interest rate on loans through interest rate ceilings, with the lowest rates set for the smallest/poorest borrowers, low central bank rates for refinance funds, encouraging banks to cross-subsidize by charging high rates to nonpriority borrowers and low rates to priority borrowers, and direct interest subsidies to lenders.
3. They reduced lending risks and costs through detailed loan targeting, crop and loan guarantees, joint liability lending to groups of borrowers, and technical assistance to lenders to help improve institutional efficiency.

Many evaluations and academic studies have documented the shortcomings of "credit needs" and have argued instead for a broader "rural financial markets"[2] approach. The next sections summarize the key findings of studies that analyzed the impact of traditional credit policies and projects on borrowers, lenders, and national economies. Although there is considerable consensus, there are exceptions. An important example is the World Bank review (1993d), which reflects a continuation of the debate between agricultural projects and financial markets staff. Surprisingly, its recommendations are inconsistent with the Bank's *Handbook on Financial Sector Operations* (1993c). The conclusions found in recent reports of AID, IDB, and ADB, however, are generally consistent with most academic studies.

Impact of Credit Projects on Farms

The first place to look for credit impacts is on farms because many projects were specifically designed to influence farm operations. Clearly identifying and measuring these impacts is difficult even with new methodological tools. Analyzing impact requires comparing what a farmer did when he or she received a loan with what would have done without the loan, but this is not observable so some proxy is required for what cannot be directly measured. One frequently made assumption, clearly inappropriate, is that none of the actions undertaken after receiving a loan would have occurred without it. This implies, for example, that a farmer would have adopted none of the new Green Revolution seed-fertilizer technology without receiving a loan. But since some farmers adopt new technology without receiving formal loans, some loan funds simply *substitute* for own funds or informal loans. The "additionality" attributable to formal lending, therefore, is less than the amount of total loans made. Additionality is further reduced when borrowers *divert* loan funds to nontargeted purposes. The fungibility of credit, therefore, makes it extremely difficult to measure farm level impact. The problem is greatest when interest rates are highly subsidized so it becomes attractive for borrowers to borrow and substitute or divert the funds (David and Meyer 1980; Von Pischke and Adams 1980).

In their review of impact studies, David and Meyer (1980) concluded that the impact of short-term credit programs on utilization of seed-fertilizer technology was unclear. Because the technology was highly divisible, farmers with varying financial constraints could adopt it at different points on the modern technology function. Medium- and long-term loans, on the other hand, might influence production because they can be used to finance large, lumpy investments that are more difficult to self-finance.

The 1993 World Bank review (World Bank 1993d) tried to assess the farm impact of bank loans using information reported in forty-one credit projects completed in the previous five years. The general conclusion was favorable, but the analysis was based on weak economic analysis. Some cases seem clearer than others. The rapid expansion of shallow tubewells in Bangladesh, for example, was associated with World Bank funding. Likewise, the rapid expansion of farm mechanization in Brazil in the 1970s and 1980s was also attributed to a massive expansion of agricultural credit at heavily subsidized interest rates.

The credit experience of selected countries is revealing. Following disastrous typhoons, the Philippines implemented the large Masagana 99 program beginning in 1973 to expand rice production and bolster land reform in rice growing areas. The program involved a package of inputs, supervised credit provided without collateral, and subsidized funds rediscounted to lenders by the central bank. The lending program reached as many as 530,000 farmers at one time, but the number fell to 70,000 by the early 1980s due to accumulated defaults. An evaluation by Sacay et al. (1985) revealed how rice output was already increasing due to adoption of the new technology. They concluded that the organization expanded too quickly and could have employed much less credit, thereby minimizing the adverse effects on financial institutions.

India has also received large amounts of donor assistance to intervene in rural credit markets in pursuit of production, income, and poverty alleviation objectives. A complex structure of institutions has emerged that is tightly administered with targets, quotas, and interest rate controls (Reserve Bank of India 1989). About 30 percent of the rural families have obtained access to institutional credit, but the system performs poorly in mobilizing deposits, efficiently lending, and recovering loans. Huge subsidies are required to prop up the system, and the only way some financial institutions can survive is to cross-subsidize rural loans by charging higher rates to nonpriority customers. Studies have tried to quantify the impact on Indian agriculture.   Binswanger et al. (1989) showed how agroclimatic endowments and quality of infrastructure influenced the location of rural commercial bank branches. They concluded that the expansion of bank branches had a large impact on fertilizer demand and on farm investments, but contributed to only a 3 percent increase in aggregate crop output over the 1960–1961 to 1981–1982 period. Interest rates made little impact on fertilizer demand or aggregate output but clearly reduced long-term investment.

Another way to evaluate credit impact is to study aggregate production trends after the credit supplies and/or interest subsidies are reduced or eliminated. If credit expansion makes a large impact on production, then production should fall when lending declines. In practice it has been difficult to clearly identify any sharp short-term production declines due to credit shrinkage. (For examples, see Vogel and Larson [1984] for Colombia, and Araujo et al. [1990] for Brazil.) This result does not necessarily demonstrate a lack of impact, but it suggests that farmers have found ways to finance their operations when credit programs were changed or terminated.

There is a concern that subsidized credit targeted to specific enterprises or capital inputs could lead to resource misallocation if entrepreneurs were induced to invest in enterprises that otherwise were unprofitable or utilized uneconomic combinations of capital and labor. For example, Vogel (1984a) noted that subsidized interest rates in Costa Rica could have influenced farmers to replace labor on dairy farms by acquiring electric milking machines. The World Bank review (1993d) tried to assess the resource allocation effects of its credit projects, but the data were weak. The review noted that in the period 1978–1985 the rapid expansion in rural lending in Brazil was not matched by an increase in farm production. A subsidized credit project in Yugoslavia encouraged overinvestment in agroindustry, resulting in substantial excess capacity. But a moderately subsidized credit project in Pakistan did not accelerate tractor use beyond its economic returns, nor did it encourage excessive displacement of agricultural labor.

The World Bank review (1993d) noted the analytical problem in assessing resource allocation effects because the credit effect is difficult to disentangle from the effects of other policies. A Korean credit project contributed to an overexpansion in greenhouses for horticultural production; however, the problem was not cheap credit but the country's tariff policy, which protected producers from foreign suppliers. Most nonacademic researchers do not use data or methodologies robust enough to separate these effects. A more robust analysis used by Khandker and Binswanger (1989) in a study of district data in India showed that the additional capital investment associated with increased formal credit contributed more to a substitution of capital for agricultural labor than to increased crop output. Agricultural credit contributed to job creation in the nonfarm sector and the increased agricultural wages reduced farm labor use.

More rigorous research is needed on resource allocation before concrete conclusions can be reached about the effects of cheap credit. The problem may not be as serious as some theorists expected, but highly subsidized loans targeted to specific capital inputs may stimulate uneconomic investments and may alter farm level capital-labor ratios, especially in highly inflationary environments, when machinery is purchased as an inflation hedge.

Another important concern about cheap credit is perverse impact on income distribution. Gonzalez-Vega (1984) developed his "Iron Law of Interest Rate Restrictions" to explain how interest rate ceilings lead to credit rationing by lenders so that the rich receive most of the subsidized funds. Early studies of subsidized loans in Costa Rica and Brazil showed that farmland ownership was more concentrated than income, and the distribution of agricultural credit was even more concentrated than land ownership. Vogel (1984a) estimated that the subsidies received through agricultural credit in Costa Rica in 1974 amounted to almost 20 percent of agricultural value added. Large farmers received most of this subsidy because the largest 10 percent of agricultural loans accounted for 80 percent of the total loans made in 1974. Formal agricultural loans in Brazil expanded from less than 15 percent of agricultural GDP in the early 1960s to 84 percent in 1975. Interest rates were often negative in real terms. From 1970 to 1985, the annual interest subsidy varied from less than 1.0 to almost 20 percent of agricultural GDP. The 1970 and 1980 Censuses revealed that relatively few small farmers reported formal loans, so most of the subsidy went to the wealthiest farmers, thereby worsening the country's highly unequal income distribution (Araujo et al. 1990).

The World Bank review (1993d), however, concluded that large farmers did not capture most of the benefits of its projects, as predicted by the Costa Rican and Brazilian experiences, for two reasons. First, Bank projects often funded long-term investments for medium and large farmers, while AID projects were more explicitly small farmer oriented. Second, lender administrative procedures prevented major abuses such as occurred in Mexico, where large farmers presented themselves as poor in order to get cheap credit. These arguments are not completely convincing, however, because little evidence was presented about the size distribution of borrowers. When some groups are targeted as priority borrowers for subsidized loans, there are powerful incentives for nonpriority groups to obtain loans. When this demand is coupled with unscrupulous or overworked bank officials, or if they perceive that the priority borrowers are too risky, the lenders have powerful incentives to concentrate their portfolios with less risky nonpriority borrowers.

The transaction costs of borrowing and lending may influence loan patterns. A large portion of the costs of making and recovering loans is invariant with loan size, so the per unit lending cost is higher for small loans than large loans. In the absence of interest rate controls, lenders would prefer to charge higher interest rates for small loans to recover lending costs. Donor-supported programs, however, usually require that lenders charge small borrowers lower rates, resulting in various types of lender rationing to discourage small borrowers. Rationing introduces cumbersome and time-consuming procedures so the noninterest borrowing costs for small loans are frequently higher than the interest charges. Survey data from eight countries revealed that borrowers of large loans incurred transaction costs that varied from less than 2 percent of interest charges to almost 60 percent, while small loan transaction costs varied from 13 to 245 percent (Meyer and Cuevas 1992). Some small farmers choose to borrow from informal lenders with high interest rates but low transaction costs (Ladman 1984). Liberalizing interest rates may improve loan distribution, but at high rates moral hazard and adverse selection problems[3] may occur (Stiglitz and Weiss 1981).

Impact of Credit Projects on Lenders

The studies reviewed in the preceding subsection showed that the impact of traditional credit projects on farmers is ambiguous and difficult to measure, but the negative impacts on lenders are clearer and the focus of much criticism. Several evaluations reveal poor performance of development finance institutions used as important conduits for donor funds (McKean 1990). Many agricultural development banks have failed, others have been recapitalized because of losses, and most rely on continuous subsidies. Agricultural cooperatives and rural credit unions have a checkered record, and commercial banks frequently try to minimize their agricultural exposure. The World Bank review (1993d) concluded that 77 percent of the institutions supported by bank agricultural projects had a good image, but only 44 percent had good financial positions by the end of the projects. Many institutions had been assisted by the Bank for several years.

The crucial variables affecting institutional viability are operating costs, loan recovery rates, and the rate of inflation relative to interest rates. The impact of seemingly small problems can be devastating. Assume, for example, that an institution recovers 95 percent of the principal and interest due on loans, that operating costs are only 5 percent, and that the nominal interest rate on loans is below the inflation rate by only five percentage points. If the institution lends out all of its money at the beginning of the year, the real value of its funds at the end of the year will be about 85 percent of the beginning value. If all funds are lent out in all subsequent years, by the end of year five, the real value of the capital will have fallen to less that 50 percent of the original value.

Many institutions are not viable. Loan default is often the largest problem but good data are scarce and unreliable. In the mid-1970s, AID (Donald 1976) and the World Bank (1975) tried to assess the problem. In most programs studied, delinquency rates were as high as 50 percent of amounts due. Some agencies had even higher delinquency, but it was concealed through refinancing of unpaid loans. The early repayment studies focused on the borrowers' inability to repay, while later studies analyzed how project design influenced loan recovery. The World Bank review (1993d) found that out of thirty-five completed projects, fourteen reported collection rates of 90 percent or more, five had rates between 50 and 70 percent, and nine had rates below 50 percent. Furthermore, thirteen reported declining collection trends, nineteen reported level trends, and only three reported improving trends. The review emphasized that loan delinquency is not default. For example, although collection rates varied between 50 and 60 percent in India, estimates of default ranged from 5 to 20 percent. The difficulty is that a large amount of resources are spent on loan recovery, and a supposedly stable relationship between delinquency and default may suddenly deteriorate.

Several reasons contribute to loan recovery problems. The early studies emphasized that natural calamities make it impossible for borrowers to repay. A more systematic problem, however, is the negative impact of government- and donor-funded projects. First, lenders tend to be rewarded for making, not recovering, loans, and this leads to lax record keeping and weak collection efforts. Second, subsidized interest rates create opportunities for political intrusion into who gets cheap loans and who must repay. Third, the screening criteria for targeted loans may cause lenders to make loans that do not meet their normal lending criteria. Aguilera-Alfred and Gonzalez-Vega (1993) found that loans made by the Dominican Republic Agricultural Development Bank from government or donor funds had a lower probability of repayment than those made following its own lending criteria.

High operating costs damage the viability of lenders even if they recover most loans. Many credit projects establish narrow interest rate margins to maintain low lending rates, but the costs of reporting and documenting the use and impact of cheap funds is often high. Cuevas and Graham (1984) found that lender transaction costs for a government and a private bank in Honduras far exceeded the authorized 3 to 4 percent. Lending costs using donor funds were nearly five times the cost of using own funds. Ahmed and Adams (1988) found that the Agricultural Bank of Sudan was limited to charging 7 to 9 percent on loans when its administrative costs averaged 10 to 15 percent.

Another reason for the lack of viability is the neglect of deposit mobilization. Financial institutions, that neglect savings mobilization are incomplete institutions and this affects their delinquency and default rates (Vogel 1984b). When lenders deal with their borrowers also as savers, they obtain information useful for loan screening. Furthermore, borrowers are more likely to repay and lenders more likely to exert more effort in recovery when loan funds come from local savers. Sacay et al. (1985) noted that a "dole-out" mentality of borrowers in the

Philippines contributed to the low recovery rate in government-sponsored lending programs. Savings mobilization can provide a more secure flow of funds so lenders avoid the feast-famine syndrome associated with donor or government funds. Borrowers perceive the lender to be a more secure source of future loans, and this is a strong motivation to repay. AID-supported savings projects in the Dominican Republic, Honduras, and Peru had a positive impact on loan recovery (AID 1991).

Finally, some participating financial institutions have collapsed because of a hostile economic environment (Chew 1987; Lieberson et al. 1985; Meyer et al. 1992). Political disruptions, wars, and civil conflicts have damaged economic activities and created uncertainties that stymied investment and production. The macroeconomic policies pursued in several countries have been a major disincentive for agricultural growth (Krueger et al. 1988). The terms of trade have turned against producers of major traded commodities for long periods, and some of the new technologies are neither as available nor as profitable as assumed in credit projects. Financial institutions are affected in several ways when policies and market trends are negative for agriculture. First, farmers and agribusinesses are poor customers for loans, so lenders make few loans with high lending costs. Second, some reliable customers are forced to default on their loans. Third, the financial institutions are discouraged from developing innovations to reduce lending costs for a dispersed and expensive agricultural clientele. Fourth, the amount of rural savings available for voluntary deposit mobilization is reduced.

The lesson learned is that many credit projects have had a negative impact on financial institutions. Many institutions supported by the World Bank have made limited progress toward improved credit management, and their financial viability is questionable (World Bank 1993d). These problems have caused donors to shift from large subsidized agricultural credit projects to supporting structural adjustment loans for correcting policy distortions, and to NGOs experimenting with alternative delivery systems for lending to microenterprises and women. The guidelines given for designing financial sector activities in AID (see Chew 1987; Lieberson et al. 1985; and AID 1988) and the World Bank (1993c) emphasize that projects should not only supply credit to selected sectors of the economy, but simultaneously serve as a catalyst for development of the financial sector.

Impact of Credit Projects on National Economies

Little evidence is available to assess the impact of credit projects on the national economies of developing countries. The World Bank review (1993d) concluded that agricultural credit projects have provided an easy mechanism to disburse foreign exchange because 96 percent of the funds approved for on-lending in the forty-one projects studied were actually disbursed. The positive impact on developing countries of receiving this foreign exchange might outweigh some negative sector-specific effects of credit projects. This argument ignores the question, however, of whether or not the large investments in agricultural credit projects were the most profitable these economies could have undertaken. Donor resources have an opportunity cost, and the empirical evidence suggests that the long-term benefits of these credit projects are questionable. The abandonment of traditional credit projects implies that skepticism exists among the donors about the benefits.

Only one detailed cost-benefit analysis of credit has been located for a developing country. Binswanger and Khandker (1992) used district-level data for India for the period 1972–1973 to 1980–1981 to conclude that the extra agricultural income attributed to agricultural credit exceeded government costs by only about 13 percent. Using less favorable assumptions, the benefits could fall below costs. Furthermore, the study did not assess the impact on future operations of the credit system that experienced steadily rising loan default. A limitation of the study is that the positive impact of credit on production may have masked a decline in area cropped if, for example, poor land went out of intensive cropping at the same time that credit facilitated intensive cropping on the remaining land.

A comprehensive cost-benefit study of the macroeconomic effects of credit projects will always be elusive because the fungibility of loans makes it difficult to quantify the real benefits received by borrowers. Funds diverted from production to consumption expenditures, for example, may have a large, but difficult to measure, social benefit for poor households because of improvements in nutrition, education, or health. On the other hand, credit projects that have led to political intrusion in financial institutions and the acceptance of high levels of loan default may represent large social costs by destroying the integrity of financial institutions and the sanctity of loan contracts. It would also be difficult to quantify the negative impact on households that are barred from borrowing today because of their failure to pay past loans granted as political favors.

Analysis of Successful Cases

Although many credit projects have failed, some financial activities have been successful. Von Pischke and Rouse (1983) identified six fairly successful African smallholder projects. They included the Caisse Nationale de Credit Agricole in Morocco, the Cooperative Savings Scheme in Kenya, credit unions in Cameroon, savings clubs in Zimbabwe, group credit in Malawi, and rotating savings and credit associations in several countries. The factors of success were favorable economic conditions, emphasis on simple traditional rural institutions and savings mobilization, and a scale of operations consistent with the routine transactions of rural people. The Grameen Bank is famous for successfully making thousands of small loans to poor people, mostly women, in Bangladesh (Hossain 1988). Several institutions in Indonesia in total serve even more poor people than the Grameen Bank. Chaves and Gonzalez-Vega (1996) argued that their success is due to both a hospitable environment and effective organizational design reflecting concern for institutional viability. An important distinction between the two country experiences is that most loans are made to individuals in Indonesia while the Grameen Bank uses groups for most lending.

The Indonesian experience in transforming failing financial institutions is instructive. Patten and Rosengard (1991) analyzed the transformation of the Badan Kredit Kecamatan (BKK) and the unit *desas* (village units) of the Bank Rakyat Indonesia (BRI). The BKK program was set up in the early 1970s to provide loans to rural people deemed too poor to save. By 1989 it had more than 500,000 loans outstanding, was covering all costs, and was financially viable. The unit *desas* were set up in the early 1970s to speed the adoption of Green Revolution technology. As occurred in the Philippines, the program experienced mounting arrears and operating deficits, so it was redesigned in 1983–1984. By mid-1990, the unit *desas* had more than 1.8 million loans outstanding, had more than 7 million savings accounts (so savings exceeded loans), and were consistently profitable. These two successes are attributed to a clear objective of creating viable institutions and careful attention to institutional design.

Yaron (1992) analyzed these two Indonesian institutions plus the Bank for Agriculture and Agricultural Cooperatives (BAAC) in Thailand and the Grameen Bank. He calculated a Subsidy Dependence Index (SDI) to determine the increase in average on-lending rate required for the institution to operate without subsidy. The results based on operations in the late 1980s showed that the unit *desas* had reached subsidy independence, while the BKK and BAAC were improving and had a moderate SDI of 20 to 30 percent. The Grameen Bank was also improving but had a SDI of 130 to 180 percent.

AID's savings mobilization projects in the 1980s in Honduras and the Dominican Republic were successful in designing incentives for financial savings (AID 1991). Prior to the projects, credit unions and agricultural development banks were floundering in both countries. They faced a shortage of funds, interest rates were not adjusted for inflation, and loan delinquency and default rates were high. Through policy dialogue, the projects succeeded in changing attitudes toward interest rates, resulting in positive rates of return for savers, and branches were opened in rural areas to reduce saver transaction costs. Improved interest rates and reduced transaction costs resulted in a large increase in deposits, so the institutions were able to resume lending. Loan recovery then improved because borrowers were willing to repay loans when they discovered that with improved liquidity the institutions could make new loans.

Several East Asian countries have been more successful than most developing countries in using subsidized interest rates, directed credit, and other financial market interventions to stimulate growth and modernization. The World Bank (1993b) offers explanations for this experience. The financial sector interventions were designed, first, to encourage financial savings and, second, to channel them into activities with high social returns. Compared to other countries, several East Asian countries achieved a better balance between the need to limit competition to assure bank solvency and to maintain low banking spreads. Credit subsidies were limited in size, and stringent standards were applied in the selection of subsidized projects. Funds were usually used for the purpose intended, and there were few loan losses. Where interventions did not work successfully, as in Indonesia, the problems have been similar.

In contrast with Northeast Asia, credit allocation decisions in many developing countries were motivated by political and noneconomic considerations. Projects were designed with conflicting objectives . . . the very large rents that could be obtained from subsidized credit were a strong incentive to corrupt practices . . . projects were prone to poor appraisal and disbursements without proper documentation . . . producing high loan losses and eventually large-scale failure of directed-credit programs. (World Bank 1993b, 287)

Informal finance often has succeeded where formal finance failed to operate successfully in hostile economic environments and has provided useful services to rural people. Several cases demonstrate the positive role played by informal finance and why it is time to reassess the negative image often held by policymakers (Adams and Fitchett 1992). Informal financial arrangements often solve problems too difficult for formal institutions. For example, in the Philippines agrarian reform beneficiaries are able to pawn their cultivation rights to secure loans for off-farm investments and emergency expenditures (Nagarajan et al. 1992). The formal system, however, cannot accept these rights as collateral for loans.

EVALUATION OF AGRICULTURAL MARKETING SERVICES

Agricultural Output Marketing Services Assisted by Donors

Donor organizations assist agricultural marketing services less than many other areas of project assistance. From 1980 to 1986, the major bilateral and multilateral technical and financial assistance agencies, including AID, the European Union (EU), IDB (Inter-American Development Bank), IFAD (International Fund for Agricultural Development), OPEC (Organization of Petroleum Exporting Countries), the World Bank, and others, made capital commitments to agriculture amounting to $12.5 billion with only 8 percent of that amount allocated to agricultural marketing services (Meissner 1989). Most project assistance for marketing services from donor organizations is focused appropriately on a few commodities—particularly grain and commercial crop marketing, livestock marketing, and, to a limited extent, fruit and vegetable marketing.

A review of the types of marketing service assistance included in project components indicates a heavy emphasis upon "marketing hardware," such as market facilities, storage facilities, postharvest facilities, agroindustry and processing, and roads and transport. Little emphasis was placed upon assistance for "marketing software," such as research, extension, price discovery, risk bearing, financing, market information, grades and standards, contracts, and increasing market competition (World Bank 1990, 27). "Marketing software" assistance can be low cost yet very important. Studies have found that small merchants and farmers can perform grain storage functions very efficiently; their investment cost for comparable facilities is 50 to 100 percent of the government cost (World Bank 1990, 41). Yet merchants generally have great difficulty obtaining bank credit to finance the construction of facilities and purchase of commodities. A recent study concludes that "trade finance mechanisms in much of the developing world are rudimentary or nonexistent" (Wenner et al. 1993, 47).

The type of marketing service selected for project assistance needs to be appropriate for the recipient country. In some instances, the equipment is too capital intensive or too technologically advanced for the country. An example is high cost, specialized bulk grain handling and silo storage facilities when low-cost flat warehouses and bag handling are more appropriate (World Bank 1990). Grain storage projects in India, Bangladesh, Brazil, and elsewhere were justified on the grounds of significant losses in traditional storage (from 17 to 21 percent). The projects' designers argued that bulk storage of grain in large facilities was more economical and would reduce significantly postharvest losses. Recent research has found that losses in traditional storage are much lower than previously thought (1.5 to 4.5 percent) and that bagged storage is more economical and flexible (World Bank 1990, 4). The recalculated economic rates of return (ERR) for the India and Bangladesh projects decreased from an original ERR of 25 percent to an ERR of 8.5 percent using the highest justified "without project" postharvest loss estimate of 5 percent. Adjusting for actual cost overruns reduces the ERR to 7.2 percent, and moving to more realistic postharvest loss estimates would reduce the actual ERR to a very low level (World Bank 1990, 41). Given the low recalculated ERR, it is very likely that the World Bank would not have considered the recalculated ERRs as bankable projects.

Large investments in wholesale markets and rural markets in Latin America, Asia, and other areas were also justified on the basis of reducing food losses and marketing margins by improving performance of the food marketing system (Harrison et al. 1974; World Bank, 1990). Many of these donor projects financed the construction of facilities that are owned and operated by the public sector. The calculated ERRs for some of these markets were most likely overestimated for reasons similar to those for the grain storage facilities (World Bank 1990).

The appropriateness of livestock project assistance in Africa has been especially troublesome because of a conflict between a nomadic type of production and the desire to modernize this production and to promote the use of more permanent pasture systems (Johnston et al. 1987, 159). A Kenya livestock development project found problems of animal health and disease control in the marketing of animals that needed to be herded long distances from the rangeland to the consumption points. Bolivia and Brazil livestock development projects found that the main negative factors were government controls on the price of beef, export restrictions, and marketing and processing problems (World Bank 1990).

Timeliness and Accessibility of Markets

Access to markets continues to be a serious problem for many farmers, especially small farmers, in most developing countries. It is argued that improving access to markets is an important way to increase the participation of farmers in the market economy and to improve their ability to sell their output and buy farm inputs and consumer goods at more favorable prices. In most cases marketing service assistance from donor agencies has attempted to improve market exchange and access through public sector projects designed to build rural roads, storage facilities, wholesale and retail markets, market information services, and cooperative marketing. An evaluation of marketing projects with public sector and cooperative marketing components found the following problems: (1) inefficient and inexperienced management; (2) inadequate record keeping and stock controls; (3) late arrival of purchasing teams in the production area; (4) insufficient cash resources to purchase the product, and late and incorrect payments to producers for their products; (5) poor financial controls, inadequate accounting and auditing, and financial irregularities; (6) inadequate transport resources and logistic management; (7) overstaffing and high costs of operations; (8) unfavorable impact of government pricing policies on operating margins; and (9) difficulty of providing adequate rewards and penalties to management for its performance (World Bank 1990, 34–35).

AID and other donors have assisted the development of market information services in many countries. Daily, weekly, and monthly price information services for basic foods at the retail, wholesale, and farm level and quantities marketed have been initiated and continue to operate in countries such as Brazil, Chad, Colombia, Costa Rica, Ecuador, Indonesia, Kenya, Korea, Mali, the Philippines, Taiwan, Tunisia, and Thailand. Some of these services are being established through AID projects with Michigan State University and the Agricultural Marketing Improvement Strategies Project (AMIS).

These services have helped to improve market arbitrage through better information about when and where to market products, but there is room for improvement (Holtzman et al. 1992). These authors conclude that some of the services need to improve the accuracy and timeliness of the information. Most of the services need a stronger orientation to the prospective users of the information, such as private sector users and policymakers. Designing a workable system for these two different users is not easy. A very important, but missing, component from most of the market information services is outlook information about anticipated supply and demand and current stocks which would serve the private and public sector well as an early warning system for imports and/or exports.

Profitability and Return of Market Services

Creation of profitable markets—where the participants have the incentive to invest, to assume risk, and to expect a satisfactory return on investment—is probably the single most important consideration in project success or failure.

Research has found that producers are rational and will respond to economic incentives, and that producer prices in developing countries are typically distorted to levels below prices in developed countries (Peterson 1988). Based on the estimated long-run supply elasticities (in the range of 0.90 to 1.19), higher prices will increase production substantially. Thus governments that intervene in markets to depress producer prices have an adverse effect on food production (Krueger et al. 1988).

Government policies affecting prices include overvalued or undervalued exchange rates, price ceilings, pan-territorial or uniform pricing, pan-seasonal pricing, marketing margin controls, high import and export taxes, parastatal marketing monopolies, and high sales taxes. For example, a large number of African and Central and South American countries (Ghana, Niger, Mozambique, Tanzania, Argentina, Brazil, the Dominican Republic, Guyana, and Ecuador) have used overvalued exchange rates in combination with other polices to depress producer prices in an attempt to control inflation and reduce food costs in urban areas (Wolgin 1990; World Bank 1990, 1991). As a result of lower producer prices and profitability, agricultural production and exports stagnated. In contrast, governments in some Asian countries such as Hong Kong, Korea, Malaysia, Singapore, Taiwan, and Thailand have used a stable macroeconomic environment with lower inflation, more appropriate exchange rates, and more competitive markets to promote agricultural production and exports with more favorable prices (World Bank 1990, 1991). Prices supported above world levels reduce national income by denying consumers access to lower-cost imports.

Price instability caused by thin or poorly performing markets, rainfall variability, or disease and pests can also reduce and/or eliminate the incentives to produce. Price instability is a problem for grains and other storable products as well as for the highly perishable products such as fruits and vegetables. Governments frequently intervene in markets to stabilize prices through minimum price purchase and storage operations for grains. The costs of these operations have usually been very high relative to receipts, causing large deficits that had to be paid by the government. Most of these operations have been conducted through government-owned parastatal marketing boards. Increased reliance upon trade to stabilize grain prices is more cost effective than government purchase and storage operations for many countries (Abbott, 1985).

Issues of Public or Private Sector Delivery of Services

Until very recently, donors have preferred to work with public sector organizations for the delivery of marketing services in developing counties. The performance of these organizations has been very disappointing to the users, the government, and the donors (World Bank 1990, 1991). High costs, poor management, misuse of funds, poor service, and large operating deficits are some of the problems that have appeared in most of the projects assisting public sector organizations in marketing. Reducing government intervention in markets is viewed as necessary to improve market performance (Krueger 1978; World Bank 1991, 1993a).

Wolgin (1990) analyzes the experience of AID in agricultural market liberalization in Mali, the Gambia, Madagascar, Zambia, Togo, Uganda, Mozambique, and Niger. His main conclusions are that (1) the biggest impact from market liberalization is the reduction in marketing costs, increasing real incomes of both producers and consumers; (2) in most liberalization experiences, real consumer prices have fallen; (3) most government monopolies were honored only in the breach, and illegal parallel markets existed in most areas (Zambia is an exception) prior to liberalization (nevertheless, the illegality of these markets substantially increased transaction costs and marketing margins); (4) despite suppression, poverty, sparse populations, and war, there exists a broad trading community ready to enter into the input and commodity markets in most countries; and (5) most liberalized markets are competitive, with marketing margins reflecting real costs of transportation and assembly. None of these cases demonstrates the existence of a rapacious, oligopolistic private trading system (Wolgin 1990, 34).

Analysis of Successful Cases

Policy reform of agricultural marketing services includes reducing the role of public sector marketing, encouraging private sector activity, restructuring of the institutions providing the services, reforming agricultural exchange rates and price policies, and reducing or eliminating subsidies. Several of these policy reforms are being implemented successfully in the cases illustrated here and in other developing countries. Some examples follow:

In Tanzania, various marketing reforms have been implemented since 1984, including the reintroduction of cooperatives, the abolition of crop purchasing authorities (1984), a more tolerant attitude toward private traders (e.g., the elimination of restrictions on buying and transporting grains), a more clearly defined and restricted role for the grain-marketing parastatal (NMC), and legalization of private sector purchases from and sales to the NMC, cooperative unions, primary societies, and farmers. A preliminary assessment shows that all these steps have had a very positive effect as could be expected in a country that had been operating substantially below its production possibility. (Lele and Christiansen 1989, 22)

Ecuador has successfully pursued policy and regulatory reform of agricultural marketing services in the 1980s to deal with a stagnating economy and agricultural export sector. The exchange rate reform of the 1980s illustrates a change from an inward-oriented development policy based on import substitution to an export oriented and market oriented development policy. In May of 1982, free market rates for the "sucre" were more than 50 percent above official and intervention rates. Policymakers embarked on exchange rate reform that included a 33 percent devaluation of the "sucre" in mid-1982 mini-devaluations from 1982 to 1984, another major devaluation in 1985, a shift to floating rates in 1986, a return to fixed rates in 1988, and a managed float after August 1988. (Bejarano et al. 1993, 2)

Marketing reforms have focused on the three parastatal monopolies and twenty-five mixed government/private marketing companies in Ecuador. ENAC is a price stabilization body for major grains and cotton, and EMPROVIT is a state enterprise that sells basic foods at official prices to consumers. E. N. Semillas is the national seed company. Like most parastatals, these have many problems of high cost, poor service, and operating deficits. The government of Ecuador in the last few years has reduced the role of these parastatals by privatizing many of their functions and attempting to sell off the facilities. Agricultural production, exports, and marketing of the private sector have responded positively to the policy and structural changes (Abbott 1985).

An assessment of grain storage in Ukraine and Russia was completed to improve the storage of grains in the New Independent States (NIS), giving emphasis to the emerging private sector and the need for low-cost storage in the agricultural producing regions. The assessment found that, as in many other countries, the reported postharvest losses of up to 40 percent were impossible to document (Borsdorf et al. 1992). Physical losses are considered to be much lower. Improvements in grain storage, drying, handling, and conditioning are needed, but the institutional barriers are large. The study also found that individual private farmers have no storage facilities and must either sell grain at harvest or rent storage in the state elevator system or at state/collective farms. The public sector has sufficient capacity under its control, but the capacity is substandard. In Russia one of the most significant factors affecting grain storage is the conflict between the state and the farmers concerning the price the state is willing to pay farmers for wheat required to be delivered under state order. The study concludes that the state monopoly on storage and purchasing must be broken if privatization and competitive markets are to succeed.

The success of nontraditional exports from some countries is an excellent example of what can be done through changing the marketing system. Nontraditional exports or high-value foods (HVFs) include products such as fresh and processed fruits and vegetables, meats, fish, dairy products, and vegetable oils. Changing consumer demand in importing countries has driven the growth of these developing country exports. During the 1980s, the value of trade in HVF increased 4 percent annually for items such as fresh vegetables and fresh meat to over 11 percent annually for dairy products and shellfish. Exports of HVF by middle- and low-income countries totaled $52.5 billion in 1990 compared to traditional exports of only $26.3 billion for coffee, cocoa, tea, sugar, cotton, and tobacco (Jaffee 1993).

The successes are examined in a study of fifteen commodity system success stories from nine countries (Jaffee 1993): (1) Mexican fresh tomatoes; (2) Kenyan specialty and "off-season" vegetables; (3) Israeli fresh citrus; (4 to 6) Chilean temperate fruit, processed tomatoes, and fish products; (7 and 8) Brazilian frozen concentrated orange juice and soybean products; (9 and 10) Argentine beef and soybean products; (11 to 13) Thai poultry, tuna, and shrimp; (14) Chinese shrimp; and (15) Taiwanese high-value processed foods.

These successes exhibit several lessons valuable for donor agricultural marketing technical assistance projects.   Each commodity system faced very favorable international market conditions during the take-off stage and for many subsequent years.   Most of the commodity systems faced favorable macroeconomic policies at the time of their initial take-off.   Several common ingredients needed for the competitive response to a favorable market were (1) favorable natural endowments, (2) strong human capital, (3) well-developed physical infrastructure, and (4) the capacity to develop and/or adapt imported production and processing technology.   In nearly all cases, the private sector played a dominant, if not exclusive, role in commercial production, processing, and trading activities.   In the vast majority of cases, governments have provided facilities and services which have either public good properties, externalities, or large economies of scale.   Export diversification often depends upon prior or parallel domestic market development.   The study concluded that government interventions should be generally geared toward encouraging competitive and flexible export marketing structures and not provide favorable treatment to some (e.g., monopolies) and exclude others (Jaffee 1993, 57–60).

EVALUATION OF AGRICULTURAL INPUT MARKETING SERVICES

Agricultural Input Marketing Services Assisted by Donors

Farmers require efficient input marketing services that can deliver the right product at the right time, in the right amounts, at a convenient place, and for a reasonable price.   Agricultural inputs and the associated marketing services have received a great deal of attention from developing countries and donor organizations in an effort to improve land and labor productivity.   Frequently, the agricultural input marketing services have been developed to deliver a package of inputs that farmers buy to obtain the expected gains in productivity.   Credit to finance farmer purchases was often an essential part of this input package.

The main institutional models employed for input marketing services include private retailers, agricultural banks, cooperatives, government institutions such as parastatals, and nongovernment organizations (NGOs).   A survey of input marketing in the 1980s in thirty-nine countries examined the frequency of government and private sector control (control was defined as 80 percent or more of the activity) and showed the very strong tendency for government control of procurement and distribution (World Bank, cited in Abbott 1993).   The countries reported 64 percent government control for fertilizer supply, 61 percent control for seed supply, 47 percent for chemical supply, and 42 percent for farm equipment supply.   Private sector control was only 11 percent, 11 percent, 17 percent, and 22 percent, respectively.   The remainder was mixed government and private sector involvement.

The appropriateness of agricultural input marketing services is best illustrated in crop technology development and distribution.   Widespread gains in food crop productivity have occurred from improved varieties, especially irrigated rice, wheat, and maize varieties in many countries of Africa, Asia, and South America. Widespread productivity gains comparable to these three examples have not been achieved for other crop products or for livestock products. A major difficulty with developing appropriate technology is the weak research base in most developing countries. Few countries have the human and institutional resources to conduct scholarly research for an extended period of time to discover technologies that work. Developing countries have had to depend upon technology developed by the international research centers (CIAT [International Center for Tropical Agriculture], IRRI [International Rice Research Institute], ICRISAT [International Crops Research Institute for the Semi-arid Tropics], CIMMYT [International Maize and Wheat Improvement Center], etc.) for local application or on technology developed for more advanced countries that can be adapted to local conditions (Oehmke and Crawford 1993).

AID has supported a number of fertilizer market liberalization programs in Asia, Africa, and Central and South America designed to reduce government fertilizer subsidies, reduce or eliminate fertilizer price and marketing margin controls, reduce government parastatal distribution of fertilizer, and increase private sector marketing of fertilizer and other inputs. These programs were recently examined in Malawi, Kenya, Cameroon, and Guinea (Wolgin 1990). This examination concludes that (1) private marketing is substantially more efficient than public sector marketing, and the efficiency gains of privatization can amount to 25 percent of the total cost; (2) private markets are competitive and efficient; (3) privatization is extremely complicated and difficult; and (4) not all donors have bought into the AID view of (reducing) fertilizer subsidies and marketing. Some donor programs actually work at cross purposes to what AID has been trying to achieve, making the task of donor coordination much more important and more difficult (Wolgin 1990, 37).

Timeliness of Delivery of Agricultural Input Marketing Services

If appropriate technology is developed and available within the country, the technology may fail due to the lack of timely delivery to the farmer. In modern, input-intensive, biological production processes, the timely availability of inputs is essential. A large number of factors can affect the timeliness of deliveries. Credit is important to finance the purchase of input packages for farmers and for merchants. The inefficiencies of the banking system can cause credit delays, so the farmer cannot buy the input when needed. Merchants can and do finance some fertilizer sales to farmers, but their ability to obtain bank financing greatly reduces the amount of informal finance. Bad weather, poor roads, and ineffective transportation systems can delay the delivery of inputs.

A study of fertilizer policy in Africa identified the following supply constraints associated with the timely delivery of fertilizers: macroeconomic factors, such as shortages of foreign exchange to import fertilizer; budgetary problems of parastatals to finance imports and distribution; import licensing systems; lack of working capital for importers, wholesalers, transporters, and retailers; price controls and fixed marketing margins; poor transport facilities, remote production areas; and a weak cooperative sector (Lele, Christiansen, and Kadiresan 1989, 47).

Profitability of Agricultural Input Marketing Services

The importance of profitability of input use should not be underestimated. The market system depends upon returns (profitability) to determine the allocation of resources.   For example, a farm-level benefit-cost ratio of 2.0 or more is considered necessary for the widespread adoption of fertilizer.   Profitability must be at least that high to assume the increased risk associated with fertilizer use (Lele, Christiansen, and Kadiresan 1989).   This profitability level has been obtained for the Green Revolution varieties but not for many traditional crops. The profitability of using improved varieties or hybrid seeds is a similar problem for input marketing. "It has been demonstrated many times during the past 25 years that truly superior seeds will almost sell themselves.   Marketing difficulties, however, are encountered when the seed represents a solid, demonstrable, but only modest improvement over the seed presently planted by cultivators (e.g., yield advantage of less than 20 percent)" (Pray and Ramaswami, cited in Abbott 1993, 312). Although no empirical estimates are available, demand is likely to be very inelastic for the truly superior seed and very elastic for the not superior seed. Because of the large potential demand for increased use at a lower price, governments frequently sell inputs at low and controlled prices or subsidize the sale of these inputs.   Both approaches have implications for market intervention, government costs, input costs, equity to users, and private sector participation.

Analysis of Successful Cases

Bangladesh illustrates successful structural and policy reform in input markets. Government of Bangladesh (GOB) policy has emphasized growth of competitive markets and increased private sector participation in marketing and distribution of fertilizer, irrigation equipment, fuel, improved seeds, and pesticides since 1978. Until 1978, the Bangladesh Agricultural Development Corporation (BADC) controlled all aspects of the importation of fertilizers, purchase of fertilizers locally from the domestic manufacturer Bangladesh Chemical Industries Corporation (BCIC), transportation, storage, financing, wholesale and retail sales, and pricing. Many problems of pricing, subsidies, financing, inefficiencies of distribution and warehousing, high costs, shortages of supplies, and complaints of poor service emerged during the BADC era (IFDC 1990, 1992).

With AID assistance in 1978, the GOB began work to reform the fertilizer sector and to increase private sector participation in the fertilizer market. Major accomplishments as of the mid-1980s include the following: (1) About one-third of the original 130 local warehouses had been closed and BADC's fertilizer points of sale would be reduced by 55 to 60 percent; (2) in the Chittagong Division, farmer access to fertilizer points of sale had greatly increased; (3) prices paid by farmers for fertilizer under the NMS (New Marketing System) were lower than under OMS (Old Marketing System); (4) a new class of private wholesalers had developed as intermediaries; and (5) despite the change in the system and a local drought, fertilizer sales in the Chittagong Division, as a percentage of national sales, remained unchanged (World Bank, cited in Abbott 1993, 303).

More change has occurred since the mid-1980s. Private sector market share in total national sales of all fertilizers increased to over 84 percent in 1990–1991 from 61 percent in 1989–1990 and from nearly zero when the program began (IFDC 1990, 1992). Private firms now handle all urea marketing and since March of 1989 have been allowed to buy urea directly from factories for the same price as BADC. At the same time, private firms were allowed to take delivery of imported fertilizer directly from ships at the ports. In a major policy reform, the GOB allowed private sector imports of fertilizer (previously BADC controlled all imports) for the first time in June of 1991. Fertilizer retail and wholesale price controls have been eliminated, but the GOB retains control of the domestic price of imported materials, which are currently subsidized by setting the domestic price about 23 percent below the cif cost or import parity price. Private sector merchants of irrigation and agricultural equipment have become increasingly important in the economy since the GOB reforms to encourage privatization in 1978.

Ghana is an example of structural reform in progress with some positive benefits already observed. In Ghana, modern agricultural inputs (fertilizer, agrochemicals, seeds, and machinery) have been heavily subsidized to increase agricultural productivity and production and to compensate for low producer prices (Jebuni and Seini 1992). Parastatal companies were organized to monopolize the importing, distribution, and sale of the subsidized modern inputs. In 1983 the government of Ghana initiated the Economic Recovery Program to restore economic growth. The program included macroeconomic stabilization and structural adjustment. The key policy changes included several devaluations of the exchange rate to more realistic levels, price and income policy to restore producer price incentives, tight fiscal and monetary policy, removal of subsidies on modern agricultural inputs, and privatization of the import, distribution, and sale of inputs.

Agrochemicals are now largely handled by the private sector. Subsidies have been eliminated and prices have been uncontrolled for some time. Several major companies import and distribute chemicals; however, availability is restricted to dealers in large towns because effective demand is small. The Ghana Seed Company, a candidate for privatization, has not operated since 1989. A national seed service has been established to supervise the seed industry. Private seed growers have been registered in all major ecological zones and will be assisted to produce and market certified seeds to farmers. The Ministry of Agriculture machinery services to farmers have been eliminated. The tractors and combines have been sold to private farmers. In real terms farmers have benefited because they now pay 70 percent less for plowing than in 1980 and 30 percent less for carting (Jebuni and Seini 1992).

Cameroon has initiated a Fertilizer Subsector Reform Program (FSSRP) with assistance from AID designed for implementation from 1988 to 1992 (Blaine et al. 1991). The FSSRP emphasizes economic liberalization and privatization of the fertilizer sector. This includes elimination of the parastatal monopoly of the imports and distribution of fertilizer, phasing out of a fertilizer subsidy, and establishment of a free-market system by the end of the program.

Importing and distributing of fertilizer is being liberalized as Cameroon moves toward privatization of this industry. However, the state is still phasing out a fertilizer subsidy and needs to phase out preferential interest rates for fertilizer importers and distributors. Fertilizer sales have remained about the same since liberalization. Liberalization has been beneficial and positive by stopping the waste, corruption, and inefficiencies of the parastatal company and by reducing the government's subsidy bill by about U.S. $14 million in only two years. Farmers have been protected from large price increases as the subsidies are being withdrawn by the efficiency gains from the private sector imports and distribution.

The FSSRP has found that, like many other projects, policy reform is a process that requires dialogue, flexibility, expertise, networking, patience, and management intensity. Market reforms may lead to the failure of some firms; however, the benefits will be greater efficiency and economies of scale. Reforms must be carried out in a comprehensive, orderly manner. Reform of the input side of a productive sector such as fertilizer will probably be difficult to complete without reform of the output marketing sector, such as coffee and cotton (Blaine et al. 1991).

In biological technology transfer, the Zimbabwe hybrid seed program has achieved success, with over 90 percent maize hybrid adoption by producers and notably higher yields than for neighboring countries. The success of hybrids is attributed to breeding as well as good government support services—input delivery, credit access, favorable prices, and extension (Lesser 1992). Commerce is heavily regulated, but the restrictions are being removed. The government regulates the entire marketing system, including prices, movement, and storage for maize, wheat, and white sorghum. New competition includes CIMMYT (1985), Pioneer Overseas Corporation (1988), Cargill Zimbabwe (1991), and Dekalb Hybrids (1991–1993 joint with Seed-Coop). Seed-Coop has a monopoly on seed production, but private firms compete strongly on quality control, better service, and improved distribution. Seed price controls have become a thorny issue as high inflation has reduced the real price of seed from 1987 to 1989. Declining profits for seed companies and farmers are a problem (Lesser 1992, 2–16).

CONCLUSIONS AND IMPLICATIONS FOR AID INVESTMENTS

This chapter presents the conclusions for credit, input, and marketing services and the implications for future agricultural investments in developing countries.

The literature reviewed seems clear: *There is a preferred sequencing of investments in agricultural services. The first priority is to develop an appropriate environment within which agriculture will function.* This environment includes at least three key dimensions. The first is policy environment. Policies that directly or indirectly affect agriculture must be reasonably conducive for agricultural production and marketing. Prices, exchange rates, trade policies, and monetary and fiscal policies must provide producers with reasonable prospects for making an economic return if they adopt new technology, make investments, and increase production. Otherwise, they will not take risks, adopt new technology, and try to increase production beyond subsistence levels. The second dimension is infrastructure. Agriculture cannot perform well unless rudimentary infrastructure is in place. There is little value in supplying credit or modern inputs if farmers lack the roads, bridges, and transportation required to acquire inputs and transport their harvests to market. Subsidized credit or inputs cannot compensate for nonexistent infrastructure. The third dimension is technology. Appropriate technology must be available for farmer use. The economic returns from using production inputs depend on the response that farmers obtain from their use. Traditional technology offers little scope for a dramatic reallocation of or increase in resource use.

Agricultural services generally represent the second priority for government support once a favorable productive environment has been created. At this stage, governments and donors can usefully make key sector-specific investments in the public goods required to support private firms engaged in farming or marketing agricultural inputs and products. For agriculture, this includes investments such as establishing prudential regulation and supervision of financial institutions, enforcement systems for contracts and property rights, market grades and standards, and market and credit information systems. Investments are also needed in research and extension systems, in training of credit and marketing specialists, and in human capital generally. Furthermore, since private firms may underinvest in new innovations because of a lack of information or risk perceptions, there may be a role for governments and donors to accelerate development by financing or conducting experiments in new credit and input delivery systems, institutions, and technologies.

Serious methodological problems in conducting impact studies make it difficult to quantitatively demonstrate the effects of policies and programs. *But the returns from many donor-funded projects appear to be fairly low, and certainly lower than expected by the project designers.* There is evidence that many projects have failed to provide a sustainable increase in the supply of agricultural inputs, credit, and marketing services. It is hard to demonstrate conclusively that aggregate output has been seriously affected when credit and marketing services disappeared once projects ended. Project completion reports often note serious problems in implementation that presumably influence their rate of return. Financial institutions have often been weakened by participation in tradition and credit projects. Many agricultural services projects have failed due to the urban bias of many policy environments. Firms and institutions supplying agricultural services cannot grow and become self-sustaining unless agricultural producers can prosper. Rarely do strong support institutions exist where agriculture is weak.

A second cause for failure was poor design of agricultural credit, input, and marketing projects, and especially the frequent failure of agricultural development banks and cooperatives. In spite of the large amount of funds spent on agricultural projects, there are few examples of successful delivery systems for financial or marketing services in developing countries. A third important problem for many sector-specific investments is that they fall into the public goods domain and require continuous government funding. Some government and donor projects have failed not because of poor design but because their sustainability required public funding that was not continuously available because of inadequate revenue collection. Reforms in public administration must accompany sector-specific investments to ensure that necessary revenues are available when donor funding is terminated.

The cost of credit, seeds, fertilizer, and marketing services normally should be paid by the user. Therefore, farmers should expect to pay these costs and are willing to do so when they are clearly profitable. Generally, *private sector firms are best equipped to supply inputs, credit, and marketing services that can be sold for a profit.* The weak performance of government banks and parastatal marketing boards suggests that governments often do a poor job in delivering many services. This is particularly true in countries too weak to resist strong rent-seeking groups and political intrusions in the operation of governmental agencies. On the other hand, some research, extension, and market regulation are public goods with high social payoffs. It is difficult for private firms to provide these services and charge users for them to recover costs, so they are the appropriate domain for the public sector. The exception is where private markets fail to provide socially desirable market services, such as for poor farmers. It is appropriate for governments and donors to support experiments leading to new institutions or instruments better designed to serve these groups, with the expectation that the private sector will eventually adopt them. The task of establishing and enforcing financial regulations is a public service often properly performed by government.

Some agencies or organizations have a clear advantage in providing agricultural services compared to others. Commercial banks have the best record in providing sustainable financial services, and in some cases cooperatives and credit unions have been successful in developing countries. Credit unions have been particularly successful in the mobilization of savings from poor people. Most NGO credit programs are highly subsidized, however, and have questionable long-term viability without continuous subsidization. Private firms generally have a better track record than government agencies in providing efficient and timely input and marketing services. Several private firms have also been effective in providing technical assistance to farmers in conjunction with the products they sell.

Some cooperatives have been successful in providing services, but many have failed. While cooperatives frequently command great patron loyalty and serve as a useful yardstick to measure the performance of the private sector, cooperatives have generally lacked the initiative and dynamism required for a highly successful agriculture in developing countries. Cooperatives are more susceptible to political manipulation than are private firms, and state-owned enterprises are even more susceptible. A useful approach in many instances is to let cooperatives compete head-to-head with private firms, with neither being subsidized nor sheltered by the public sector.

Historically, government agencies have provided the basic infrastructure of transportation and communication, and research, education, and extension services. Today, more and more of these functions are considered to be candidates for privatization. An unanswered question is how well poorer farmers will be served in completely privatized systems. Governments will continue, however, to play a key role in setting the "rules of the game" for the private sector through regulatory and supervisory activities. A debatable point is the extent to which NGOs can substitute for the government in providing public goods.

In closing, there is a large scope for U.S. investment in agricultural services in several of the low-income, emerging market economies. Experience has shown that where the basic economic environment is conducive for agriculture, the United States can help to finance sector-specific investments and design the technology and institutions necessary to provide agricultural support services in a market economy. The provision of agricultural inputs, credit, and marketing services will be especially important in those developing countries that have exploited their agricultural frontiers and must now tackle the difficult task of improving agricultural productivity.

NOTES

1. A longer version of this chapter listed in the reference section is available from the authors.
2. Dale Adams may have been the first person to use this terminology in The Ohio State University *Newsletter on Rural Financial Markets and Policy*, No. 1, Oct.–Dec. 1974.
3. These problems refer to potential losses that lenders face due to the risk of choosing borrowers who are likely to default or who engage in actions after getting a loan that increase their probability of default.

REFERENCES

Abbott, John. March 1985. "Agricultural Marketing Mechanisms and Institutions: Their Performance and Limitations." AGREP Division Working Paper No. 94. Washington, D.C.: World Bank.

———. 1993. *Agricultural and Food Marketing in Developing Countries: Selected Readings.* Tucson: The University of Arizona Press.

Adams, Dale W. 1974. *Newsletter on Rural Financial Markets and Policy*, The Ohio State University, No. 1, Oct.–Dec.

————. January 1988. "The Conundrum of Successful Credit Projects in Floundering Rural Financial Markets." *Economic Development and Cultural Change* 36 (2): 355–68.

————. December 1990. "U.S. Funded Rural Finance Activities in Latin America and the Caribbean 1942–1990: A New Strategy for the 1990s." ESO 1709. Columbus: Department of Agricultural Economics, The Ohio State University.

Adams, Dale W, and Delbert A. Fitchett, eds. 1992. *Informal Finance in Low-Income Countries*. Boulder, Colo.: Westview Press.

Adams, Dale W, and Douglas H. Graham. 1981. "A Critique of Traditional Agricultural Credit Projects and Policies." *Journal of Development Economics* 8 (1981): 347–66.

Adams, Dale W, Douglas H. Graham, and J. D. Von Pischke, eds. *Undermining Rural Development with Cheap Credit*. Boulder, Colo.: Westview Press, 1984.

Adams, Dale W, and Robert C. Vogel. 1986. "Rural Financial Markets in Low-Income Countries." *World Development* 14 (4): 477–87.

Agency for International Development. 1988. *A.I.D. Policy Paper on Financial Markets Development*. Washington, D.C.: USAID.

————. 1991. *Mobilizing Savings and Rural Finance: The A.I.D. Experience*. Washington, D.C.: USAID.

Aguilera-Alfred, Nelson, and Claudio Gonzalez-Vega. 1993. "A Multinomial Logit Analysis of Loan Targeting and Repayment at the Agricultural Development Bank of the Dominican Republic." *Agricultural Finance Review* 53 (1993): 55–64.

Ahmed, H. Ahmed, and Dale W. Adams. 1988. "Transaction Costs in Sudan's Rural Financial Markets." *Savings and Development* 1 (Supplementary Issue): 1–12.

Ahmed, Raisuddin, and Cynthia Donovan. November 1992. "Issues of Infrastructural Development: A Synthesis of the Literature." Washington, D.C.: International Food Policy Research Institute.

Araujo, Paulo F. C. de, Ricardo Shirota, and Richard L. Meyer. 1990. "Brazilian Agricultural Credit Policy Revisited in the Eighties." *Savings and Development* 14 (1): 101–116.

Asian Development Bank. February 1993. "Agricultural Credit Policy Paper." Draft paper. Manila: ADB.

Bejarano, Xavier, David R. Lee, and Duty Greene. July 1993. "Exchange Rate Reform and Its Effects on Ecuador's Traditional Agricultural Export Sector." Working Paper in Agricultural Economics. Ithaca, N.Y.: Department of Agricultural Economics, Cornell University.

Binswanger, Hans, and Shahidur Khandker. August 1992. "The Impact of Formal Finance on the Rural Economy of India." Policy Research Working Paper Series No. 949. Washington, D.C.: The World Bank.

Binswanger, Hans P., Shahidur R. Khandker, and Mark R. Rosenzweig. March 1989. "How Infrastructure and Financial Institutions Affect Agricultural Output and Investment in India." Working Paper Series No. 163. Washington, D.C.: The World Bank.

Blaine, Dianne, Michael Fuchs-Carsch, David Hess, and Jane Seifert. June 1991. "The A.I.D. Economic Policy Reform Program in Cameroon." A.I.D. Impact Evaluation Report No. 78. Washington, D.C.: USAID.

Borsdorf, Roe, Larry Dirksen, Virgil Eihusen, and Roger Wolfe. October 1992. "An Assessment of the Storage of Grains in Ukraine and Russia." Kansas State University Technical Assistance Report No. 129. Manhattan, Kans.: Food and Feed Grains Institute.

Chaves, Rodrigo A., and Claudio Gonzalez-Vega. 1996. "The Design of Successful Rural Financial Intermediaries: Evidence from Indonesia." *World Development* 24 (1): 65–78.

Chew, Siew Tuan. June 1987. "Credit Programs for Small Farmers: A Project Manager's Reference," A.I.D. Evaluation Special Study No. 47. Washington, D.C.: USAID.

Cuevas, Carlos E., and Douglas H. Graham. 1984. "Agricultural Lending Costs in Honduras." In *Undermining Rural Development with Cheap Credit*, ed. Dale W. Adams, Douglas H. Graham, and J. D. Von Pischke, 96–103. Boulder, Colo.: Westview Press.

David, Cristina C., and Richard L. Meyer. 1980. "Measuring the Farm Level Impact of Agricultural Loans." In *Borrowers & Lenders: Rural Financial Markets & Institutions in Developing Countries*, ed. John Howell, 201–34. London, U.K.: Overseas Development Institute.

Donald, Gordon. 1976. *Credit for Small Farmers in Developing Countries*. Boulder, Colo.: Westview Press.

Gonzalez-Vega, Claudio. 1984. "Credit-Rationing Behavior of Agricultural Lenders: The Iron Law of Interest-Rate Restrictions." In *Undermining Rural Development with Cheap Credit*, ed. Dale W. Adams, Douglas H. Graham, and J. D. Von Pischke, 78–95. Boulder, Colo.: Westview Press.

Harrison, Kelly, Donald Henley, Harold Riley, and James Shaffer. November 1974. "Improving Food Marketing Systems in Developing Countries: Experiences from Latin America." Research Report No. 6. East Lansing: Latin American Studies Center, Michigan State University.

Holtzman, John S., Richard D. Abbott, Carol Adoum, Patricia Kristjanson, Thomas Wittenberg, Charles J. D. Stathacos, Ismael Ouedraogo, Christine Erbacher, Nicolas Kulibaba, and Kimberly M. Aldridge. September 1992. "Agribusiness Development in Sub-Saharan Africa: Suggested Approaches, Information Needs and an Analytical Agenda." Volume 1: *Synthesis* and Volume 2: *Case Studies*. Agricultural Marketing Improvements Project (AMIS). Bethesda, Md.: Abt Associates and Post Harvest Institute for Perishables, University of Idaho.

Hossain, Mahubub. 1988. "Credit for Alleviation of Rural Poverty: The Grameen Bank in Bangladesh." Research Report No. 65. Washington, D.C.: International Food Policy Research Institute.

Inter-American Development Bank. February 27, 1984. "Summary of Evaluations of Global Agricultural Credit Programs." Draft paper. Washington, D.C.: IDB.

International Fertilizer Development Center. 1990. "Farmers' Survey Report." Fertilizer Distribution Improvement Project II, Funded by USAID. Dhaka, Bangladesh: IFDC.

———. 1992. "Annual Report 1990–91." Fertilizer Distribution Improvement Project II, Funded by USAID. Dhaka, Bangladesh: IFDC.

Jaffee, Steven. 1993. "Exporting High Value Food Commodities: Success Stories from Developing Countries." World Bank Discussion Paper 198. Washington, D.C.: World Bank.

Jebuni, Charles D., and Wayo Seini. October 1992. "Agricultural Input Policies Under Structural Adjustment: Their Distributional Implications." Cornell Food and Nutrition Policy Program Working Paper 31. Ithaca, N.Y.: Cornell University.

Johnston, Bruce F., Allan Hoben, Dirk W. Dijkerman, and William K. Jaeger. April 1987. *An Assessment of A.I.D. Activities to Promote Agricultural and Rural Development in Sub-Saharan Africa*. A.I.D. Evaluation Special Study No. 54. Washington, D.C.: USAID.

Khandker, Shahidur R., and Hans P. Binswanger. August 1989. "The Effect of Formal Credit on Output and Employment in Rural India." Working Paper Series No. 277. Washington, D.C.: World Bank.

Krueger, Anne. 1978. *Foreign Trade Regimes and Development: Liberalization Attempts and Consequences.* New York: Columbia University Press.

Krueger, Anne O., Maurice Schiff, and Alberto Valdés. September 1988. "Agricultural Incentives in Developing Countries: Measuring the Effect of Sectoral and Economywide Policies." *World Bank Economic Review* 2 (3): 255–71.

Ladman, Jerry R. 1984. "Loan-Transactions Costs, Credit Rationing, and Market Structure: The Case of Bolivia." In *Undermining Rural Development with Cheap Credit*, ed. Dale W. Adams, Douglas H. Graham, and J. D. Von Pischke, 104–19. Boulder, Colo.: Westview Press.

Lele, Uma, Robert Christiansen, and Kundhavi Kadiresan. 1989. "Fertilizer Policy in Africa: Lessons from Development Programs and Adjustment Lending, 1970–87." Managing Agricultural Development in Africa (MADIA) Discussion Paper No. 5. Washington, D.C.: World Bank.

Lele, Uma, and Robert E. Christiansen. 1989. "Markets, Marketing Boards, and Cooperatives in Africa: Issues in Adjustment Policy." Managing Agricultural Development in Africa (MADIA), Discussion Paper No. 11. Washington, D.C.: World Bank.

Lele, Uma, Nicolas Van De Walle, and Mathurn Gbetibouo. November 1989. "Cotton in Africa: An Analysis of Differences in Performance." Managing Agricultural Development in Africa (MADIA) Discussion Paper No. 7. Washington, D.C.: World Bank.

Lesser, W. November 1992. "Agribusiness and Public Sector Collaboration in Agricultural Technology Development and Use in Sub-Saharan Africa: A Synthesis of Field Studies." Agricultural Modeling Improvement Strategies Project (AMIS). Washington, D.C.: USAID/AFR/ARTS/FARA.

Lieberson, Joseph M., Katherine A. Kotellos, and George G. Miller. October 1985. "A Synthesis of A.I.D. Experience: Small-Farmer Credit, 1973–1985." A.I.D. Evaluation Special Study No. 41. Washington, D.C.: USAID.

McKean, Cressida S. July 1990. "Development Finance Institutions: A Discussion of Donor Experience." A.I.D. Program Evaluation Discussion Paper No. 31. Washington, D.C.: World Bank.

Meissner, Frank. May 1989. "Effective Food Marketing: A Tool for Socioeconomic Development in the Third World." *Food Policy* 14 (2): 90–96.

Meyer, Richard L., and Carlos E. Cuevas. 1992. "Reduction of Transaction Costs of Financial Intermediation: Theory and Innovations." In *Savings and Credit for Development*, 285–317. Report of the International Conference on Savings and Credit for Development, Klarskovgärd, Denmark, May 28–31, 1990. New York: United Nations.

Meyer, Richard L., Douglas H. Graham, and Carlos E. Cuevas. December 1992. "A Review of the Literature on Financial Markets and Agribusiness Development in Sub-Saharan Africa: Lessons Learned and Suggestions for an Analytical Agenda." Report to the Africa Bureau, USAID, ESO 2008. Columbus: Department of Agricultural Economics, The Ohio State University.

Meyer, Richard L., and Donald W. Larson. July 1996. "Issues in Providing Agricultural Services in Developing Countries." ESO 2323. Columbus: Department of Agricultural Economics, The Ohio State University.

Nagarajan, Geetha, Cristina C. David, and Richard L. Meyer. October 1992. "Informal Financing through Land Pawning Contracts." *Journal of Development Studies* 29 (1): 93–107.

Oehmke, James F., and Eric W. Crawford. 1993. "The Impact of Agricultural Technology in Sub-Saharan Africa: A Synthesis of Symposium Findings." MSU International Development Paper No. 14. East Lansing: Department of Agricultural Economics and Department of Economics, Michigan State University.

Patten, Richard H., and Jay K. Rosengard. 1991. *Progress with Profits. The Development of Rural Banking in Indonesia.* Sector Studies No. 4. San Francisco, Calif.: ICS Press.

Peterson, Willis L. December 1988. "International Supply Response." *Agricultural Economics* 2 (4): 365–374.

Reserve Bank of India. 1989. *A Review of the Agricultural Credit System in India.* Bombay, India: Report of the Agricultural Credit Review Committee.

Reusse, E. November 1987. "Liberalization and Agricultural Marketing: Recent Causes and Effects in Third World Countries." *Food Policy* 12: 299–317.

Sacay, Orlando J., Meliza H. Agabin, and Chita Irene E. Tanchoco. 1985. *Small Farmer Credit Dilemma.* Manila, Philippines: Technical Board for Agricultural Credit.

Schmidt, R. H., and Erhard Kropp, eds. 1987. *Rural Finance, Guiding Principles.* Deutsche Gesellschaft fur Technische Zusammenarbeit (GTZ): Eschborn.

Stiglitz, Joseph E., and Andrew Weiss. June 1981. "Credit Rationing in Markets with Imperfect Information." *American Economic Review* 71 (3): 393–410.

Vogel, Robert C. 1984a. "The Effect of Subsidized Agricultural Credit on Income Distribution in Costa Rica." In *Undermining Rural Development with Cheap Credit,* ed. Dale W. Adams, Douglas H. Graham, and J. D. Von Pischke, 133–45. Boulder, Colo.: Westview Press.

————. 1984b. "Savings Mobilization: The Forgotten Half of Rural Finance." In *Undermining Rural Development with Cheap Credit,* ed. Dale W. Adams, Douglas H. Graham, and J. D. Von Pischke, 248–65. Boulder, Colo.: Westview Press.

Vogel, Robert C., and Donald W. Larson. 1984. "Illusion and Reality in Allocating Agricultural Credit: The Example of Colombia." In *Undermining Rural Development with Cheap Credit,* ed. Dale W. Adams, Douglas H. Graham, and J. D. Von Pischke, 49–58. Boulder, Colo.: Westview Press.

Von Pischke, J. D., and Dale W. Adams. November 1980. "Fungibility and the Design and Evaluation of Agricultural Credit Projects." *American Journal of Agricultural Economics* 62: 719–726.

Von Pischke, J. D., and John Rouse. 1983. "Selected Successful Experiences in Agricultural Credit and Rural Finance in Africa." *Savings and Development* 7 (1): 21-43.

Von Pischke, J. D., Dale W. Adams, and Gordon Donald, eds. 1983. *Rural Financial Markets in Developing Countries: Their Use and Abuse.* Baltimore, Md.: Johns Hopkins University Press.

Wenner, Mark D., John S. Holtzman, and Gary Ender. September 1993. "Agribusiness Promotion in Developing Countries: Policy Regimes and Institutional Support." Agribusiness Policy Analysis Project, Phase II (APAP) Collaborative Research Report No. 351. Cambridge, Mass,: Abt Associates.

Wolgin, Jerome M. August 1990. "Fresh Start in Africa: A.I.D. and Structural Adjustment in Africa." Washington, D.C.: USAID.

World Bank. May 1975. "Agricultural Credit Sector Policy Paper." Washington, D.C.: World Bank.

————. 1990. "Agricultural Marketing: The World Bank's Experience, 1974-85." Washington, D.C.: Operations Evaluation Department, World Bank.

————. 1991. *World Development Report 1991: The Challenge of Development.* New York: Oxford University Press.

————. July 1993a. "Agricultural Sector Review." Washington, D.C.: Agriculture and Natural Resources Department, World Bank.

————. September 1993b. *The East Asian Miracle: Economic Growth and Public Policy.* New York: Oxford University Press.

————. 1993c. *Handbook on Financial Sector Operations* 1st Edition. Washington, D.C.: Operations Policy Department, World Bank.

————. June 29, 1993d. "A Review of Bank Lending for Agricultural Credit and Rural Finance (1948–1992)." World Bank Report No. 12143. Washington, D.C.: World Bank.

Yaron, Jacob. January 1992. "Successful Rural Financial Institutions." World Bank Discussion Paper No. 150. Washington, D.C.: World Bank.

6

Asset Distribution and Access: Land Tenure Programs

Virginia A. Lambert with Mitchell A. Seligson

INTRODUCTION

Land is a fundamental asset needed for agricultural production. Donors have invested in less developed countries to influence the distribution of and access to farmland in order to increase agricultural productivity, improve the quality of rural life, and reduce rural unrest.

U.S. involvement in land reform began immediately after World War II, with major and generally successful reforms in Japan, Taiwan, and South Korea. Beginning in the 1960s, in response to the Cuban Revolution, redistributive land reforms were implemented in Latin America under the Alliance for Progress. Later, with the spread of economic liberalism and disappointment with these post-Cuban Revolution reforms, investment shifted to broaden access to land through market mechanisms and to strengthen tenure security through land titling and registration. Increasing concern for the environment is pushing a new set of land tenure issues to the forefront.

This review of the impact of donor investments to improve agricultural asset distribution and access over the past thirty years shows near universal agreement that family-size farms are more efficient than large farms, but that distortions in land markets often prevent land distribution from moving in the direction of optimal efficiency. Either redistributive land reform or elimination of market distortions is necessary to increase efficiency, but both of these approaches invariably run into opposition from powerful forces within the country. The review also shows that gross inequalities in land distribution have been a highly destabilizing force in rural areas, associated with numerous instances of rural rebellion in the developing world. At the same time, many land reforms have failed to quell insurgency or to affect the underlying inequalities reflected in income. Finally, the review shows that an effective land tenure program must be crafted in response to the complex of factors that defines the agrarian structure of each country. No single formula will work for all countries at all times. Knowledge of the existing land tenure structure is a sine qua non for any intervention in this area.

Until the mid-1980s, the United States had been the principal international proponent and supporter for land tenure programs and as a result has amassed an impressive breadth of experience in this area. Although USAID support for land tenure interventions has waned in recent years, its expertise in this vital area of agricultural development remains.

This chapter first expands on definitional issues and delineates the evaluation literature on which the synthesis is based and then summarizes the motivations for land reform by outlining the historical pattern of investment in agrarian structure.   It next draws on academic literature to examine the theoretical relationships between agricultural growth and agrarian structure. Finally, it examines empirical evidence of the effectiveness, in both political and economic terms, of various interventions intended to change the agrarian structure.

DEFINITIONS

The 1978 AID "Agricultural Development Policy Paper" identified five essential elements of agricultural development. "Asset distribution and access" (land tenure and local participatory institutions) was defined as "the relative equality of the distribution of assets, particularly land, and the effectiveness of local participatory institutions, including local government, cooperatives, and other farmer organizations, in ensuring access to productive inputs through enforcement of land tenure security, water rights, etc." (AID 1978, 26). Asset distribution and access concerned agrarian structure—the institutional framework determining distribution of and access to resources—thereby describing an arena for investment rather than a type of investment. Successful investments were expected to improve equity and equality of opportunity (particularly for the rural poor) and increase agricultural production and productivity.

The complexity and variation of agrarian structure across regions is well known and, technically, no ideal structure holds for all times and places:

There is nothing inherently good or bad, right or wrong about land tenure systems as such. While ideological arguments on the best ways of organizing agriculture continue, no tenure system can be adjudged best in the abstract. Any judgments concerning a particular system must take note of the institutional and technological conditions in the society and the stage at which that society lies in the transformation from an agrarian to an industrial economy. Our judgments should also consider what specific groups and individuals in that society are attempting to accomplish. (Dorner and Kanel 1970, 3)

In characterizing agrarian structure, the literature focuses on land tenure. Land tenure is the bundle of rights that determines how land is owned and operated and the behavior flowing from that institutional pattern. Land reform is a basic restructuring of the land tenure system (Thiesenhusen 1989). The AID *Spring Review of Land Reform* (1970) characterized land reform or land tenure reform as "(1) land ownership redistribution; and/or (2) granting land users secure, long-term tenancy at fair rents, both in areas where at least modest amounts of social infrastructure already exist"[1] (Lachman 1970).

Some analysts distinguish between land reform, the redistribution of land and property rights, and agrarian reform, the complex of changes in rural structure that accompany land redistribution. The term *agrarian reform* sometimes is used explicitly to call attention to the necessity for investments in services for farmers, land titling and registration, and rural infrastructure, as well as for redistribution of assets. In this chapter, the term *land reform* means programs based on land redistribution, with the understanding that broad structural change and *agrarian reform* must necessarily accompany land reform.

While land reform was the principal type of land tenure investment in the 1960s, later programs increasingly focused on tenure security and land market operations. Tenure security, the assurance of continuing access to resources, is a characteristic of both customary and formal tenure systems. In private property systems, tenure security ultimately rests on legal documentation and the state's guarantee of ownership rights. Land titling programs involve the issuance of private property titles to holders of plots of land, and registration refers to the recording of these titles by the state (Stanfield 1990).

Economic theory suggests that over time, efficient land markets will optimize land distribution and access and obviate the need for land reform. In less developed countries, however, distortions in land markets inhibit the participation of landless peasants and small farmers. To counter these distortions and increase market efficiency, donors have supported programs (1) to increase the supply of land accessible for peasants to purchase (e.g., through land banks or land purchase/sale programs),[2] and (2) to increase the effective demand for land by peasant producers (e.g., through credit schemes or mortgage guaranty programs).[3] Systems to tax agricultural land, which base tax rates on the value of the land under optimal use, also seek to open land markets and increase productivity.

Land settlement projects expand the land under cultivation. "New lands settlement is defined as the spontaneous and sponsored settlement of areas which are largely uncultivated at the time of their occupation" (Scudder 1984, 1). These integrated rural projects involve not only land distribution but extensive infrastructure construction and institution building. The settlements are often on public land and usually involve virgin areas or reclaimed land.

Other interventions to modify the distribution of and access to land include land consolidation, limitations on sales, restrictions on rentals, and privatization and decollectivization. There are no broad-based evaluations of these programs, though they may be more pertinent to decision making in the 1990s than those reviewed in this chapter. For example, restrictions on sales and land use through zoning regulations are primary interventions used in conjunction with environmental programs. Privatization and decollectivization have taken on new importance with the shift from socialist to market structures in Eastern and Central Europe and the Newly Independent States.

MOTIVATIONS FOR LAND REFORM: A HISTORICAL SYNTHESIS

Land reform is not an invention of the great revolutions of the twentieth century. Elias Tuma (1965) has shown that it dates back at least twenty-six centuries and possibly earlier. In spite of this protracted history, there is no clear consensus on its costs and benefits, because most reforms have been motivated by distinct and often conflicting objectives.

Consider the Mexican Revolution. One of its major outcomes was a major land reform. But this land reform actually occurred in reaction to an earlier reform instituted at the end of the nineteenth century, imposed from above by the government of Porfirio Díaz to stimulate agricultural development by privatizing communally held property. Entire indigenous communities lost land they had farmed for centuries, and they were forced either to become wage laborers on the sugar plantations that expanded onto the land they had once farmed or to migrate to other parts of Mexico in search of work. The Díaz reform, through its impact on the peasant, is widely seen as the central motivation behind the Mexican Revolution of 1910 (Womack 1969).

The Mexican case illustrates nicely the widely conflicting motivations for land reforms over the centuries. On the one hand are reforms designed to modernize agriculture. In some cases these reforms focus on changing the nature of land tenure (e.g., privatizing communal land), while in others they are directly confiscatory, taking land from what are viewed as "inefficient" small holders and recombining the properties into what are seen as "efficient" large estates or plantations. Although these reforms are nearly always justified in terms of improved agricultural efficiency, in many cases the real motivation is to take property from a less powerful group and turn it over to one more powerful.

On the other hand are reforms explicitly designed to redress inequalities in the distribution of land assets, as in numerous twentieth-century cases of peasant uprisings, including the Mexican Revolution of 1910, the Russian Revolution of 1917, the Chinese Revolution of 1949, the Bolivian Revolution of 1952, the Cuban Revolution of 1959, and the Nicaraguan Revolution of 1979.[4] In each of these cases, a major land redistribution program was put in place either during the insurrection or soon after its conclusion. Numerous other cases of peasant uprisings did not result in full-scale revolution, but land was a central issue and such uprisings remain an element in the post–Cold War world, as in the January

1, 1994, Zapatista peasant uprising in southern Mexico, where demand for land was a central issue.

The success or failure of land reform must be assessed in relation to the motivation for the reform. Reforms brought about by peasants who demand land cannot be judged by the same criteria as those designed "from above" to enhance productivity.

U.S. Interests in Land Reform

Throughout its thirty-year involvement with land reform, the United States has been concerned with equity as often as with productivity. Until a marked shift in 1986, U.S. policy explicitly saw land reform in terms of its equity implications.[5] So strong was the belief in the role of equity in land reform that it constituted a central tenet of U.S. policy in the two post–World War II guerrilla wars with the most direct U.S. involvement: Vietnam and El Salvador. In both cases, agricultural productivity took second place to counter-insurgency concerns.

The logic behind U.S. support for redistributive land reform in El Salvador is presented by the Rand Corporation (Schwarz 1991, 44):

El Salvador's land redistribution program, designed by American experts, financed by American economic aid, and largely implemented by American organizers and technicians, has been, along with America's attempt to improve the armed forces' respect for human rights, the heart of the U.S. effort to transform the conditions that motivate the insurgency. . . . From the beginning, land reform, initiated by the reformist civilian-military junta that prevailed briefly in 1979 to 1980, was seen primarily as a *political* tool. Even American advisers who doubted its economic utility stressed that it was a political necessity in the war against the guerrillas for the peasantry's hearts and minds.

A less official but highly knowledgeable source, Roy Prosterman, was directly involved in designing land reform programs in both Vietnam and El Salvador. He argues that land reform can help avoid "at least half a dozen great civil conflicts, otherwise overwhelmingly likely, which might well carry a combined death toll in the millions, and beyond even that, would bring individually small but cumulatively significant risks of a direct superpower confrontation" (Prosterman and Riedinger 1987, 1). With the Cold War behind, such counter-insurgency-based reforms will be far less common in the future. But the specter of Mexican instability brought on by the uprising in Chiapas demonstrates that such reforms may not have been permanently removed from the U.S. foreign policy agenda.

U.S. interest and support for land reform has had three distinct phases, described next.

Phase 1. Immediately following World War II, the United States saw land reform as a major tool to build democracy in Asia. The United States supported reforms in Japan, Taiwan, and South Korea to stimulate the growth of "yeoman farmers," who were perceived at the time as representing the backbone of democracy. Those reforms have been linked by many scholars to the rapid economic growth that emerged in the 1950s and 1960s in all three countries and to their ability to avoid severe income inequality. The protracted period of authoritarian rule in Taiwan and South Korea also demonstrates, however, that reform is not a sufficient condition for the emergence and stability of democracy. Support for land reform beyond Asia was limited during this first phase.

Phase 2. The Cuban Revolution in 1959 radically altered the U.S. position on land reform, and the emergence of a strategic alliance between Cuba and the Soviet Union forced a rethinking of U.S. policy toward Latin America. The Kennedy administration developed a new strategy that promised massive foreign assistance on the condition that recipient governments implement structural economic transformations. A direct statement of U.S. faith in land reform was made in the 1961 Charter of Punta del Este for the Alliance for Progress, which proposed, among other things, land reform as a precondition for U.S. financial aid to Latin American countries. Following this accord, agrarian reform agencies were formed in virtually every Latin American country, and reform efforts were begun in most.

These land reforms, stimulated by the fear both in the United States and in Latin America of further communist takeovers, were limited in scope. The reform agencies, even with the best intentions, ran into a head wind of landlord opposition that was successful in blunting the reforms through budget restrictions, protracted legal battles in the courts, and, at times, threats and violence to intimidate peasants and land reform technocrats. In addition, U.S. policy lacked domestic political support because land reform threatened the property interests of U.S. companies operating overseas, particularly in Central America. Thus these Alliance for Progress reforms were limited in depth and scope.

Despite growing opposition to land reform in the United States, the Nicaraguan Revolution of 1979 again stirred fears of communist takeovers in the region. As a direct result, the United States began to provide strong support for land reform in neighboring El Salvador to win over the peasants from the growing insurgency. That was the last case in which the United States became directly involved in a major land reform program.

Comparing the first and second phases of U.S. involvement in land reform, it is clear that the pre-Castro reforms were more successful. The historical circumstances of World War II were critical to the success of land reform in Asia, since the war destroyed Japanese colonial administration and its system. It was replaced by a strong political power backed by military forces. No such preconditioning circumstances existed with the Alliance for Progress. In addition, reforms in Asia generally did not involve redistribution of land but rather a change in tenure status. In these "land-to-the-tiller" reforms, small farmers continued to farm the same land they had farmed for generations, but as owners rather than tenants.   Also, in Taiwan and other areas of Japanese colonial rule, political opposition to dislocation was reduced because the expropriated landowners were foreigners (Dorner and Thiesenhusen 1989).

In Latin America, the pre-Castro reforms were the most successful.   The reforms in Mexico (1930s) and Bolivia (1952) were driven by populist forces in the context of national revolutions.   Powerful state action pushed forward difficult reforms that displaced the native landed elite and redistributed hacienda land to landless peasants.   Castro's land reform, the most extensive of any ever undertaken in Latin America, also emerged in the context of a national revolution and expropriated numerous foreign-owned properties as well as large estates owned by Cuban nationals.

Phase 3.   Until the mid-1980s, land reform had been considered one of the tools available to increase land access and improve agriculture. The 1979 AID Policy Determination on Land Reform included redistribution of land ownership as one option among others for reform (cited in Montgomery 1984).

The policy shifted, however, under the influence of the Reagan administration. Initially, intervention was justified to stimulate the growth of small farms and, by extension, the growth of small business. By 1986, the AID Policy Determination on Land Tenure did not mention land reform or redistribution as potential interventions, and instead shifted attention toward land titling and registration and land markets.

AID supports those LDC policies and programs which lead to a general, country-wide reliance on market forces in the valuation and distribution of land ownership and land use rights. AID will also support programs that broaden the opportunity for access to agricultural land, promote tenure security, and stimulate productive uses of land to ameliorate the barriers to market entry that exist in some LDCs. (AID 1986, 2)

Not only U.S. policy shifted. Even though the World Bank had amassed considerable data that supported the conclusion that small farms were more efficient than large farms, the Bank concluded that the way to increase the number of small farms was through the rental market rather than reform (Binswanger, et al. 1993, 48). Despite the continuing need for and potential benefits of land reform in parts of the world, because of the weak financial and political feasibility of reform, other policy options may have more impact than land redistribution.

Accordingly, both USAID and multilateral funds for land reform have diminished since the mid-1980s, and investments in land tenure have shifted toward land titling and registration and projects to increase market efficiency. Other options for investment include support for land settlement (and resettlement) schemes, land consolidation, tenancy reform, and land taxation.

THEORETICAL CONCERNS

The following discussion lays out the theoretical rationale underlying five interventions in agrarian structure: redistributive land reform, land titling and registration, land market interventions, land taxation, and land settlement and resettlement. The inverse relationship between farm size and agricultural productivity is the main economic rationale underlying investments in redistributive land reform. Tenure security is the underlying economic rationale for investments in the other four areas.

Farm Size and Productivity: The Economic Rationale for Land Reform

Much evidence shows that small farms are more productive than large farms in developing countries. Large estates all over the developing world tend to be highly inefficient compared to small or family farms. Redistributive land reform, therefore, makes sense as an intervention to spur agricultural growth. The hypothesis that small farms generally have a higher value of output per unit of land and capital than do large farms has been tested empirically most extensively by Berry and Cline (1979). They analyzed the relationship for a sample of about thirty countries and concluded that

in practically all of these countries the large farm sector . . . uses its land less intensively than the small farm sector . . . based on the percent of farm area under cultivation. . . . A second set of statistical tests using cross-country data finds no evidence of faster growth of agricultural output in countries with larger average farm size. . . . Nor is the agricultural growth rate related, positively or negatively, to the degree of concentration in the distribution of land. Finally, . . . farm output and employment per area of available land are higher in countries with smaller average farm size and more equal distribution of land. (Berry and Cline 1979, 40)

In addition, they tested the relationship with internal production data from Brazil, Colombia, the Philippines, Pakistan, India, and Malaysia. "For all six countries with intensive data sets, the statistical tests . . . confirm the negative relationship between farm size and output per unit of land area available. This negative relationship holds, even when removing the influence of land quality" (Berry and Cline 1979, 126).

Additional empirical research has refined the measures of production and structure and verified the causal mechanisms. (See, for example, Sen 1981; Carter 1984; Carter and Jonakin 1987; Thiesenhusen and Melmed-Sanjak 1990; and Binswanger et al. 1993.) The inverse relationship has been confirmed uniformly across a variety of agricultural systems and geographical locations.

In the late 1960s, institutional economists developed a theoretical argument to explain this empirically observed inverse relationship and the potential contribution of optimal size to economic growth, equity, and particularly, poverty alleviation. On the supply side, because output per unit of land is greater on smaller holdings, land reforms that redistribute land from large estates to small farms should boost aggregate production. The creation of relatively small family farms (or cooperative forms of tenure) also should provide employment for excess rural labor, thereby relieving the pressures for urban migration. On the demand side, incomes of the rural majority should increase as a result of land reform, stimulating increased demand for industrial goods and growth of the manufacturing sector (Dorner 1992).

The predicted results have not always materialized, however. First, the process is highly disruptive if it forces the relocation and resettlement of the former owners as well as the new owners. Second, it may well remove from the farms those with the most knowledge about successful agricultural production on that land. Third, the new farm owners may have no loyalty to the region to which they have been assigned and even less knowledge of its political and social environment. Fourth, land reform may negatively affect the business climate, producing a net outflow of investment and entrepreneurial skills. Fifth, the owners may resist the reform through legal means, tying up the program in the court system for decades, or through illegal intimidation and attacks on the new settlers.

Tenure Security

A second important theoretical relationship underlying interventions in agrarian structure is the positive relationship between tenure security and agricultural productivity. Theoretically, a person secure in his or her access to land will work the land more intensively, make long-term capital investments, exhibit greater concern for soil conservation, and practice more effective stewardship than someone with tenuous ties to the land, because he or she personally will realize the benefits of these investments over the long term.

Tenure security is a more important issue in land-scarce than in land-abundant regions, and it increases in importance over time in areas where population growth puts pressure on arable land resources. Security varies along a continuum, from holding land under the most tenuous conditions as a squatter, to holding fully titled and registered private property. Traditional or customary tenure in both private and communal property systems may provide considerable security, depending on locally accepted and enforced tenure rules (Stanfield 1990).

Land titling and registration. In private property systems, security of tenure is maximized through registered titles backed up by the legal system. In theory, fully registered titles contribute to investment and productivity because they allow the land to be used as collateral for credit. Legally registered titles are thought to increase tenure security by reducing land disputes and by providing a forum in which to resolve disputes that do arise. Land titles also facilitate land transfers in the land market by guaranteeing that the owner has the right to sell the land and by standardizing information for buyers and sellers. Titles also may be used to protect owners when external factors (such as roads, irrigation systems, discovery of oil) change land values, because owners with title are likely to be less vulnerable than those without. The price of titled land, as a result of all of these factors, is often higher than the price of land not securely held.

On the other hand, land titling and registration programs have no impact on land distribution, positive or negative, and therefore do not address the fundamental equity question. Also, titling and registration are costly and therefore more likely to be available to large rather than small landowners. Large landowners, in turn, may use the additional advantages of titles to accumulate more land through the land market.

Land markets. There are two theoretical reasons to focus on land market interventions. First, the complexities of tenure systems and social and economic systems across cultures, regions, and nations make it unlikely for planners to select an optimal tenure structure to apply through land reform. Second, perfectly competitive markets allocate resources, including land resources, to their optimal use (Stringer 1987).[6] Even less than perfectly competitive markets can increase efficiency in resource use and agricultural production.

Although land markets are imperfect everywhere, they are generally more distorted in less developed countries than in industrialized ones (Stringer 1987). In Latin America and countries with a strong dual structure of landholding (*latifundia* and *minifundia*), small and large properties are transferred in separate markets. Small farmers do not have access to the large farm sector, and when large farms enter the market they are rarely sub-divided. Land market interventions are designed to facilitate the subdivision of extensive large farms into intensive small farms and also to allow suboptimal farm units to be expanded.

Not all researchers believe land markets can achieve these benefits. In a World Bank paper Binswanger et al. (1993) hypothesize that coercion and imperfections in labor and credit markets and the inclusion of expected capital gains in land prices mean the value of land will exceed capitalized agricultural profits. A person without savings or capital who must take out a mortgage at market interest rates and whose only income from the land is from agricultural production can pay for the land only by reducing consumption, or, in effect, subsidizing the cost of his or her own occupation of that land.

Small farmers face an additional disadvantage in the land market if transaction costs are fixed. Further, in systems without insurance, small landowners are more likely than wealthier landowners to face distress sales (Binswanger and Elgin 1988; Carter and Mesbah 1990). Large farmers also tend to benefit more than small farmers from agricultural subsidies, such as special credit lines and tax breaks.

Land market interventions may not be effective if they are undertaken as isolated activities rather than as part of a broad land strategy. Dorner and Saliba (1981, 1) state that land market interventions are "most effectively applied in situations where redistribution *via* expropriation and tenure reform has already proceeded, where a relatively egalitarian landholding structure already exists, and where the land market can be made, with the aid of these lesser instruments, to work more efficiently in the interests of both productivity and equality." Binswanger and Elgin (1988) argue that neither redistributive land reform nor redistribution through market mechanisms can be effective in a distorted environment that favors large farmers with benefits such as unequal income tax exemptions or access to credit. Thus, a precondition for the success of these programs is elimination of these distortions. A comprehensive title and registration system may be another precondition for land markets to function effectively.

Land taxation. Taxes on agricultural land have been proposed not only as a source of revenue but also as a tool to influence land distribution and to increase agricultural production. The nonrevenue functions of land taxation have been in use since the mid-1800s, and they have received donor funding in less developed countries since the 1950s.

In theory, a fixed tax on all land, productive or not, based on land values in optimal use would encourage owners of large, unproductive farms to sell their land or to use it more productively. Tax exemptions or credits for productivity-related improvements would also encourage more intensive land use. Alternatively, a progressive land tax could be applied which would be based on some measure of farm size and farm productivity and presumably would offer a stimulus to subdivide large, unproductive farms for sale to landless or land-poor farmers.

Land taxation requires a reliable cadaster. A cadaster also provides important information needed for the land market, natural resource management, and land reform, but it is costly to construct and maintain. As a practical matter, taxation systems have rarely been used for equity adjustments. Most taxation systems, even those that are explicitly progressive, are manipulated by the rich and powerful for their own benefit and harm the poor.

Land settlement. Land settlement projects are different from the other interventions because they do not deal with distribution of and access to existing resources but rather with bringing new resources into production. Colonization of new lands has been on the agenda of governments for centuries. As population densities have increased throughout the world, colonization schemes have become more attractive. Even without government intervention, spontaneous land settlement in frontier areas can serve as a safety valve for overpopulation.

Government- and donor-sponsored settlement on government-owned or reclaimed lands has been advocated as an alternative to or component of redistributive land reform. According to the World Bank (1985), the principal goal is increased agricultural production. During the 1970s and 1980s, most of the increase in agricultural production in the less developed world was due to opening new land to farming rather than to increased productivity. In many cases, absorption of excess rural population has been a goal. Equity objectives (improved income and standard of living for the settlement households) are usually implicit.

On the other hand, land colonization schemes may do more damage than good. First, it is argued that unpopulated land is a myth. Increasingly, colonization schemes are situated on lands of ethnic minorities, especially the Indian populations of Latin America, because indigenous rights to those properties are not recognized. Second, "unsettled lands" are often located in fragile environments where colonization could do substantial damage while bringing only limited and ephemeral production gains.

EMPIRICAL EVIDENCE

What is the empirical evidence associated with the theoretical claims made for and against investments in land reform and tenure security? This section begins by examining evidence on the relationship between land reform and political stability, because political stability has been the primary motivation for virtually all U.S. interventions in land reform. Political stability is a vital precondition for economic growth, including agricultural growth. Next, the results of selected evaluations of land reform programs are summarized, beginning with evaluations of the 1970s, the decade following strong U.S. support for redistributive reform, and followed by evaluations of the 1980s. Finally, evaluations of interventions designed to improve tenure security are reviewed.

Land Reform and Political Stability

U.S. intervention in land reform since Castro's revolution has been designed, in part, to serve as a counter-insurgency strategy to deprive guerrilla groups of a peasant following. Unfortunately, the lessons learned from the postWorld War II land reforms in Asia and the pre-Castro reforms in Mexico and Bolivia seem to have had little to do with more contemporary situations in Vietnam, El Salvador, and Iran. In all three cases, land reform did not accomplish its intended objectives and indeed may have exacerbated the problems of political instability.

Vietnam.[7] Land reform was initiated in South Vietnam in 1956 but was restricted both in geographical area and number of properties affected. In 1968 the pace of reform accelerated dramatically, and over 100,000 titles were distributed. In 1969 land rents were frozen by the government, and in 1970 a major land-to-the-tiller law was passed. By 1974 almost 1 million titles had been granted covering 1.1 million hectares—44 percent of the total farm area of the country.

By any measure, the land reform in South Vietnam was massive and would appear to provide an excellent case against which to test the thesis that such reforms enhance political stability and quell insurgency. Yet, as is well known, in 1975, one year after the conclusion of this massive reform, South Vietnam fell and was absorbed by the North. That land reform did not affect the outcome of the war would seem to suggest that land reform does not work as a counterinsurgency strategy. Others argue, however, that the reform was "too little, too late," and had it been implemented earlier would have succeeded.

El Salvador. The land reform in El Salvador was decreed in 1979 just as the civil war was commencing. It involved three distinct phases: Two phases involved expropriation of large properties and the third was a land-to-the-tiller program. According to Prosterman, the magnitude of the El Salvador reform was close to that of Vietnam, affecting approximately 30 percent of all land in farms and nearly 200,000 farmers (Prosterman and Riedinger 1987, 157).[8]

It is difficult to argue that the El Salvador reform was either too little or too late, yet the reform did not head off the civil war that began simultaneously and continued for twelve years. On the other hand, although the reform did come at the beginning of the insurgency, many powerful elements within the military strongly opposed the reformist junta that briefly held power in 1979 and was responsible for the land reform decree. The reform also was strongly opposed by business elites, some elements of the Church, and large landlords. In 1980 alone "over 500 peasant leaders, dozens of land reform officials, and hundreds of peasant union and cooperative members were assassinated" (Schwarz 1991, 45–46). Schwarz also reports that by 1983 thousands of beneficiaries had been killed.

Iran.[9] In the early 1960s, the shah of Iran, under pressure from the Kennedy administration, launched his so-called Landless White Revolution, which in effect accelerated the land reform begun in the 1950s. By 1967, according to official sources, land had been redistributed to about 520,000 families, or about 15 percent of peasant families. Here again, the reform could not be considered too little or too late, yet it did not immunize the regime from dissent nor, ultimately, save it from being overthrown by opposition forces, no doubt because the government continued its repressive policies that served to exacerbate opposition (Green 1982).

These three cases of major land reforms give little support to the proposition that land reform has an important counterinsurgency role. In all three cases, there was a presumed direct association between *land* inequality and revolution, although a more powerful predictor of revolutionary activity may be *income* inequality. When income inequality is included in a cross-national multiple regression analysis, one finds no relationship between land inequality and insurgency, since all of the effects of land inequality are mediated by income inequality (Muller and Seligson 1987).[10]

Land reform, if carried to the point of actually affecting the distribution of income, as in Japan, Taiwan, and South Korea, can indeed make an important contribution to countering insurgency and fostering political stability. Land reform without income redistribution, however, is probably at best a temporary palliative and can escalate conflict through alienation of powerful conservative groups.

The Economic Impact of Land Reform: Evidence from the 1970s

The earliest comparative regional studies of the economic impact of land reform appeared in the late 1960s, most focusing on Latin America. Two are examined here: the 1970 AID *Spring Review of Land Reform* and a World Bank evaluation of land reform in five Latin American countries. These studies repeatedly point to the problem of comparing across diverse situations and drawing generalizations from individual cases. The economic impact of land reform varies according to the pre-reform situation, the nature of the reform, and the general economic condition of each country.

Spring Review of Land Reform. In early 1970, USAID sponsored a conference on land reform. Thirty country-specific case studies as well as theoretical background papers and synthesis documents were prepared. The review focused on (1) the extent to which land reform had been an economic, social, and political success in countries that had tried it; (2) the relative merits of land reform compared with other strategies for rural development; (3) preconditions for successful reform; (4) design of land reform programs most appropriate for achieving stipulated objectives; and (5) the role of donors, if any, in this complex and politically sensitive process.

The *Spring Review* provided strong and consistent evidence confirming that pre-reform levels of agricultural production and productivity were increased or at least maintained when farm size was reduced as a result of reform. In general, the studies also affirmed the positive impact of land reform on employment and welfare. One of the synthesis documents reported that

the most important single finding is that social and political goals of wider distribution of opportunity, power, and employment among farm people need not be in conflict with but can be consistent with increased agricultural production and efficiency. In other words, equity and productivity tend to be mutually supporting objectives of land reform. There is little basis in fact for the common assumption that land reform, in reducing the size of landholding, also reduces economic efficiency and output. Rather, empirical studies discussed in the Review showed increased production per acre in association with land reform. Further, the opportunities land reform provides for increasing employment, income distribution, and hence markets in countries with high population growth rates and increasing unemployment are significant and are often the only alternatives to despair. (Carter et al. 1970, 2)

Another synthesis document, "Economic Results of Land Reform," found that, in terms of agricultural *output*, "in most land reform countries changes in output cannot in any clear way be traced to land reform. In most of them it is clear, however, that the growth in output has been quite satisfactory, and thus no specific drawback to the economy stems from reforms as such" (Dovring 1970, 11).

In terms of agricultural *productivity*, Dovring found that

evidence on land reform as promoting or hampering productivity is in most cases even more indirect and tenuous than in the case of output. In its most precise form, the question is: does the land system established by land reform do a better job than the pre-reform system would have if it had continued, and does the reformed system allow the highest rates of increase in productivity which other systems would permit? (Dovring 1970, 14)

Based on the evidence in the case studies, he gives a "qualified yes" to smallholding reforms. For traditional large estates, no generalizations were possible because the variations in the specific cases were extreme (*colon* lands in Algeria, British-held estates in Kenya, *latifundia* in Latin America).

Land reform that involves smallholdings also has a positive effect on the demand for outputs of other sectors of the economy. Because small farms use relatively more labor than capital, requirements for heavy equipment, which would have to be imported, are reduced, while requirements for inputs such as fertilizer, which may be produced nationally, increase shortly after the reform.

Finally, land reform induces a larger proportion of incremental production that stays in rural areas as farmer income. Increased per capita output leads to higher farm consumption of both home produced food and other articles. Because land reform redistributes land, which is the main source of rural employment and income, and because it affects many people positively and only a few negatively, in an overall sense rural welfare increases.

Land reform in Latin America: Bolivia, Chile, Mexico, Peru, and Venezuela. This 1978 World Bank assessment by Eckstein et al. examines land reform in five countries: Mexico (1934–1940), Bolivia (1952–1955), Chile (1967–1973), Peru (1969–1976), and Venezuela (1965–1970). The report assesses economic impacts within the reform sector (including changes in agricultural production, welfare, and income of the affected parties) and the national economy as a whole. Like the *Spring Review*, the report is based on numerous background papers and case studies carried out between 1973 and 1975.

The five countries vary in many important respects, including pre-reform structure, scope of the reform, and postreform organization. Mexico and Bolivia predated the Alliance for Progress and were the most extensive. Venezuela relied heavily on settlement of beneficiaries on public land that was not previously farmed, so that only about 6 percent of existing farmland was affected by the reform. The most distinctive feature of the Peruvian reform was the transformation of coastal plantations to production cooperatives. Reform in Chile occurred at a later stage of development than in the other countries, because only about 26 percent of the total work force was engaged in agriculture as of 1955.

The report offers six broad generalizations (pp. i–iii):

1. In Mexico and Bolivia, traditional haciendas were extensively subdivided into small farms, affecting about half of the rural population in each country. Economic results over a relatively long period of time—since 1940 in Mexico and 1955 in Bolivia—show that

the new small farmers have increased their (low) incomes and have raised their output from the land in comparison with previous owners. At the same time, the ex-owners of large estates who had retained substantial portions of their land appear to have considerably improved their techniques and productivity after the reform. In both countries national agricultural production has been rising substantially, faster than before reform and faster than average growth rates for Latin America. (Eckstein et al. 1978, i)

2. The experience of creating production cooperatives on large estates previously cultivated with costly machinery and chemical inputs was mixed, and much of it was too recent to draw conclusions about the durability of collective arrangements. In general, though, production and income effects from reforming traditional haciendas were greater than from reforming modern estates.
3. Distributing land to new settlers on a fairly large scale in Venezuela and to settlers of newly irrigated lands in Mexico was generally successful.
4. The evaluators found unequivocal positive impacts on production within the reform sector in four of the five countries. The clearest case was Bolivia, where the effects had been positive for ten to fifteen years. In Mexico and Venezuela, it was more difficult to sort out the effect of the reform, since most of the growth, except in staple food crops, seems to have come from the larger farms and the reserve lands.[11] Peru was the exception, where the data were based on incomplete case studies from relatively recent land transfers.
5. The effects on rural income distribution were the same across the five countries: Lower-income beneficiaries gained, while high-income landlords lost. "The extent of income equalization, however, varied considerably, depending on the scope of the reform, the treatment of ex-landowners, and the economic status of beneficiaries before and after the change" (Eckstein 1978, 92). The impact was greatest in Mexico and Bolivia, where the scope of the reform was large and ex-landowners were not compensated. In Venezuela, reform beneficiaries gained because they had been landless and poor before the reform; on the other hand, wealthy private owners lost little. In Chile and Peru, reform beneficiaries were generally not the landless poor, and the impact appears to have been minimal because "the reform was limited to an incremental equalization [among families] largely within the upper ranks of rural incomes" (Eckstein 1978, 93).
6. The impact of the reform on the national economy was assessed in terms of (a) national agricultural growth, (b) productivity, and (c) change in national income distribution. Agricultural growth increased after land reform in four of the five countries.

While it is impossible to separate the direct impact of land reform on production, there is a stronger case for inferring that land reform may have served on balance as a stimulus to national production, and certainly it has not prevented the observed growth accelerations in four of the five countries even if it did not necessarily bring them about. (112)

The inverse relationship between farm size and productivity was observed in all five cases, particularly in Mexico and Bolivia. The increase in productivity that accompanied the transfer of hacienda lands to small farms was attributed to greater labor intensity on small farms and, in some cases, increased production of cash crops for the local market.

All five countries evidenced incremental equalization of rural incomes, but the impact varied depending on the scope of the reform. None of the reforms extended to all of the rural landless, although some came much closer than others, and everywhere both the percent and number of rural landless increased again after the initial decrease. Overall, the income distribution effects have been a byproduct of other forces and policies, rather than an outcome of policies designed to produce a predefined distribution of rural incomes. In drawing generalizations across all five countries, the study notes the importance of examining land reform in the particular historical context of each country:

Land redistributions tend to come about in waves, to slow down after the first impetus as administrative proceedings get bogged down in conflicts over particulars and as opponents rally their forces for resistance. A first wave may or may not be followed by later ones after various intervals. Land reform is part of a dynamic process of change rather than a one-time action. (9–10)

Doreen Warriner (1973), a British economist, documents two major positive economic impacts of land reform in Asian and Latin American countries: increased peasant incomes and increased agricultural production. She presents data illustrating the role of ancillary services (e.g., infrastructure, education, credit, and market access) in land reform. Providing reform beneficiaries with infrastructure and services, however, raises the cost of reform considerably and may, as a result, limit its scope. On the other hand, without adequate services, beneficiaries may not be able to earn enough from their new land to maintain their families. An advantage of the early successful reforms in Japan, Taiwan, and Korea was that they required little investment of this type.

Warriner distinguishes between "integral reforms" (involving both land redistribution and the provision of services) and "simple reform" (involving only land redistribution). In general, integral reforms have had a greater and more sustained impact than simple reforms.

The Economic Impact of Land Reform: Evidence from the 1980s

Evidence from the 1970s found land reform ineffective in its ability to perform a counterinsurgency role, but it presented a strong case for reform on economic grounds. More recent evaluations from the 1980s reinforce these divergent conclusions.

Five major comparative analyses show that land redistribution can yield important positive benefits to labor and the agriculture sector, but they also demonstrate that (1) land reforms, by themselves, have in most cases been of insufficient magnitude to have an impact on the economy as a whole; and (2) competing demands and direct opposition to land reform can so severely limit its scope that beneficiaries suffer from lack of services, especially credit, technical assistance, infrastructure, and market outlets. Many of the reforms were accompanied by the growth of inefficient and sometimes corrupt state agencies.

Power, distortions, revolt, and reform in agricultural land relations. The most recent in these assessments is the World Bank study by Binswanger et al. (1993). They state that while political stability is the principal motivation behind land reform programs, they also can have important economic benefits through increased efficiency. Land reform is necessary, they argue, because land markets are imperfect and fail to distribute land to the most efficient producers. Market failures, in turn, are due to policy distortions favoring large landowners and restrictions in credit availability. Accordingly, Binswanger et al. advocate a focus on macroeconomic policy reform.

Impoverished peasants cannot be expected to repay the full value of the land granted to them, because they lack financial resources to meet mortgage costs. Numerous land reform programs have failed, including those in Brazil, the Philippines, and Venezuela, because they insisted that peasants pay full compensation to landowners at market prices.   On the other hand, when compensation is paid in bonds whose interest rate is substantially below market rates, political opposition is strong and the programs are quickly terminated.

Binswanger et al. argue that land reform can succeed under situations such as (1) revolution (Russia, China, Cuba, Bolivia, Mexico, and Nicaragua) or defeat of a colonial power (Korea, Taiwan, Vietnam); or (2) use of foreign grants and large internal subsidies to finance the reform. In the United States, the Foreign Assistance Act restricts or prohibits financing operations implied by this option.

Searching for agrarian reform in Latin America. The second major cross-cutting evaluation, edited by Thiesenhusen in 1989, examines the impact of land reform in ten countries in Latin America and the Caribbean.   The volume generally supports the notion that while land reform is necessary for political reasons and wise for economic reasons, limitations on its implementation have sorely affected its performance. Thiesenhusen concludes that

the authors in this volume largely agree that reform programs to date in the region have been too small, too late, too underfunded, too dictated from above, too hierarchically organized, and too infrequently responsive to pressure from the grass roots. Since the land reforms occurred at the same time as other major structural changes (rapid population growth and urban expansion), the economic effects of the reform were of diminished importance. Relatively few peasants received land through reform, averaging about a fourth of those eligible, and in no country was more than 45 percent of the usable land involved, so that, over time, the impact on macroeconomic indicators was minimal. In sum, income and resources did not display much between-class redistribution, new jobs which were created by reform fell short of demand, and domestic markets did not widen much. Even so, more jobs were created than would have been in the absence of reform, and some income additions to the peasantry resulted. (Thiesenhusen 1989, 487–89)

Various factors help explain these limited results. Among the most important were the multiple goals of many of the reforms—social, political, and economic—that were not necessarily compatible and resulted in shifting alliances over time. In addition, recipients of land often had inadequate access to ancillary services and inputs to farm effectively. The high cost of these services together with shifting political and social agendas led to abandonment of the beneficiaries and the lands. Also, the paternalism inherent in the redistributive and postreform phases was a deterrent to building effective local organizations and led to resentment among beneficiaries. The evidence suggests that "bureaucratic" reforms without either military or revolutionary zeal behind them are likely to become bogged down.

Latin American land reforms in theory and practice: A retrospective analysis. Dorner's (1992) study reinforces many of the lessons in the Thiesenhusen study and concludes that "It is clear that the hopes and expectations raised by the Alliance for Progress were not realized." Once again, it was not fundamental errors in economic logic that doomed the reforms, but rather lack of strong commitment, insufficient political will, and, at times, insufficient resources for adequate implementation. Still, some economic impacts, besides the effects on production, can be identified.

Economic trends that have been much more directly affected by the reforms include the voluntary division of some large holdings into medium-sized, capital-intensive farms. Likewise, the number of less capitalized, small family units has increased substantially in some countries as a result of land provided directly in small units or as a result of the decollectivization of recent years. A direct result of the reforms has been to make the peasantry more heterogeneous. While these have been positive results of the reforms, some negative consequences need also be recognized. In most cases reforms were quite partial, and land was often granted to those among the peasantry who were among the better-off rather than those in the deepest poverty. Likewise, in some cases the services crucial to a productive agriculture—inputs, credit, market—were not available via the private sector and were not supplied by government, leading to land abandonment by a substantial number of the beneficiaries. (Dorner 1992)

The peasant betrayed: Agriculture and land reform in the Third World. A 1987 review of land reform in twenty-seven countries by Powelson and Stock identifies "control" as the central variable responsible for disappointing economic results of reform. Acknowledging that each country is affected by many variables other than degree of control, they nevertheless argue that the economic benefits of land reform (improved level of living in rural areas, increased agricultural production) often have not been realized because the state has used land reform as a tool to skim off agricultural surplus. Rather than allowing peasants to realize the benefits of land ownership and entrepreneurship, the state has tightly controlled reform beneficiaries and centralized decision making about land use, production and marketing, and land transfers.

The agrarian question and reformism in Latin America. The de Janvry study (1981) suggests that land reform had a positive impact on agricultural production. However, the increase in production was due to reform-induced change on lands excluded from reform rather than on farms created by reform. For pre-reform landowners, the threat or even the possibility of land reform discouraged extensive land use, but at the same time encouraged investment and technological improvement on "reserve lands," which landowners would be allowed to continue farming after the reform. These quality lands have received (according to de Janvry) the bulk of inputs from the public sector in the postreform era and have produced most of the commercial agricultural output.

In contrast, production in the reform sector has been restricted by the small size of farms created, organizational problems of group farms, the fact that, in most cases, only marginal lands were available to reform beneficiaries, and inadequacy of input and marketing services (de Janvry 1981, 211–22). Thus, the principal effect of land reform in the reform sector was political—it reduced the threat of rural political instability. Its effect on creating new markets for an expanding urban industrial sector was insignificant.

As both Thiesenhusen (1989) and Dorner (1992) note, however, if the justification for land reform is stated in terms of social welfare rather than economic growth, then the costs should be compared with those of other social programs and the benefits should be evaluated in terms of rural level of living rather than agricultural output. "One must evaluate the *relative effectiveness* of alternative ways of handling multifaceted problems. Land reform may turn out to be a 'halfway' measure. But if alternatives are only 20 percent effective, then land reform may still be a viable option" (Dorner 1992).

The Economic Impact of Other Land Access Interventions

This subsection summarizes the impact of investments in land titling and registration, land markets, land taxation, and land settlement. As in the case of land reform, however, it is difficult to isolate the independent effects of these programs on agricultural production and growth.

Land titling and registration. In an early study in Costa Rica (Saenz and Knight 1971), interviews with a cross-section of farmers showed that the more secure their claim to land, the higher their agricultural income. Another study in Costa Rica using 1974 data found that landowners with title had double the income of landowners without title, and that squatters and renters earned even less (Seligson, 1980, p. 90). Similar results were found in a World Bank study in Thailand (Feder et al. 1988), showing that titled owners had greater access to and use of credit and investment than untitled landholders.

While these cross-sectional studies showed that insecure tenure is related to lower agricultural productivity, they failed to control for the potential impact of land quality, climate, and the characteristics of landowners on production. Perhaps farmers with title farm differently or have better than those without title. A longitudinal study in Honduras, accompanying a land titling program, showed different results. Production did not increase as a result of new titles. Virtually none of the benefits of title (increased access to credit, technical assistance, investment, technology improvement, elevated land values) occurred in the areas studied (Seligson et al. 1984; Seligson and Nesman 1987, 1989; Stanfield et al. 1990). Preliminary unpublished results from a follow-up study of the same areas in 1994 confirmed the lack of impact of titles ten years after they were issued (G. Larson, personal communication).

Based on a comparative evaluation of USAID-sponsored land titling programs in Honduras, St. Lucia, and Ecuador, Stanfield (1990) found that small farmers perceived an increase in the value of titled versus untitled land, but this perception did not change behavior. There were no systematic differences between newly titled groups and control groups in the use of credit, at least during the five-year time period covered by the studies, because other factors, like farm size, that limit access of credit are not affected by presence of a title.

In communal land tenure systems like those found in parts of Africa, issues of land titling interact with those of individual tenure. Barrows and Roth (1989) examined historical data from Kenya, Uganda, and Zimbabwe to assess the impact of individualization and titling on tenure security, investment, and market operations. They concluded that titling in and of itself had little effect on investment or credit use because the key constraint was the supply of credit. Individualization occurs in response to changing economic opportunities and new technological options. Titling may be important in facilitating that process and may serve to protect farmers threatened with loss of land as change occurs.

Land markets. The empirical literature on land markets in less developed countries deals primarily with how markets function and secondarily with interventions designed to correct market distortions (Shearer et al. 1990). Like land reform, land market interventions, has been advocated as a means to increase agricultural growth by reducing market distortions and removing barriers to market access for the rural poor and landless.

Shearer et al. (1990) describe several USAID programs in land financing including the Penny Foundation land purchase/sale program in Guatemala, a mortgage guaranty fund in Honduras, and a proposed fund to allow co-owners of family land in St. Lucia to buy out other owners. In 1990 none of these programs was large enough or substantial enough to produce measurable results. In fact, the St. Lucia program was never fully implemented. The Honduras guaranty fund, which was intended to allow commercial banks to make land loans, was used very little before it expired. The Guatemala program ran into major organizational problems that threatened its continuation.

A central issue for both governments and private organizations in the implementation of such programs is the political capacity to foreclose on small, otherwise landless, farmers. To the extent a government cannot take land from a small farmer, a land bank is a drain on the national budget, and its feasibility depends on budget strength and political commitment to the program. For a private foundation, the inability to foreclose will gradually drain the capital base of the bank and end the program (AID 1989).

Land taxation. USAID studied the effectiveness of using land taxation systems in less developed countries for achieving nonrevenue goals like increased activity in the land market, intensified land use, and optimal holding size (Strasma et al. 1987). The evaluation concluded that

- Land taxation schemes that seek multiple ends (e.g., revenue, land redistribution, market efficiency) do none of them well.
- Land taxation schemes in less developed countries have been ineffective because— lacking the large expensive infrastructure required to assess, collect, and process the taxes—few people pay.
- In response to political pressures, tax rates are usually so low that the taxes are insignificant as a proportion of government revenue and do not justify the collection expense.
- Tax collection is frequently plagued with corruption.
- On the positive side, there is no evidence that land taxes (unlike export taxes, for example) discourage investment because, in general, they are so low that they do not affect incentives.

Thus, the costs of land taxation seem to outweigh their benefits in less developed countries. Also, as Binswanger et al. (1993) point out, land taxation schemes face the same political hurdles as redistributive land reform, which offers a much more direct path to achieving the same ends.

Land settlement. Successful land settlement projects increase agricultural production, benefit large numbers of low-income families, and can catalyze a process of regional development (World Bank 1985, ii). At the same time, they are costly and require substantial external financing. A central question raised is their potential for destroying fragile environments.

Effective cost recovery is an important issue in justifying these projects. Multiplier effects of employment and income generation are a central element of benefit calculation, but to realize these effects, settlement projects must be large (Scudder 1984). A World Bank review of twenty-seven settlement projects reported that "62 percent of the projects that had been audited had economic rates of return of 10 percent or better" (World Bank 1985, ii). While certainly acceptable, Scudder notes that rates of return are frequently disappointing three to five years after implementation begins, particularly relative to the estimates made in the appraisal documents. On the other hand, "while planning expectations tend to be too high in regard to the rapidity with which early returns can be expected, *they are too low in regard to possible long-term benefits*" (Scudder 1984, 2).

Overall, however, settlement has rarely been effective because of cost, relocation to remote areas, and the process of building both social and physical infrastructure. World Bank documents ranked management as the single most important variable relating to project success. Management was more effective when the inputs, tasks, and decisions were sequenced over time—which can take at least a generation for successful settlement projects (Scudder 1984, 9, 14, 34, 37; World Bank 1985, v–vi).

CONCLUSIONS AND IMPLICATIONS

Rarely does one encounter evidence so unequivocal concerning two crucial aspects of agricultural asset distribution and access as the following: First, family-size farms are more productive than large farms in most developing countries. Second, countries with large numbers of landless and land-poor farmers are primed for social instability, guerrilla war, and, ultimately, revolution. It is quite paradoxical, therefore, that in spite of the clarity of these findings, the benefits of intervening in agrarian structure are anything but clear. The first paradox is that even though large farms are inefficient and subdivision of such large farms ought to yield increases in agricultural productivity, often they do not. The second paradox is that even though programs that give land to the landless and land poor should, logically, reduce the potential for insurgency and instability, too often they have not.

Investment to change the distribution of land has fostered more impassioned debate than other donor programs intended to increase agricultural growth. Private property rights are pitted against the right of access to the means of survival. The merits of laissez-faire market mechanisms are examined relative to directed land redistribution. These considerations have had a direct impact on land reforms implemented the world over, and in many cases have prevented the logically obvious positive results of land reform from emerging. In view of these complexities and apparent inconsistencies, what conclusions can one draw about investing in agricultural asset distribution and access? Under what conditions have such investments been relatively successful?

Land reform. The evaluation literature emphasizes repeatedly that the most important precondition for land reform, and to a large extent other types of investments, is strong political will and capacity to implement change. Economic considerations are always secondary. Beyond this overriding consideration, the success of land reform in economic terms varies with the pre-reform structure, the postreform structure, and the overall structure of the economy. Generally, reforms implemented rapidly are less costly and more successful than reforms that linger. Reforms that pay full cash compensation to landlords almost always run out of resources long before they are completed. The most successful reforms have transferred landlord estates to family farms, whereby the only change was in ownership. The shift from haciendas to either family farms or cooperatives has been the most difficult. Among other factors, the political strength of the landowners and the lack of rural infrastructure, peasant organization, and services for new farmers increased the cost of reform beyond the capacity of the government to implement it. Land reform has been more successful in countries able to supply a package of ancillary services to support it.

Land titling and registration. Cross-sectional studies suggested that investments in land titling and registration systems in developing countries might increase credit use and have other positive impacts; in contrast, longitudinal studies have not found any significant benefit from titling programs. Agricultural development can take place under a private property system without an effective title and registration system, but an ineffective system may impede growth, especially when formal bank credit based on collateral becomes a regular feature of agricultural operations. Continual maintenance of the registration system is essential. Continuity is more likely in situations where lack of secure tenure is recognized as a problem by the landholders themselves and where land titles are useful in obtaining credit. Because the costs of land titling and registration systems are high, they should be implemented only when the benefits are clear and the country has sufficient resources to invest over a long period of time.

Land markets. More problematic is an uneven and discriminatory pattern of title possession—when large farmers have titles (because they have the resources to pay for them or because the system has formal built-in biases favoring large farmers) and small farmers do not. Unless small farmers are on a level playing field with large farmers, the greater economic efficiency of the former will not constitute a sufficient incentive to make the invisible hand of the market do its work. Rather, the "invisible foot" of rent-seeking behavior will distort markets at the cost of greater efficiency. Widespread distortions in the developing world favor large farmers and efforts to stimulate land markets are more likely to be effective when they are preceded by other reforms to correct policies that disproportionately benefit large landowners.

Land taxation. Land taxation as a means of influencing land use and agricultural growth has generally not been successful. The most important condition for implementing such a system is political support to enact the system with rates high enough to have an impact on landowner behavior. A second condition is an administrative system sufficiently strong to implement the legislation. The ineffectiveness of land taxation systems in many less developed countries is due to their high cost. On the other hand, under some circumstances a land taxation system may generate enough revenue to be sustainable. After all, self-financing systems exist in all industrialized countries.

Land settlement and resettlement. Population growth throughout the Third World makes it increasingly unlikely that governments will find large land areas that are not already settled. For that reason alone, settlement schemes are not likely to offer a major opportunity for agricultural growth in most countries. When settlement is an option, successful projects must be large enough and diverse enough to stimulate a long-term process of integrated area development that involves rural as well as urban elements. This implies a long period of donor support.

To what extent will future conditions be conducive to land reform? Two important factors have to be considered. First, does the political will and capacity exist to carry out reform and, in particular, to pay for it? Second, what are the objectives of the reform and what are the alternatives for achieving those objectives? As Binswanger and Elgin (1988) point out, the cost of land reform and how that cost will be covered is perhaps the most important question in terms of feasibility. Small farmers cannot pay for the land they receive. Elites are likely to resist paying for reform either through taxes or receipt of devalued bonds as compensation for expropriated land. If donor grants are not forthcoming, direct interventions to correct market and policy distortions that benefit large landowners at the expense of small farmers are likely to be more effective than land reform. In any event, without correcting these policies land reform will fail anyway.

Regarding objectives, some analysts suggest that future land reform should be evaluated more as a social program than as an economic program—and that its effectiveness in reducing poverty and unemployment should be compared to other alternatives available to Third World governments to achieve these ends. The dual objectives of increased agricultural production and improved equity of the earlier reform era, these analysts argue, should be dealt with through other investment programs.

Dorner (1992) and Montgomery (1984) examined whether donors, and particularly the United States, should continue to have a role in supporting agrarian reform. One lesson of the Alliance for Progress was that financial assistance and political pressure from the outside are not sufficient to convince an unsupportive government to implement a meaningful reform (Dorner 1992). Land reform requires an internal political commitment. Montgomery (1984) reiterates the point made in 1970 in the AID *Spring Review*: International support is only effective after the internal political decision has been taken.

U.S. assistance may be valuable in two areas. First, because the United States has been so active in this area, it can offer assistance in understanding past experiences and in carrying out crucial field research about the diversity of tenure institutions and systems. This pool of experience and research can be of great value in designing the types of interventions required to deal with emerging land tenure issues, not only in developing countries but also in Eastern and Central Asia and the New Industrial States.

Second, "land reform is not an isolated program, separated administratively and conceptually from other agricultural policies. The most obvious failures in land reform are those that have left new owners on their own after the old support system has been withdrawn" (Montgomery 1984, 224). International donors can play an important role in assisting governments and local organizations to fill this gap. Programs to improve land titling and registration and land markets will not produce the same results as redistributive land reform, at least in the short run, but they may be essential precursors to or key components of a broader reform (Binswanger et al. 1993).

NOTES

1. The *Spring Review* noted that "[this strange animal called land reform] is an animal that changes its colors, its appearance, its anatomy, and its physiology almost as often and as much as other strange animals called democracy, freedom, capitalism. Virtually every author of our analytical papers apparently felt he had to define the term. Definitions vary according to whether you favor or oppose land reform; whether you treat it as an ideological symbol, or as an achievable goal, or look at actual results" (AID 1970, 3).

2. A land bank involves government purchase of farmland as it becomes available on the open market. That land is then made available to qualifying farmers for long-term lease and/or purchase. A land purchase/sale program also involves the purchase of large farms offered for sale in the land market. After purchasing and registering the large farms and then dividing them into family size plots, such programs provide financing as well as technical assistance and production credit to peasant families who purchase the plots. The titles for the plots are transferred to the peasants purchasing them, with mortgages and payment schedules attached.

3. Two types of credit schemes have been used in land market programs: those that guarantee the seller and those that guarantee the lender (Dorner and Saliba 1981). Under the first type, the government enters sale contracts between large landowners and groups of peasant farmers as a third party, guaranteeing the landowner payment for the land purchased by the group of farmers. Under the second type (the mortgage guaranty), the government backs up loans made by credit agencies directly to peasants purchasing land.

4. The earlier cases are reviewed in Moore (1966) and Skocpol (1979). The Latin American cases since 1956 are reviewed in Wickham-Crowley (1992).

5. The U.S. position on land reform is seen in the Alliance for Progress, as articulated in the Charter of Punta del Este.

6. Conditions for a perfect land market include (1) a substantial number of buyers and sellers so that no single land purchase influences the price of land, (2) homogeneous land units so that buyers and sellers are indifferent about from whom they buy or to whom they sell, (3) buyers and sellers who have easy and equal access to market information, and (4) complete freedom of entry and exit from the market for both buyers and sellers.

7. See Prosterman and Riedinger, 1987, Chapter 5.

8. Thiesenhusen (1993) suggests that only one-fifth of the agricultural land and 10 percent of the population were affected.

9. See Muller and Seligson, 1987, p. 428.

10. However, see Midlarsky (1989), who refutes these findings, and the response by Muller et al. (1989).

11. "Reserve" land is the area a landowner is allowed to keep without fear of later expropriation. The maximum size of reserve lands varies across countries, and in some cases by crop. Landowners generally select which land is to remain in the reserve, which means that reserve land is the most productive land with the best access to water and existing infrastructure.

REFERENCES

Agency for International Development. June 1970. *Spring Review of Land Reform.* 58
vols. Washington, D.C.: USAID.
———. June 1978. "Agricultural Development Policy Paper." Washington, D.C.:
USAID.
———. May 1986. "Policy Determination. Land Tenure." PD-13. Washington, D.C.:
USAID.
———. August 1989. "A Report on Land Financing Projects and Agricultural
Production Cooperatives in Central America." Washington, D.C.: USAID.
Barrows, Richard, and Michael Roth. 1989. "Land Tenure and Investment in African
Agriculture: Theory and Evidence." Land Tenure Center Paper 136. Madison:
University of Wisconsin Land Tenure Center.
Berry, R. Albert, and William R. Cline. 1979. *Agrarian Structure and Productivity in
Development Countries.* Baltimore, Md.: Johns Hopkins University Press.
Binswanger, Hans P., Klaus Deininger, and Gershon Feder. 1993. "Power, Distortions,
Revolt, and Reform in Agricultural Land Relations." Working Paper. Washington,
D.C.: World Bank.
Binswanger, Hans P., and Miranda Elgin. 1988. "What are the Prospects for Land
Reform?" Report No. IDP-21. Washington, D.C.: World Bank.
Carter, E., E. J. Long, and E. Stern. June 1970. "Findings and Implications for A.I.D."
Spring Review of Land Reform. 58 vols. Washington, DC: USAID.
Carter, Michael R. 1984. "Identification of the Inverse Relationship between Farm Size
and Productivity: An Empirical Analysis of Peasant Agricultural Production."
Oxford Economic Papers 36: 131–45.
Carter, Michael R., and Jon Jonakin. 1987. "The Economic Case for Land Reform: An
Assessment of the "Farm Size/Productivity Relation and Its Impact on Policy."
Unpublished manuscript. Madison: University of Wisconsin Land Tenure Center.
Carter, Michael R., and Dina Mesbah. 1990. "Economic Theory of Land Markets and
Its Implications for the Land Access of the Rural Poor." In Shearer et al., "The
Reform of Rural Land Markets in Latin America and the Caribbean: Research,
Theory, and Policy Implications." Land Tenure Center Paper 141. Madison:
University of Wisconsin Land Tenure Center.
de Janvry, Alain. 1981. *The Agrarian Question and Reformism in Latin America.*
Baltimore, Md.: Johns Hopkins University Press.
Dorner, Peter. 1992. *Latin American Land Reforms in Theory and Practice: A
Retrospective Analysis.* Madison: University of Wisconsin Press.
Dorner, Peter, and Bonnie Saliba. 1981. "Interventions in Land Markets to Benefit the
Rural Poor." Land Tenure Center Research Paper. Madison: University of
Wisconsin Land Tenure Center.
Dorner, P., and D. Kanel. June 1970. "The Economic Case for Land Reform:
Employment, Income Distribution, and Productivity." *Spring Review of Land
Reform.* 58 vols. Washington, D.C.: USAID.
Dorner, Peter, and William C. Thiesenhusen. 1989. "Selected Land Reforms in East
and Southeast Asia: Their Origins and Impacts." Madison: University of Wisconsin
Land Tenure Center.
Dovring, F. June 1970. "Economic Results of Land Reform." *Spring Review of Land
Reform.* 58 vols. Washington, D.C.: USAID.

Eckstein, Shlomo, Gordon Donald, Douglas Horton, and Thomas Carroll. 1978. "Land Reform in Latin America: Bolivia, Chile, Mexico, Peru and Venezuela." Staff Working Paper No. 275. Washington, D.C.: World Bank.

Feder, Gershon, Tongroj Onchan, Yongyuth Chalamwong, and Chira Hongladarom. 1988. *Land Policies and Farm Productivity in Thailand*. Baltimore, Md.: Johns Hopkins University Press.

Green, Jerrold D. 1982. *Revolution in Iran*. New York: Praeger.

Lachman, A. June 1970. "What is Land Reform?" *Spring Review of Land Reform*. 58 vols. Washington, D.C.: USAID.

Midlarsky, Manus I. (and reply by Edward N. Muller, Mitchell A. Seligson and Hung-der-Fu). June 1989. "Land Inequality and Political Violence." *American Political Science Review* 83 (2): 587–595.

Montgomery, John D., ed. 1984. *International Dimensions of Land Reform*. Boulder: Westview Press and Lincoln Institute of Land Policy.

Moore, Barrington, Jr. 1966. *The Social Origins of Dictatorship and Democracy*. Boston: Beacon Press.

Muller, Edward N., and Mitchell A. Seligson. June 1987. "Inequality and Insurgency." *American Political Science Review* 81 (2): 425–451.

Muller, Edward N., Mitchell A. Seligson, and Hung-der Fu. 1989. "Land Inequality and Political Violence." American Political Science Review 83 (June 1989): 577–587.

Powelson, John P., and Richard Stock. 1987. *The Peasant Betrayed: Agriculture and Land Reform in the Third World*. Boston: Oelgeschlager, Gunn, and Hain and Lincoln Institute of Land Policy.

Prosterman, Roy L., and Jeffrey M. Riedinger. 1987. *Land Reform and Democratic Development*. Baltimore, Md.: Johns Hopkins University Press.

Saenz, P. Carlos Joaquín, and C. Foster Knight. 1971. "Tenure Security, Land Titling, and Agricultural Development in Costa Rica." San Jose: University of Costa Rica Agrarian Law Project.

Schwarz, Benjamin C. 1991. "American Counterinsurgency Doctrine and El Salvador: The Frustrations of Reform and the Illusions of Nation Building." Santa Monica, Calif.: Rand Corporation.

Scudder, Thayer. 1984. "The Development Potential of New Lands Settlement in the Tropics and Subtropics: A Global State-of-the-Art Evaluation with Specific Emphasis on Policy Implications." Executive Summary. A.I.D. Evaluation Discussion Paper No. 21. Washington, D.C.: USAID.

Seligson, Mitchell A. 1980. *Peasants of Costa Rica and the Development of Agrarian Capitalism*. Madison: University of Wisconsin Press.

Seligson, Mitchell A., and Edgar Nesman. May 1987. "Baseline Survey of the Honduran Small Farmer Titling Project: Descriptive Analysis of the 1985 Sample." Land Tenure Center Research Paper No. 93. Madison: University of Wisconsin.

————. August 1989. "Land Titling in Honduras: An Impact Study in the Comayagua Region." Madison: University of Wisconsin Land Tenure Center.

Seligson, Mitchell A., Earl Jones, and Edgar Nesman. 1984. "Community and Cooperative Participation Among Land Reform Beneficiaries in Honduras." *Journal of Rural Cooperation* 12 (1–2): 65–87.

Sen, A. K. 1981. "Market Failure and Control of Labour Power: Towards an Explanation of 'Structure' and Change in Indian Agriculture." *Cambridge Journal of Economics* 5: 201–228.

Shearer, Eric, Susana Lastarria-Cornhiel, and Dina Mesbah. 1990. "The Reform of Rural Land Markets in Latin America and the Caribbean: Research, Theory, and Policy Implications." Land Tenure Center Research Paper No. 141. Madison: University of Wisconsin Land Tenure Center.

Skocpol, Theda. 1979. *States and Social Revolutions.* Cambridge: Cambridge University Press.

Stanfield, David. 1990. "Rural Land Titling and Registration in Latin America and the Caribbean: Implications for Rural Development Programs." Land Tenure Center Paper No. 190. Madison: University of Wisconsin Land Tenure Center.

Stanfield, David, Alex Coles, Edgar Nesman, and Mitchell A. Seligson. June 1990. "The Honduras Land Titling and Registration Experience." Land Tenure Center Research Paper No. 191. Madison: University of Wisconsin.

Strasma, John, James Alm, Eric Shearer, and Alfred Waldstein. 1987. "Impact of Agricultural Land Revenue Systems on Agricultural Land Usage." Report prepared for USAID. Burlington, Vermont: Associates in Rural Development.

Stringer, Randy. September 1987. "Land Transfers and the Role of Land Banks in Rural Development." Land Tenure Center Research Paper. Madison: University of Wisconsin.

Thiesenhusen, William C., ed. 1989. *Searching for Agrarian Reform in Latin America.* Boston: Unwin Hyman.

Thiesenhusen, William C., and J. Melmed-Sanjak. 1990. "Brazil's Agrarian Structure: Changes from 1970 through 1980." *World Development* 18: 393–415.

Thiesenhusen, William C. 1993. "Agrarian Reform in El Salvador: A Contemporary Assessment." Typescript. Madison, WI.

Tuma, Elias H. 1965. *Twenty-Six Centuries of Agrarian Reform: A Comparative Analysis.* Berkeley: University of California Press.

Warriner, Doreen. 1973. "Results of Land Reform in Asian and Latin American Countries." *Food Research Institute Studies in Agricultural Economics, Trade, and Development* 12 (2). Stanford, Calif.: Stanford University, Food Research Institute.

Wickham-Crowley, Timothy P. 1992. *Guerrillas and Revolution in Latin America: A Comparative Study of Insurgents and Regimes since 1956.* Princeton, N.J.: Princeton University Press.

Womack, John. 1969. *Zapata and the Mexican Revolution.* New York: Knopf.

World Bank. 1985. "The Experience of the World Bank with Government-sponsored Land Settlement." Washington, D.C.: World Bank.

———. 1987. "World Bank Experience with Rural Development 1965-1986." Report No. 6883. Washington, D.C.: World Bank.

7

Investing in People

Luther G. Tweeten

INTRODUCTION

Economic growth comes from leveraging the output of raw labor with inputs of human and material capital. Investment in people is an attractive development option partly because it can be consistent with both economic equity and efficiency. This chapter mostly is about education, but investments in nutrition and health also are important components of human resource development.

OBJECTIVES

The largest expenditures for rural development in developing countries are for education and infrastructure. Chapter 4 addresses infrastructure; this chapter addresses education. The overall objective of this chapter is to ascertain the role of human resource investments for economic development mainly through agriculture. Specific objectives are

- To report the social payoff from human resource investment in agriculture and general education
- To explain why human resource investment must be a public as well as a market service
- To analyze critical problems encountered when investing in people
- To explore the role of international donors in support of human resource investment for agricultural progress in developing countries.

BACKGROUND

Elements underlying economic development can be broadly classified as natural resources, institutions, and people—the latter including raw labor, skills, and attitudes. Rainis (1988, 2–3), observing the spectacular economic progress of Hong Kong, Singapore, South Korea, and Taiwan despite high person-land ratios and few natural resources, stated that "an inescapable conclusion must be that their overall success was due primarily to their ability to exploit something they did have: their human resources." Significant human resource dimensions of their people included hard work, savings propensity, entrepreneurial strength, and the capacity to engage in risk-taking activities. Some of these are cultural but are inseparable from deliberate public and private decisions to invest in people to improve cognitive and other skills.

Widespread commitment to human resource development is apparent from commonplace statements such as "A nation's children are its greatest resource" and "investment in children's learning is the most important contribution a nation can make to a better future" (Anne Hamilton, cited in Lockheed and Verspoor 1991, xv). Conceptual and empirical analyses reviewed in this chapter give credence to such conventional impressions, but commitment to the human dimension of agricultural development is of comparatively recent origin.

Prior to the 1960s, agriculture was widely viewed as peripheral to economic development. Peasant farmers were perceived to be less than rational decision makers unresponsive to economic incentives but a source of raw labor for industrialization. People who work with their hands were not thought to need formal education. The seminal work of Nobel Laureate Theodore Schultz helped to change that image. Schultz (1964, 24–35) viewed the peasant as poor but rational, using resources efficiently to improve family well-being within constraints of capital and technology in traditional society. The challenge was to open new opportunities for productivity advances through research and diffusion of improved technology and knowledge.

Improved technology presented alternatives, reducing the risk and/or raising the level of production from available resources. Although peasants respond to price and profit incentives, the ability of producers to cope with risk and manage new technology was enhanced by human resource investments in schooling. Higher levels of human capital in agriculture helped producers evaluate technologies before adoption and adapt to the disequilibrium inseparable from rapid technological change.

Above all, human development must be viewed as part of a system, no part of which stands alone. Universal literacy is not an end in itself but is part of a synergistic system that includes education, health, nutrition, and fertility. Schooling influences and is influenced by cognitive traits of numeracy, literacy, communication, and problem solving. Schooling also influences and is influenced by noncognitive traits such as tolerance of others, civility, integrity, savings propensity, family planning, and work ethic. Farm people with enhanced cognitive skills not only made agriculture more productive, they also made better citizens, parents, nonfarm workers, and leaders.

Investments in education add to productivity and income, in part by underlying the high long-term returns to agricultural technology development and dissemination documented in Chapter 3. Economic growth fostered by broad-based education is essential for poverty reduction, improved health, and participatory government.

Primary education investment is especially redistributive toward the poor. Elementary schooling is a basic building block for further general education and vocational training. In short, elementary schooling for boys and girls is essential for *broad-based* economic development central to food security.

Education also is valued as a consumption good—albeit one that cannot be realized without economic growth to pay for it. Yet developing countries systematically underinvest in human resources, as discussed later in this chapter.

SOCIAL RATES OF RETURN TO EDUCATION

The social rate of return on schooling may be interpreted to be the highest interest rate that could be paid and just break even financing all private costs (mainly foregone earnings) plus public (mainly tax) costs of schooling. That rate of return calculated from monetary gains was summarized by the World Bank (1980, 49) for eleven low-income countries, nineteen middle-income countries, and fourteen industrialized countries (Table 7.1). Results showed striking similarities among countries, with rates of return on investment averaging 18 to 27 percent for primary schooling, 10 to 17 percent for secondary schooling, and 9 to 12 percent for higher education.[1] More recent estimates of rates of return on schooling in developing countries are few but generally consistent with rates in Table 7.1.

Table 7.1.
Social Rates of Return on Education[a]

Country Group	Primary	Secondary	Higher	Number of Countries
All developing countries	24.2	15.4	12.3	30
Low income/adult literacy rate under 50 percent	27.3	17.2	12.1	11
Middle income/adult literacy rate over 50 percent	22.2	14.3	12.4	19
Industrialized countries	17.8[b]	10.0	9.1	14

Notes: [a]Costs include forgone earnings (what the students could have earned had they not been in school) as well as both public and private outlays. Benefits are measured by income before taxes.
                 [b]For U.S. males; from Tweeten and Brinkman 1976, 127.

Source: World Bank 1980, 49.

Knight et al. (1992) show rates of return for primary education of 19 percent for the earlier or "experienced" cohort but of only 12 percent for the later or "marginal" cohort in Kenya. For secondary schooling, returns averaged 14 percent and 13 percent for the experienced and marginal cohorts, respectively. Returns are lower for marginal cohorts of workers, who are forced to take lesser jobs after better jobs are filled by earlier "experienced" cohorts. Diminishing returns to human factors of production also would be expected to reduce rates of return as human capital accumulates over time, although that effect is not apparent. In the United States, for example, returns to higher education seem to have increased relative to returns to primary and secondary (common) schooling despite the rising ratio of investment in higher education relative to investment in common schools.

Another criticism is that firms use higher education merely as a screening device to hire able workers. That is, firms use diplomas as devices to select employees, not for what they learned in school, but to locate inherently able and motivated employees—traits required to obtain a diploma. Because, it is argued, the employers do not utilize the specialized skills obtained at great cost, rates of return to education are overestimated. These arguments cannot be resolved. However, it is notable that the returns continue to be favorable on investments in people in developing countries under a wide range of circumstances that cannot be explained by "creaming" or "screening" alone. And studies such as by Knight et al. (1992), which are critical of past studies and attempt to correct their bias, also show favorable returns to schooling.

Based on rates of return, primary and, to a lesser extent, secondary education should have the highest claim on incremental public resources for education in many developing countries to promote broad-based development. Knight et al. (1992) estimated that raising education in Tanzania to the quantity and quality of that in Kenya would raise Tanzania's earnings 13 percent and erase Tanzania's current shortfall of mean income below that of Kenya.

Dougherty and Psacharopoulos (1977, 454) found that education contributed 0.5 percent to annual growth rates of seventeen developing countries in the 1970s. The paradox is that these numbers and the high rates of return in Table 7.1 indicate economic inefficiency—Dougherty and Psacharopoulos (1977, 457) estimate that developing nations were forgoing as much national income by investing too little in education as they were spending on education.

Returns to Schooling of Farmers

Relatively few studies have examined the payoff from primary education for persons engaged in agriculture. A review (World Bank 1980, 48) of ten studies found that four years of primary education raised farm output 13 percent on average if complementary inputs were available and 8 percent if complementary inputs were not available (Table 7.2).

Returns on specific projects can deviate far from the average. For example, the World Bank (1980, 51) reported that agricultural extension, using the "training and visit" approach, helped raise the proportion of high-yielding wheat and paddy varieties from less than 2 percent to 40 percent of acreage planted in a single year in West Bengal (World Bank 1980, 51).

Tweeten and Brinkman (1976, 126, 136) found that returns to elementary and secondary schooling were comparable for farm and nonfarm white males. They also found frequent low returns to higher education among those who remain in agriculture. The same conclusions may hold in developing countries for those who lack access to improved inputs or to the scale and scope of agricultural resources essential to realize the benefits of advanced schooling. As agriculture becomes more commercialized, these shortcomings diminish and returns for higher education are likely to rise for those who remain in agriculture as well as for those who utilize their investment in other occupations.

Table 7.2.
Farmer Education and Productivity

Study	Estimated Percentage Increase in Annual Farm Output Due to Four Years of Primary Education Rather than None
With complementary inputs[a]	
Brazil (Garibaldi), 1970	18.4
Brazil (Resende), 1969	4.0
Brazil (Taquari), 1970	22.1
Brazil (Vicosa), 1969	9.3
Colombia (Chinchina), 1969	-0.8
Colombia (Espinal), 1969	24.4
Kenya, 1971–1972	6.9
Malaysia, 1973	20.4
Nepal (wheat), 1968–1969	20.4
South Korea, 1973	9.1
Average (unweighted)	13.4
Without complementary inputs	
Average (unweighted)	8.1

Note: [a]Improved seeds, irrigation, transport to markets, and so on.

Source: World Bank, 1980, p. 48.

Returns to Donor Investment in Human Resources

The U.S. Agency for International Development invests in human resources in numerous ways. It donates food to starving people. It supports school feeding programs that encourage youth from poor families to stay in school. It also uses food aid to operate food-for-work programs building schools and other infrastructure. It sometimes sells food for local currencies in developing countries and uses the proceeds to fund training and other investments in people.

One study (Pinstrup-Andersen and Tweeten 1971) indicated on average that food aid to developing countries was worth about half the value of untied cash aid in the 1960s but also had low opportunity cost to the U.S. government because the alternative was to accumulate costly stocks or pay American farmers not to produce. The dated Pinstrup-Andersen and Tweeten study begs the question of what is the rate of return on current food or cash aid. When food aid is decisive to keep children in school, it can bring returns as high or higher than the returns to education cited in Table 7.1.

Proceeds from food aid sold in the recipient country are often used to fund indigenous agricultural research and extension. In other cases USAID funds agricultural research and extension directly rather than through food aid. Much of that aid is to develop the human resources essential for successful indigenous research and extension. Such investments on average are expected to earn the high rates of return shown in Chapter 3. Such aid is especially important because, despite the high return, investment in people to operate successful agricultural research and extension would have been forgone by developing countries because those countries lacked the wealth, long-term perspective, and political will essential for funding such efforts.

Even where aid is only a transfer payment of food or other assistance consumed by very low income people, the return is high because the marginal utility of income is high for the poor (Tweeten and Mlay 1986). Food aid is at best a temporary expedient, however. The longer-term objective is to raise income through human and material capital formation so that countries are self-reliant and no longer in need of food aid. Unless a country is severely short of food supplies and people are acutely short of food, food is not the preferred form of aid.

Many who have worked with USAID view training programs in agriculture and other areas as the agency's single greatest accomplishment. In Chapter 2 Simmons and Kent observed that training of host country nationals, both overseas and in-country by teams of expatriate advisors, was a centerpiece of most USAID projects. Peter McPherson, former Administrator of USAID, addressing the International Banquet of the American Agricultural Economics Association on August 7, 1995, emphasized that the greatest contribution of the Agency to development was providing advanced training, much of it abroad. As evidence of that priority, he noted that the number of trainees went from 8,000 to 18,000 per year while he was Administrator from 1981 to 1987.

Summarizing results of a major USAID-funded project in Peru, Professor John Timmons (1981, 8) stated that "in retrospect, the training program, embracing training components outside as well as inside Peru, was probably the most effective and lasting part of the program even though its cost in funds was relatively small."

This Iowa-Peru Program funded by USAID and extending from 1961 to 1977 provided educational training for forty-four long-term participants and nineteen short-term participants in the United States and in Third World countries. Additional hundreds of Peruvians were provided on-the-job training through contributions of the Iowa Mission Staff members.

Concluding Comments

1. In developing countries, rates of return are higher to elementary than to secondary or higher education, but even returns on the latter are comparable to returns in the private sector and higher than returns of many other public investments.
2. True social rates of return might be higher than those shown in Table 7.1 if externalities (benefits not showing up in wages and salaries) were accounted for in calculating rates of return.
3. The major cost of schooling in many circumstances is earnings forgone while in school. These costs can be high in rural regions of developing countries, where young people lend a critical hand at harvest.
4. Despite earnings forgone while in school, private rates of return to individuals usually exceed social rates of return because taxpayers subsidize education. Still, individuals underinvest in schooling in developing countries due to tradition, weak capital markets, and other reasons.
5. Primary education promotes broad-based economic development because it raises future earnings of children of high- and low-income families alike while costs, especially taxes, usually are disproportionately paid by families with higher incomes. Although the same cannot be said of secondary or higher education (because the principal recipients are children from higher-income families), one must recognize that public higher education provides the skilled human resources essential to obtain the high social rates of return available from agricultural research and extension. The key for the public sector is to invest where returns are high and to complement rather than compete with the private sector.

HUMAN RESOURCE DEVELOPMENT AS A PUBLIC SERVICE

Public expenditures for education usually account for 4.5 to 7 percent of GDP in developed countries and 2.5 to 7.5 percent of GDP in developing countries (MacKenzie 1991, 107). Governments typically pay 90 percent of the direct costs of schooling. They apparently view schooling as a *public* service (good) rather than a *market* service (good) to be allocated solely by the private sector guided by supply, demand, and prices. At issue is the validity of that view that education not be left solely to market forces. This section makes the case that a public role is justified on economic grounds because education displays externalities, capital market failure, nonrivalness, economies of size, nontransparency, and merit service characteristics that argue against sole reliance on markets.

Externalities

Externalities justifying public investment in human capital were noted earlier and include creation of a sense of national identity and social cohesion. These benefits are not captured as profits by private firms or as wages and salaries by individuals. Dasgupta (1995, 5) has shown that statistically, even in poor countries, political and civil liberties go together with improvements in other aspects of life, such as schooling, income per person, life expectancy at birth, and infant survival rate. He concludes (p. 5) that such liberties are desirable in themselves and also empower people to flourish economically. Education interacts with social, economic, and demographic variables, both as a cause and effect. Most of that interaction with education is favorable to the well-being of people.

Capital Market Failure

Capital markets function imperfectly for education. Lenders would like collateral in case of default, but public attitudes and laws preclude using people as collateral. Lenders and parents who fund schooling make sacrifices by forgoing consumption or other investments. Economists call these sacrifices high discount rates or "high opportunity costs" of schooling. The public sector is likely to have a lower discount rate because it has fewer alternative, high-return investments and can average out the risks. Under such circumstances schooling investment left solely to individuals and families falls short of optimal investment for society.

Nonrivalness

Education transfers knowledge. Once knowledge has been developed, use of that knowledge by one person does not diminish the stock of that knowledge available to others. Once painstakingly assembled, knowledge needs to be distributed as widely as possible to obtain maximum social payoff—subject, of course, to costs of dissemination. The combined benefits of shared learning are greater than the sum of its parts. A person isolated from educated people would sacrifice much of his or her benefits of education both in production and consumption.

Economies of Size

Costs per unit of education often decline as class and school size increase—at least to a point. In many communities, only one school can operate at lowest cost per student by achieving economies of size. The result is a natural monopoly.

Marginal cost pricing ordinarily maximizes net benefits, but such pricing does not cover all costs when unit costs are declining. The community may prefer a public school to a private school, which either would lose money and fail with marginal cost pricing or would gain excess profit with monopoly pricing.

Transparency

People cannot make wise investment decisions if they cannot judge the quantity or quality of the education services they are receiving. Thus governments intervene with public schools to ensure quality. Public schools also are in disarray for lack of a clearly defined mission or output. Without a measure of output and how teachers and other inputs contribute to that output, it is impossible to provide incentives essential for effective and efficient schooling. One alternative is greater use of testing, rigorous standards, and external assessment to judge and ensure quality from private and public schools.

Merit Services

Individuals may be too poor to pay for school or may be discouraged by parents from attending school so they can work at home. Some services may be profitable to individuals, but, left to markets, individuals acting alone may not obtain enough of the service to maximize the well-being of society. Individuals may not act in the public interest because they lack knowledge of or reap only a part of the rewards from education. The nation may feel a compelling need for universal literacy to serve national welfare. Issues of equity, externalities, and market failure all figure in these arguments for public schools or for public subsidies to private schools.

If a merit service serves a compelling national interest in equity as well as economic efficiency, broad-based development through investment in human resources seems to work. Persson and Tabellini (1991) found a strong positive relationship between economic growth and economic equity, the latter evidenced by greater equality of income. Borsu and Glejser (1992, 1237) concluded that economic growth is not hindered by economic equity, but growth and equity are hindered by protectionism and low schooling in developing countries. However, the first stage of development of very poor countries does seem to vindicate Kuznet's law that economic growth generates greater income inequality.

Comments

The preceding considerations argue for a public role in provision of education, but there is growing recognition that sole reliance on the public sector to operate and regulate schools has serious drawbacks. Schools not subject to market competition develop bureaucratic, rigid, inefficient structures. Teacher or school performance measured by value added (contribution to student achievement) is not rewarded; indeed, it is unlikely even to be measured. I now turn to issues of how to allocate schooling inputs to induce best outcomes.

OTHER ISSUES ENCOUNTERED WHEN INVESTING IN PEOPLE

The high rates of return found for schooling veil difficult issues confronting those who would invest wisely in people. Questions include (1) where to place the incremental unit of investment, and (2) the role of donors.

Where to Place Incremental Investment in Education

Studies such as those reported in Tables 7.1 and 7.2 showing favorable aggregate payoffs, stand in contrast to schooling production functions, showing at best a weak relationship between student achievement (or other schooling outcomes) and specific schooling inputs. Compared to developed countries, developing countries face more serious issues of how to raise funds and less serious issues of how to use funds effectively, because even basic needs are often glaring. Still, educators do not know much about how best to use funds for education beyond basic inputs.

The dilemma is dramatically illustrated by the numbers in Table 7.3. Only 9 percent of 152 production function studies in the United States of educational achievement as a function of the teacher-pupil ratio found the expected positive, significant coefficient. Only 7 percent of the studies including teacher education, only 9 percent of the studies including facilities, and only 11 percent of the studies including administration found the expected positive and significant coefficient of these variables explaining student achievement in the United States The percentages were higher but still unimpressive for teacher salary, teacher experience, and expenditure per pupil (Table 7.3).

Statistically significant coefficients with the expected signs were found more frequently in developing countries. Although only 27 percent of the studies found that a higher teacher-pupil ratio had a significant and positive impact on achievement, some 50 percent or more of the studies revealed that expenditure per pupil, teacher education, and facilities had a significant, positive impact on student achievement (Table 7.3). Experience and salaries of teachers were positive and significant predictors of student achievement in only about one-third of the studies where these variables were included in developing countries. These numbers hardly rouse enthusiasm for pouring funds into any particular schooling input.

It is not surprising that the education level of teachers is more closely related to student achievement in developing countries (where teachers often have little schooling) than in developed countries (where teachers usually have twelve years or more of schooling). Although the education and experience of teachers are not strongly related to performance of students, it is notable that teachers' salaries are widely based on academic degrees and experience and not on teachers' value added to student achievement. Other uses of incremental schooling funds often

Table 7.3.

**Summary of Estimated Expenditure Parameter Coefficients from Studies of
Educational Production Functions in the United States and in Developing Countries**

	United States		Developing Countries	
Input	Number of Studies	Statistically Significant, Expected Sign	Number of Studies	Statistically Significant, Expected Sign
	(No.)	(%)	(No.)	(%)
Teacher/pupil ratio	152	9.2	30	26.7
Teacher education	113	7.1	63	55.6
Teacher experience	140	28.6	46	34.8
Teacher salary	69	15.9	13	30.8
Expenditure per pupil	65	20.0	12	50.0
Administration	61	11.5	na	na
Facilities	74	9.5	34	64.7

Source: Harbison and Hanushek 1992, 18, 24.

give greater promise of better schooling than do financial rewards for teachers'
degrees and experience.

More recent studies of input-output characteristics of schooling in developing
countries confirm results reported in Table 7.3 but add new insights:

1. *Based on an extensive study in poor and rural northeast Brazil, Harbison
and Hanushek (1992, 197) concluded that good teachers are extremely important
for student achievement.* Specifically, teachers who know their subject matter
were found to be better performers. However, consistent with results for the
United States in Table 7.3, the authors found that neither teachers' schooling levels
nor experience were systematically related to student performance. The authors'
summarization (p. 199) is sobering: "Teaching may be more art than science. The
conclusion is only that it is foolish to choose among prospective teachers solely on
the basis of credentials and experience."

2. *Inadequate schooling facilities, equipment, and supplies compromise
education in many developing countries.* Students often lack textbooks and basic
writing materials. Harbison and Hanushek (1992) estimated that an additional
dollar spent on these items would return $4.03 to $6.95 in lower overall costs of
schooling completion in northeast Brazil.

3. *School operation issues are strikingly similar in developed and developing
countries.* For example, Harbison and Hanushek (1992, 207) concluded that in no
case is it necessary to distinguish between schooling in northeast Brazil and
schooling in the United States, despite their disparate situations. Both countries
pay teachers based on their education and years of service rather than
performance. In both countries, attempts to reward merit have encountered strong
opposition from teachers' groups or unions.

4. *The principal predictors of schooling achievement are socioeconomic status of parents (income, occupation, education) and IQ of the student.* Characteristics of schools typically account for less than 5 percent of variation among students in academic achievement tests. Class size within a reasonable range is not very important, except where individual attention is important such as remedial reading. The importance of school variables such as class size is often understated because samples are too small or too homogeneous to show statistical significance. Nonetheless, tinkering with schools alone cannot reverse the fortunes of economically depressed areas or nations.

This widely supported conclusion does not mean that schooling performance cannot or should not be improved. It does not mean that specific interventions cannot bring favorable benefit-cost ratios. It does mean that schooling must be part of a multifaceted approach to economic development encompassed by the *standard model* outlined in Chapter 9, on food security.

5. *Schools make little use of economic incentives.* Prices bear only a tenuous relationship to marginal costs. Greater effort to match actual incremental cost with student fees would make sense, especially in higher education. For example, students do not much like being taught college courses with television, but passing the savings to students could make such cost cutting more palatable.

6. *Equity and efficiency considerations frequently conflict in human resource development.* Subsidized secondary and higher education especially benefits middle- and upper-income classes, which could have paid their own way (Behrman and Schneider 1992, 13). An exception is broad-based elementary schooling, which by reaching the poor can serve both equity and economic efficiency.

In Brazil, for example, a disproportionately high 23 percent of the public education budget goes to higher education, but higher education accounts for only 2 percent of the student population (World Bank 1994, 23). In Latin America, white-collar employees account for 15 percent of the total population but 45 percent of enrollment in higher education (World Bank 1994, 23). Unit costs of higher education are much higher than of primary education—fifty times as high in anglophone Africa, for example (MacKenzie 1991, 108). If, as often is the case, the costs are paid by the public sector but benefits are reaped by youth from high-income families, investment in higher education is income regressive.

7. *Students, especially in secondary and higher education, are some of the wealthiest members of society, as measured by the present value of expected future earnings.* Means testing of higher education tuition coupled with surcharges on future earnings are possible ways to increase equitability in school funding. Such measures can increase economic efficiency along with equity by freeing funds to support education for those too poor to afford schooling.

8. *Public education outlays are often poorly distributed among fields of study.* In Latin America many students are trained in law and liberal arts when engineers and business graduates are needed. In Eastern Europe and the former Soviet

Union, many students are trained in mathematics, physics, or engineering when the nation especially needs people trained in law and business administration.

9. *In some countries unemployment is considerable among secondary and higher education school dropouts and graduates.* For example, unemployment among those with graduate degrees was 19 percent in the Philippines in 1990, 16 percent in Egypt in 1986, and 16 percent in Jordan in 1991 (World Bank 1994, 20). On the one hand, this is the result of high earnings expectations relative to opportunities and of the sizable gains to individuals who spend more time in job search. On the other hand, unemployment and underemployment of such school leavers highlight the need for attention to the supply-demand balance, especially in specific skills in developing countries. When schooling outruns the demand for skills, resources are wasted.

Governments can influence the supply-demand balance in constructive or destructive ways. In constructive ways, government can encourage students to enroll in high-demand occupations, such as business administration and engineering. In contrast, pressures on governments to serve politically important but frustrated unemployed higher education graduates sometimes motivates an economically destructive response: The public sector serves as employer of last resort. The result can be an unaffordable government financial burden, make-work jobs, low employee moral, "moonlighting" on a private job while a "phantom" government employee, diversion of students from challenging fields of study whose graduates are prized by the private sector, and diversion of the work force to the public sector from more productive private sector activities.

10. *International comparisons suggest that human capital investments are excessively skewed toward males relative to females (Behrman and Schneider 1992, 18).* Girls frequently do not share proportionately in schooling for cultural, religious, or other reasons.

It would be difficult to overemphasize the importance of educating women. That importance is buttressed by women's role in development: "Rural women account for more than half the food produced in the developing world, [and] as much as 80 percent of the food produced in Africa" (Thompson 1995, 2).

Many parents in low-income countries do not invest in their daughters' schooling because girls are expected to marry into someone else's family, bear children, and remain home with their children while the husband earns the living for the family. But educated women not only earn more income, they also have fewer, healthier children, who in turn obtain more and better schooling and income. Societies discouraging parents and educators from schooling girls (perhaps because women are not accepted in the labor force) pay a large economic cost in lost income and excessive birth rates.

Behrman and Schneider (1992, 15) conclude that returns to human capital investments are high for schooling of females. The importance of women in raising children and creating their aspirations, controlling birth rates, and establishing good family health and nutrition argue for schooling equality for broad-based economic development.

Summers (1992) gives examples of estimated payoffs from educating an extra 1,000 girls in Pakistan in 1990 at a cost of $40,000:

- Reduce future infant deaths of these mothers by sixty (saving the same number of mothers by health care intervention was expected to cost $48,000).
- Avert 660 births because more educated mothers have fewer children (reducing 660 births by typical family planning programs would cost $43,000).
- Avoid deaths of four mothers in childbirth because of fewer births and fewer deaths among educated mothers giving birth.

After noting that rates of return typically exceed 20 percent on schooling investment in girls, Summers (p. 132) concludes that such education "may well be the single most influential investment that can be made in the developing world."

11. *Improper economic policies create inadequate education policies.* Countries that have mismanaged their economies, especially those going through structural adjustments, have experienced lower monetary rewards and deteriorating working conditions for teachers. For example, an able Ph.D. faculty member of Makerere University in Uganda who was acting head of the Agricultural Economics Department was earning $14 per month when I visited the campus in 1990. Other faculty were doing no better. In Nigeria real salaries in 1992 were 10 percent of those in 1978 (World Bank 1994, 18). Teachers in the former East Bloc and former Soviet Union in 1995 were earning very small salaries in absolute terms and in relationship to pay a decade earlier. Very low pay brings low morale, poor performance, and falling quality of education, in part because teachers' energies are diverted to second jobs essential to sustain their livelihood.

Schooling incentives and outcomes are a function of the state of the economy. Unwise macroeconomic policies bring poor public and private performance and salaries. A strong private economy not only offers student rewards for education but also provides the tax base essential for sound schooling. Regarding Indian schooling, Behrman and Schneider (1992, 22) note that "of even greater importance [than schooling policies reform] is the unfettering of possibilities for individuals to obtain returns from their human resources through radical deregulation of the economy."

12. *Schooling failures have roots in political failure.* Public officials often have their own agenda, such as attention to their personal wants and to special interest constituencies. Without reform, planning horizons are too short for public officials to be concerned with rural schooling or the general welfare. Policies of the status quo, however bad, serve some who are likely to be in key positions of authority. Thus political reform must often precede economic and schooling reform.

Health Service

Health services in developing countries are treated in detail elsewhere (see World Bank 1993; Jamison 1993; Tomich et al. 1995). Here, attention is on the economics of basic health delivery in low income countries.

Public health measures can be highly cost-effective in reducing mortality and morbidity. The World Bank estimates that minimal packages of critical clinical services and public health interventions can be provided for all citizens in low income countries for as little as $12 per capita (Jamison 1993, 4). Even sub-Saharan Africa which spent 4.5 percent of its GNP or $24 per capita on health in 1990 (in sharp contrast to 10 percent of GNP and nearly $2,000 per capita in industrialized countries) can afford basic cost-effective interventions.

Numerous issues confront the design of health care services in developing countries. One issue is whether health services are market or public "goods." Health services clearly have a public good component. Immunization not only benefits the person immunized, it cuts down transmission of diseases to those not immunized. Nutrition education for pregnant and lactating mothers can reduce the number of infants whose mental development is retarded by malnutrition. People who receive (and, perhaps, pay for) education on preventing the spread of the HIV virus benefit other people.

A second issue is the formal level of health services provided by the public. One thing is clear: in poor countries, services must be inexpensive and rationed. Even developed countries cannot afford universal access to free health services. Given limited resources for health services, it makes sense to pursue cost effectiveness defined usefully by the World Bank as cost per Disability Adjusted Life Year (DALY). Because children have greater life expectancy than adults, DALY puts a high premium on services that reduce mortality and morbidity among children and at low cost per child. DALY places a high premium not only on treating infants and children but also pregnant and lactating women because of their role in reducing infant mortality and morbidity.

Cost-effectiveness of health measures can be high — just $1 per DALY for vitamin A supplement for children under age 5 (Tomich et al., 274), $10 per DALY for measles immunization, and $25 for a combination of diphtheria, pertussis, tetanus, polio, tuberculosis, and leprosy immunization. If a DALY is valued at a very conservative $200 (per capita annual income in many low income countries), the benefit-cost ratio for vitamin A supplement is $200:$1. Few investments in people can match that! Needs for services vary from country to country, depending on income, diets, common diseases, and culture (World Bank 1993, 72). Thus each situation needs evaluation on its own merits, but the following ten measures frequently are cost-effectively administered through community health clinics:

1. Immunization
2. Oral rehydration (including packets and education for home use)

3. Nutrient supplements, especially vitamin A, iron, iodine, and folic acid where deficiencies are common
4. Antibiotics for pneumonia
5. Family planning measures, including education
6. Nutrition and hygiene education
7. Breast feeding education, including importance of colostrum milk
8. Treatment for parasites
9. Treatment for sexually transmitted diseases
10. Environmental sanitation education (waste and water)

The list is not exhaustive and could include provision for protein diet supplements and education on the hazards of tobacco, alcohol, and hard drug use. However, countries may not be able to afford some of these basic services.

Schools, hospitals, and the community share responsibility with health clinics to provide for the above health services. For example, human waste disposal and sanitary water supplies may need to be addressed at the community level.

DALY also places a premium on preventative rather than curative services. To illustrate, modest outlays for HIV prevention education programs can save many lives whereas even unlimited outlays are as yet unable to cure AIDS.

The Role of Donors

The United States has been the largest donor of all countries and the World Bank the largest donor of all institutions to improve education in developing countries. Contributions have not been large, however. In the 1981–1986 period, the United States accounted for $26 million or 14 percent of the world's bilateral aid for primary education (Lockheed and Verspoor 1991, 211). Food aid administered through the U.S. Agency for International Development was another component of American assistance to education in poor countries.

The World Bank lent $5.5 billion for education from 1985 to 1990, and $1.3 billion of this was for primary education. Whether such aid is large or small is subjective, but Schultz (1989, 22) judged that "although the levels of the [World] Bank's economic intelligence about schooling is high, the loans and credits provided by the Bank to augment the stocks of human capital consisting of schooling have been and continue to be negligible."

Given limited budgets for investing in people, donors need to sharpen the geographic and programmatic focus of assistance. Several suggestion are offered next.

1. *Underinvestment in people is a universal problem, but the focus of concern to international development agencies can narrow to Sub-Saharan Africa and selected other low-income countries, such as Haiti.* Asia traditionally has had the largest number of illiterates, most of them in agriculture, but needs less outside help for several reasons. One is that, because of institutional reform, economic development is now proceeding at breathtaking speed in China and to a lesser extent in Southeast Asia and India, which have over 2 billion inhabitants and large

numbers of poor and illiterate. Current economic development in these countries mostly is not broad based but potentially provides the base of domestic resources to finance human resource development in rich and poor regions alike. Second, Asia has a core of educational institutions that have demonstrated excellence from primary to higher education, turning out world-class scholars and technicians. That core of academic excellence and financial resources can be broadened and deepened as resources become available through indigenous economic development without drawing on major donor assistance.

2. *Agencies such as the World Bank and USAID are not in a position to provide across-the-board funding of education and health services, but donors can provide help at critical points.* One is technology and training. Donors can encourage countries to adopt educational policy reform promoting high-quality, broad-based, cost-effective education utilizing private providers and private funding, where possible, to augment public schooling. Examples include advise on devolution of school control and funding to local districts financed by local property taxes. Examples of cost-effective health services were listed in the previous section.

As indicated earlier, one of the greatest contributions of USAID is to help train a few key people in critical skills required for successful operation of the economy. Examples are key administrators providing leadership in schools in developing countries, key researchers providing the base for research to improve agricultural production practices and technology, and key instructors, such as those teaching other teachers, researchers, and health service providers. These individuals need to be selected for higher education based on merit rather than political or family connections.

3. *Primary schooling must receive top priority for available funds.* As indicated earlier, we know too little about how schooling inputs relate to schooling outcomes. But enough is known of characteristics of successful schools in developed and developing countries to act.[2] Expenditures for school supplies and textbooks and for training of teachers are not good predictors of student achievement in many developed countries but are lacking and decisive for education in many developing countries. Successful schools everywhere possess essential elements: (a) strong expectations that students will work hard in school and on homework, (b) commitment of parents to educational achievement, (c) student discipline and rigorous, enforced regional or national academic standards, (d) rigorous instruction in reading, spelling, mathematics, and science but with enough history, literature, and the like to ensure cultural literacy, (e) repeated writing and rewriting of essays that integrate learning and develop creativity, (f) maximum recognition of student achievement, and (g) competent and enthusiastic administrators helping to upgrade teaching quality and with ability to recognize and hire competent teachers and release incompetent teachers.

Learning value added is highest in schools where teachers care about students and treat them with respect, but expect and obtain maximum *effort* from students. This encompasses skill in the basics, homework, longer school days and school years, and keeping extracurricular distractions such as sports in proper perspective. Good schools complement fundamentals through projects that require innovation and initiative and foster interactions between teachers and parents—encouraging the latter to provide enrichment by, for example, reading to preschool children. The above elements for successful learning do not require high wealth but they require enough resources to supply basic learning materials, facilities, and salaries to attract and hold able teachers.

4. *It would be premature to conclude that the higher rates of return for primary than for further education shown in Table 7.1 warrant deferring secondary and higher education until quality primary schooling is achieved by all youth in a country.* A few cognitively gifted youth going on to receive an advanced degree and a career in crop or animal science may generate much higher social rates of return than those shown in Table 7.1. Key individuals receiving secondary and higher education provide skills and leadership essential to high payoffs for those with only primary education. The process is self reinforcing. That is, investment in an appropriate mix of schooling in an atmosphere supportive of economic activity brings economic development in turn providing the base to support more investment in education. Favorable payoffs from schooling provide adult role models, motivating youth to attain more depth and breadth of schooling.

5. *Donors can encourage constructive diversity in institutions.* For example, not every postsecondary student needs to be educated in a research university. Cost-effective alternatives include vocational-technical institutes, polytechnic colleges, distance learning, and short courses. Distance learning includes correspondence courses that have been successful in South Korea, Brazil, Kenya, and the Dominican Republic. Television, VCR, satellite, and fiber optic communication can enrich learning and reduce the frictions of space that once isolated rural areas. Some distance learning may be of university quality, with opportunities to transfer credits to universities. Other distance learning can promote productivity gains in immediate employment.

The most cost-effective vocational training usually is on-the-job training in the private sector. Any public vocational-technical training is best closely coordinated with potential employers to develop skills in demand. Excellent examples of successful alliances between the private and public sectors for effective vocational training come from such diverse settings as Cincinnati, Ohio; Germany; Chile; and Singapore.

6. *The government can establish mechanisms for accreditation, oversight, and evaluation of private institutions.* Competitive bidding for research projects financed by the public sector can at once provide cost-effective research and support for faculty in private educational institutions. Private higher education often can meet such needs at lower cost than public institutions, especially if private institutions can draw funds from private charitable giving.

7. *Donors can encourage countries to diversify funding sources.* It is appropriate for parents and student to pay as much of the costs of higher education as possible. Fees can be raised for all students, with loans provided for needy

students. These loans can be repaid out of career earnings. An alternative is a surcharge on future earnings of students receiving loans for higher education. Provision of assistance to individual students rather than to institutions is a force for improvement because the market rewards excellence when students with vouchers choose the best institutions. For students to make wise decisions, they need information on the quality of programs and institutions and on job opportunities. The government need not necessarily be the accrediting agency; private accrediting agencies and professional associations often can do a better job at lower cost.

8. *Private rather than public sector provision of meals and lodging often can reduce education costs while improving service.* Student fees can supplement college budgets and faculty pay, but too much reliance on such measures can compromise the mission of public institutions. The World Bank (1994, 7) suggests that 30 percent of recurrent expenditures for public higher education should come from private sources such as student fees.

If the government removes public funding equal to any additional support institutions garner from the private sector, such institutions will have no incentive to replace public support. This means that incremental private support must add to overall support and not be offset completely by higher taxes or lower subsidies from government.

9. *Few countries can afford strong programs in all useful fields of higher education.* Graduate training and research programs are often best organized on a regional basis, with each country within the region providing a few strong programs. Or an institution of higher learning may serve several countries. The University of the South Pacific and the University of the West Indies are examples of universities serving regions. Centers of academic excellence in the developing world—the Indian Institute of Technology and Management, the Korean Advanced Institute of Science and Technology, the National University of Singapore, and the University of the Philippines at Los Banos, for example—all have international missions and policies to promote global contacts (World Bank 1994, 68–69). Regional universities are especially well situated to use sound management practices, such as international advertising and recruitment for positions, international review of candidates for promotion, international evaluation of academic units, partnerships with foreign institutions (universities), overseas training of faculty, and home country research topics for students who train abroad.

10. *The European model (locating agricultural research under the central government's Ministry of Agriculture separate from institutions of higher education) is followed by many developing countries but bears reexamination.* Donors can learn from the American land grant tradition, emphasizing the integration of teaching, research, and extension in institutions of higher learning. researchers are encouraged to keep up with their academic discipline when they teach, teachers are encouraged to be more relevant when they are exposed to real problems through research and extension, and extension personnel can elevate

their outreach by utilizing research results and subject matter from their teaching and research contracts.

11. *In many situations, funding for agricultural research and extension is an excellent means to raise returns to human capital.* Funding is often most adequate for structures and least adequate for recurrent (operating) costs. This conclusion holds for general schooling and for agricultural research and extension. Teachers with adequate school buildings may have no funds for textbooks; agriculture extension services may have no funds for transportation or teaching material. The recurrent budget is inadequate despite very high returns. Of all high-return public service opportunities, outlays for adaptive research are often most limited. That is because research fund cutbacks have no immediate political repercussions and because payoffs are long term and lost output is not immediately apparent to the politically influential. These high-payoff but chronically underfunded indigenous public services are strong candidates for donor support.

12. *A related issue is the brain drain of host country scientific and technical experts to international agencies and foreign private employment.* This robs developing countries of some of their best human capital critical for progress. Donors can help keep trained people at home by providing training specifically for host country needs which may stop short of a Ph.D. degree. Second, donors need to pay more attention to continuity of host country employment for trained personnel, perhaps taking major financial responsibility to assure continuity of research on, for example, crop varieties adapted to local conditions.

13. *Official Development Assistance (ODA) for health measures in Sub-Saharan Africa is modest averaging $2.50 per capita in 1990.* Thus donors are unlikely to pay a sizable part of health expenditures, but ODA can be critical in paying for basic health care items that must be imported. Use of indigenous community health organizations, paraprofessionals, volunteer workers, and user charges can ease financial burdens of health care.

14. *Finally, American support of human resource investments to raise agricultural productivity can expand commercial demand for American agricultural exports.* U.S. agricultural exports have nothing to gain from having more Haitis or North Koreas but have much to gain from having more economic success stories such as Taiwan or South Korea. As recently concluded by the International Food Research Institute (Pinstrup-Andersen et al. 1994, 4),

Development aid for agriculture in general and agricultural research in particular is a win-win proposition. It helps developing countries grow while creating export markets for donor countries. Although donor countries may not be able to ensure that they will capture all the benefits from expanded export opportunities, development assistance builds commercial ties between donors and recipients, raising the likelihood that developing countries will buy their imports from the donor country.

NOTES

1. The lower bound of 18 percent for primary schooling in developed countries is from Tweeten and Brinkman (1976) for all U.S. males.

2. A simplistic way for a school to ensure high achievement test scores is to matriculate only students of high socioeconomic status, but that selectivity must be avoided in favor of broad-based education. The practice is inconsistent with the goal of broad-based development. To reward schools for high performance but discourage "creaming," school evaluation requires control for socioeconomic status so that performance can be judged on *value added* to students' achievement.

REFERENCES

Behrman, Jeri, and Ryan Schneider. 1992. "Empirical Evidence on the Determinants of and the Impact of Human Capital Investments and Related Policies in Developing Countries: Implications for India." *Indian Economic Review* 27 (1): 1–23.

Borsu, A., and H. Glejser. 1992. "Do Protection, Schooling, Product per Head, and Income Distribution Influence Growth?" *European Economic Review* 36: 1235–39.

Dasgupta, Partha. June 1995. "Population, Poverty, and the Local Environment." *Ag Bioethics Forum* 7: 1–5.

Dougherty, Christopher, and George Psacharopoulos. 1977. "Measuring the Cost of Misallocation of Investment in Education." *Journal of Human Resources* 12: 446–59.

Harbison, Ralph, and Eric Hanushek. 1992. *Education Performance of the Poor.* New York: Oxford University Press.

Jamison, Dean. 1993. "Investing in Health." *Finance and Development* 30 (September): 2–5.

Knight, J. B., R. H. Sabot, and D. C. Hovey. 1992. "Is the Rate of Return on Primary Schooling Really 26 Percent?" *Journal of African Studies* 1: 192–205.

Lockheed, Marlaine, and Adriaan Verspoor. 1991. *Improving Primary Education in Developing Countries.* New York: Oxford University Press.

MacKenzie, G. A. 1991. "Education." In *Public Expenditure Handbook: A Guide to Public Expenditure Policy Issues in Developing Countries,* ed. Ke-young Chu and Richard Hemming. Washington, D.C.: Government Expenditure Analysis Division, International Monetary Fund.

Persson, T., and G. Tabellini. 1991. "Is Inequality Harmful for Growth? Theory and Evidence." Working Paper 91-155. Berkeley: University of California.

Pinstrup-Andersen, Per, Rajul Pandya-Lorch, and Mattias Lundberg. 1994. "Commentary: International Assistance to Developing-Country Agriculture Expands Export Markets." IFPRI Report 16: 1–4. Washington, D.C.: International Food Policy Research Institute.

Pinstrup-Andersen, Per, and Luther Tweeten. 1971. "The Value, Cost, and Efficiency of American Food Aid." *American Journal of Agricultural Economics* 53: 431–40.

Rainis, Gustav. 1988. "The Evolution of Policy in a Comparative Perspective: An Introductory Essay." In *The Evolution of Policy Behind Taiwan's Development Success,* ed. K. T. Li. New Haven, Conn.: Yale University Press.

Schultz, Theodore W. 1964. *Transforming Traditional Agriculture.* New Haven, Conn.: Yale University Press.

————. 1989. "Investing in People: Schooling in Low Income Countries." *Economics of Education Review* 8: 219–23.

Summers, Lawrence. 1992. "The Most Influential Investment." *Scientific American* (August): 132.

Thompson, Robert. 1995. "Women: Catalysts for Change, Leaders of the Future." *Seeds* (Summer): 1–8. Morrilton, Ark.: Winrock International.

Timmons, John. September 1981. "Final Report on Iowa State University and University of Iowa Technical Assistance Program in Peru." Monograph No. 13. Washington, D.C.: U.S. Agency for International Development.

Tomich, Thomas, Peter Kilby, and Bruce Johnston. 1995. *Transforming Agrarian Economies*. Ithaca, NY: Cornell University Press.

Tweeten, Luther, and George Brinkman. 1976. *Micropolitan Development*. Ames: Iowa State University Press.

Tweeten, Luther, and Gilead Mlay. 1986. "Marginal Utility of Income Estimated and Applied to Economic Problems in Agriculture." Agricultural Analysis Project Report B-21. Stillwater: Department of Agricultural Economics, Oklahoma State University.

World Bank. 1980. *World Development Report, 1980*. Washington, D.C.: International Bank for Reconstruction and Development.

———. 1993. *Investing in Health*. World Development Report, 1993. Washington, D.C.: International Bank for Reconstruction and Development.

———. 1994. *Higher Education: The Lessons of Experience*. Washington, D.C.: International Bank for Reconstruction and Development.

8

Investing to Protect the Environment of Agriculture

Donald G. McClelland

INTRODUCTION

Global population could double and food demand could triple in the next half century, requiring food production to increase over 2 percent annually on average. Most of that increase in population and food demand will be in developing countries. Because most of the world's arable land is being cultivated and because millions of acres are being lost to urban and other nonagricultural development, to degradation associated with irrigation (falling water tables, waterlogging, and salt buildup), and to erosion, it follows that increased production will need to come from higher yields rather than more area cropped.

Chapter 3 showed the payoff from technology development and diffusion to raise yields. This chapter reports payoffs from efforts under USAID either directly or indirectly intended to reduce degradation of land—a natural resource that food producers and consumers can ill afford to lose. Land degradation also is an environmental concern figuring in the loss of animal and plant species and in damage to water, air, and habitats.

LAND DEGRADATION

Between 1975 and the year 2000, the world will lose an estimated 155 million hectares of *high*-potential land (including high-potential cropland, grassland, and forest land). This represents about 22 percent of total high-potential land (Buringh and Dudal 1987, as reported in Craswell 1993).

During the twenty-five-year period ending in the year 2000 for three land use potentials (high, medium, and low), *high*-potential land will decrease for all three land use classes (cropland, grassland, and forest land). Medium- and low-potential land will increase for cropland and grassland but will decrease for forest land. In fact, all three classes of productive forest land—high, medium, and low potential—are expected to decline over the twenty-five years from 800 to 360 million hectares, a decrease of 55 percent.

Much of this forest land is being converted to cropland, usually of medium or low potential. In Southeast Asia, especially, in the last three decades, millions of hectares of valuable and productive tropical forest land have been converted to cropland and grassland of low or zero production potential. At the same time, high-potential cropland has been degraded to medium- and low-potential cropland. For example, in sub-Saharan Africa millions of hectares of cropland have been lost as a result of overexploitation caused by reduced fallow periods between crops. Acreage devoted to grassland in all three land classes is expected to remain about constant. However, the production potential of grasslands has been reduced as a result of overgrazing.

Soil degradation and losses of productivity are occurring faster than new land is being brought into production.[1] It is equally apparent that loss and degradation of land, coupled with increased population, has resulted in a reduction in productive land per capita (Netherlands, Ministry of Foreign Affairs 1993). Because the remaining productive land is under increasing pressure, agricultural production will continue to expand onto marginal and environmentally fragile lands. It will become even more difficult to increase food and fiber production to keep pace with population growth while protecting the natural resource base.

Oldeman et al. (1991) have identified four major causes of soil degradation: deforestation, overgrazing, agricultural activities, and overexploitation. Deforestation is the main cause of soil degradation in Asia and South America, accounting for 41 percent in both regions. In contrast, deforestation is nil in North America and accounts for only 14 percent of soil degradation in Africa. Overgrazing is the main threat to soil stability in Africa (49 percent); it explains from 26 to 30 percent of degradation in other regions. Agricultural activities account for 24 to 27 percent of soil degradation in Africa, Asia, and South America. Overexploitation causes the least amount of soil degradation in the four areas considered: North America (4 percent), South America (5 percent), Asia (6 percent), and Africa (13 percent).

These data suggest the need to tailor conservation programs to foster local solutions to local problems. For example, sustainable agriculture programs in parts of South America and Asia should focus on deforestation whereas those in Africa should focus on overgrazing.

Statistics cited by Lal and Pierce (1991) underscore concerns over continued deforestation and soil degradation:

- Soil erosion has irreversibly destroyed an estimated 430 million hectares worldwide, which is about 30 percent of presently cultivated land area.
- The rate of land degradation is 5 to 7 million hectares per year, and may increase to 10 million hectares per year by the year 2000.

- Soil degradation of one type or another affects one-third of the earth's land surface, according to some estimates.
- Natural soil erosion is 9.9 billion tons per year; human induced erosion is 26.0 billion tons per year.
- In 1986 per capita arable land was 0.3 hectares. Yet an estimated 0.5 hectares are needed together with a modest level of production inputs to produce an adequate diet, suggesting that current needs are not being met.
- Per capita arable land is expected to decline to 0.23 hectares by the year 2000, and to 0.15 hectares by 2050. This raises the question of how the world will satisfy its food needs in the future.
- The rate of change in per capita grain production increased by 13 percent per decade in the 1950s, decreased by 2 percent per decade in the 1980s, and is projected to decrease by 7 percent per decade in the 1990s.

While worldwide trends in resource degradation are clear, specific actions needed to halt or reverse those trends in a particular country are not so clear. The biophysical characteristics of land degradation are manifested in many ways, including soil erosion (due to wind and water), loss of soil fertility (due to leaching and acidification), loss of plant cover (the main effect of desertification), loss of moisture holding capacity (largely due to loss of organic matter), development of impermeable subsurface layers (hardpans), and loss of microflora and plant diversity.

Moreover, the social and economic circumstances under which farmers operate are as important as, and often more complex than, the biophysical problems they face. In fact, many view soil erosion and land degradation as a multifaceted social, rather than biophysical, problem (Blaikie 1985). Among the socioeconomic factors affecting farmers is population growth, which increases the demand for land on which to grow crops. This often leads to deforestation or shorter fallow periods. Continuous cropping, in turn, increases the demand for fertilizer to maintain soil fertility. At the same time, short-sighted economic policies often encourage clearing new land for cultivation rather than protecting and improving land already under cultivation. Population pressures also encourage overgrazing of arid land, causing desertification. Insecure land tenure arrangements discourage farmers from making long-term investments so often needed to conserve resources. Farmers are sometimes not even aware of the benefits of protecting their resource base. Finally, low general productivity causes general poverty, which precludes investments in technology development and diffusion that would raise productivity and release pressures of population on land.

USAID SUSTAINABLE AGRICULTURE PROGRAMS

In the 1960s and early 1970s, USAID agriculture programs were directed toward increasing food production to meet the developing world's rapidly expanding population. USAID agriculture programs continued to evolve, so they now encompass the much broader concept of *sustainable* agriculture, which, according to the Consultative Group on International Agricultural Research "should involve the successful management of resources to satisfy human needs while maintaining or enhancing the quality of the environment and conserving natural resources" (CGIAR 1988, ix).   It is now generally understood that programs to halt soil erosion and land degradation must include viable technical packages, appropriate government policies and economic incentives, secure land tenure, farmer education and community participation, and adequate infrastructure and support systems.   USAID surveyed five countries to determine the impact of its investments in sustainable agriculture. In each country, technologies had been introduced not only to increase agricultural production but also to reduce soil erosion (thereby achieving both economic and environmental benefits).   In most countries, USAID also supported complementary interventions, such as promoting education and awareness, strengthening institutions, and improving the policy environment. But among all the interventions, the introduction of appropriate technologies was fundamental in helping to explain the relative success or failure of the sustainable agriculture programs.   It is important to understand at the outset what these diverse technologies were designed to accomplish.

Four technologies were supported in the Gambia:

- Saltwater intrusion dikes stop salt intrusion from the saline estuaries of the Gambia River, thereby reclaiming formerly saline soils for agricultural production.   In addition, they impound the runoff water at the mouth of the small streams flowing into the saline estuaries. This raises the freshwater table in the swamplands farthest from the estuary and, by flushing out the salts, reduces the salinity of the soils closest to the estuary.
- Water retention dams capture rainfall runoff, impounding some of the water that flows into the streams immediately after it rains. This raises the water table and creates additional areas for flooded rice production closest to the dams. It also increases moisture availability for rice production further from the dams. Unlike saltwater intrusion dikes, water retention dams do not increase cultivable land area by reclaiming saline soils.
- Contour berms are mounds of earth about one meter high and two or more meters at the base that run along the topographic contour of the field. They control upland erosion by stopping water from flowing downslope, and they allow rainfall runoff that otherwise would be lost to infiltrate into the soil.
- Grass waterways are usually built, along with contour berms, on upland fields. Grass is planted along the waterways to hold the soil in place, thereby preventing soil loss and damage to fields by stopping gully erosion, which often accompanies heavy rains.

Three technologies were introduced in Mali:

- Rock lines were constructed along the contour of the slope and, like the contour berms in the Gambia, controlled rainfall runoff and reduced soil erosion.

- Environmentally sound alternatives to the use of chemical fertilizers (which cause soil acidity) were introduced, and fertilizer subsidies were reduced to encourage farmers to use these organic, rather than chemical, fertilizers. The alternatives involved stabling animals, improving corrals, and developing composting and manure pits.
- Improved (streak-resistant) maize varieties were introduced, which provided more reliable yields but required lower fertilizer and pesticide applications than the varieties previously used.

Three quite different technologies were supported in Jamaica under two different projects: the Integrated Rural Development Project (IRDP) and the Hillside Agriculture Project (HAP):

- IRDP used heavy earth-moving equipment to construct terraces, ditches, and waterways (often made of concrete) to control soil erosion on steeply sloping terrain.
- In contrast, HAP gave farmers perennial tree seedlings (primarily coffee and cocoa), which, when planted on steep hillsides, not only helped to control soil erosion but also provided farmers with a source of income. Trees protect watersheds by (1) reducing the flow of water over the soil; (2) blunting the forces of wind and rain; and (3) contributing to the buildup of organic matter on the soil surface. Tree *roots* protect watersheds by (1) holding the soil in place; (2) providing channels that increase the percolation of water into the soil; and (3) binding the soil to prevent its loss from gravity and waterflow.
- HAP also introduced more direct soil conservation practices, including (1) individual plant basins combined with plant material left on the soil surface to reduce sheet erosion, increase water infiltration, and supply organic matter to improve soil fertility; (2) ditches, grass or wooden barriers, and reinforced contours, which, in addition to reducing erosion and improving infiltration, channel excess water off the field; (3) gully plugs, which reduce water velocity in the vertical channels that drain water from the fields and roads; and (4) tree cuttings placed along contour lines to reduce erosion.

The sloping agricultural lands technology (SALT) was introduced in the Philippines:

- SALT involves the cultivation of crops in "alleyways" between hedgerows of leguminous trees planted along the hillside on the contour. The leguminous trees (like the perennial trees in Jamaica) and nitrogen-fixing cover crops halt soil erosion on the hillsides. Over time (three to eight years, depending on the slope of the hillside and the degree of erosion), soils in the alleyways level into terraces. The biomass of the hedgerows improves soil fertility on the terraces and increases crop yields.

Five practices (or technologies) were introduced in Nepal:

- Building dams in gullies and planting grass and vegetative cover on eroded agricultural land to check further erosion.
- Allowing marginal rainfed land to regenerate.
- Rehabilitating common lands with multipurpose trees and fodder grasses to increase biomass that could be used for compost.
- Stall feeding livestock to permit farmyard manure to be collected and used to improve soil fertility.
- Recycling waste water to irrigate off-season vegetables as cash crops.

In general, USAID's programs in sustainable agriculture had significant positive benefits, but their *socioeconomic* impact was easier to document than their environmental impact. None of the sustainable agriculture programs had been designed to measure biophysical or environmental impacts stemming from the adoption of improved practices. This was partly because most USAID projects operated within a relatively short time frame, while most environmental programs, by their nature, require a relatively long period to demonstrate impact. Consequently, the evaluation teams relied on secondary data and proxy indicators to assess environmental impact. The findings reported next were based on personal observations, interviews with farmers and program implementors, and previously conducted studies, which usually did not focus on the actual impact of the program.

Socioeconomic Impact

In the Gambia, the economic impact of the soil and water conservation program was impressive. Within one to two seasons, average rice yields increased by 108 percent, from 1.3 to 2.7 tons per hectare. In one village, women confirmed that they were able to harvest from one plot what they typically had harvested from three plots before the saltwater intrusion dike was constructed. In Njawara, rice was harvested on plots that had not been cultivated for over a decade. In upland areas, too, the construction of contour berms and antierosion measures resulted in increased production of millet, sorghum, corn, and peanuts.

Increased production contributed to increased incomes and improved food security. For example, the increased water retention made possible by the conservation infrastructure allowed women to grow vegetables, a source of cash income, during the dry season following the rice harvest. Both men and women uniformly and repeatedly pointed out that the saltwater intrusion dikes allowed families to eat for months without purchasing rice or other food stuffs, and the money saved could then be used to meet other needs.

There were social benefits as well.   For example, the conservation infrastructure effectively ended flooding in the village of Njawara.   Women, who were the primary beneficiaries of the new income-earning activities, regained control over subsistence production in their traditional fields.

In Mali, millet and grain sorghum yields increased by at least 10 percent in fields where rock lines had been constructed.   Even though there were significant labor costs in building the rock lines, the internal rate of return (IRR) to investing in the technology was estimated between 45 and 95 percent, depending on the method used to transport the rocks.

In Jamaica, the economic impact was substantial.   Coffee production increased from less than the national average (about twenty boxes per acre) to almost thirty boxes per acre.   Likewise, cocoa production increased from between eight and ten boxes per acre to about thirty boxes per acre.   Another analysis concluded that after four years coffee production increased by 21 percent and cocoa production increased by 45 percent.   In large part, these yield increases were due to increased availability of external inputs (principally fertilizers and pesticides) and improved practices recommended by HAP.   The extent to which the increased production translated into increased income varied, depending largely on world market prices for coffee and cocoa and the foreign exchange rate.

The HAP program also had an important social impact.   Perennial trees provide an annual source of income over a long period of time, fifteen to twenty years.   Therefore, the social security of the beneficiaries of the program improved in direct relation to the number of additional perennial trees that were planted and resuscitated.   This was important because the beneficiaries (both men and women) were generally older than the population at large, as reflected by the fact that the average age of Jamaican farmers is fifty-five years.

In the Philippines, also, the economic impact of the soil conservation program was positive.   Despite the space taken up by hedgerows under SALT, net production per unit of land steadily increased on the newly terraced land to levels obtained before erosion began.   Yields were much greater than those obtained under bush-fallow cultivation of comparably degraded lands in other parts of the Philippines.   Farmers implementing SALT realized yield increases of an estimated 300 percent after several years of cultivation.   The increased yields allowed farmers to satisfy their subsistence needs on less land, and the "extra" land could then be used for planting fruits, vegetables, and other cash crops.   As a result, the net income of farmers who switched from slash and burn practices to hedgerow cultivation typically increased by about $400 per hectare.

Even though SALT required more labor, the return to the technology was 25 percent greater than with traditional slash and burn technology.   When additional economic benefits are taken into account (for example, the potential for livestock production and crop diversification), the economic incentives for adopting SALT are even greater.

In Nepal, improved water management enabled farmers to double- and triple-crop their fields, and this resulted in a doubling or tripling of yields. Increased yields permitted farmers to shift from subsistence crops to cash crops and other market-oriented enterprises, which contributed to increased incomes. Additional income permitted increased savings and investment at both the household and community levels. At the community level, savings were pooled and invested in infrastructure, such as public buildings and elementary schools.

Reforestation activities also contributed to improved household welfare. For example, the time women used to spend collecting fuelwood, fodder, and grass could—thanks to reforestation—be reallocated to agricultural production, food preparation, and child care. The amount of time saved can be substantial: One study found that a hill woman in a deforested area in Nepal spends, on average, 2½ hours a day, every day, foraging.

Environmental Impact

The saltwater intrusion dikes and water retention dams introduced in the Gambia had a significant, positive environmental impact for lowland rice farmers. The impact was most dramatic where salinization had made fields impossible to cultivate, and the dikes and dams reversed this situation. In all, the saltwater intrusion dikes and water retention dams protected critical portions of 15 percent of the lowland rice-growing areas of the country. The benefits of the conservation structures introduced to upland farmers were less striking, reducing soil erosion and flooding on about 1 percent of the upland farming areas.

Of the three conservation technologies reviewed by the evaluation team in Mali, the installation of rock lines in farmers' fields had the greatest environmental impact. They resulted in decreased soil surface erosion, increased water retention, improved soil cover buildup, and increased crop yields in areas adjacent to the rock line. Although quantitative data on results were limited to the number of meters of rock lines installed, the positive impact of the technology was consistent with that found in other Sahelian countries, with conditions similar to those found in Mali.

In Jamaica, perennial trees were planted on steep hillsides susceptible to soil erosion. More than 1 million coffee and cocoa trees were planted and more than 2 million trees were resuscitated on more than 6,500 acres, affecting more than 9,500 beneficiaries. In addition, HAP introduced structures to control soil erosion, including more than 3,100 chains of ditches; 1,000 gully plugs; more than 1,300 chains of grass barriers; 2,100 chains of wooden barriers; and nearly 3,500 plant basins. It is clear that these interventions helped reduce soil losses on highly erodible steep lands, but, as in Mali, there were no direct measures of reduced erosion.

Adoption rates of SALT practices in the Philippines varied considerably, depending on the particular site. At most of the sites visited by the evaluation team, the technology resulted in increased terrace formation and soil stabilization, clear environmental benefits.

The evaluation team in Nepal did not gather much quantitative data to evaluate environmental impact. However, the team observed farmers using multipurpose trees and fodder grasses and legumes to stabilize slopes and provide animal fodder. Community-based groups practiced afforestation to increase overall vegetative cover and protect land surrounding springs and irrigation canals. In addition, farmers were using manure obtained from stall feeding livestock to improve soil fertility, which had a direct environmental impact.

KEY PROGRAM ELEMENTS

Each of the five country case studies sought to explain program impact in terms of four interventions which USAID had supported to one degree or another in each country. These interventions were designed to introduce or promote (1) specific soil and water conservation technologies (as described previously); (2) improved education and awareness, (3) training and institution building, and (4) an appropriate policy environment. The relative importance of each intervention is examined.

Technological Change

Improved technology is generally crucial in changing farming practices so that they are more conducive to soil conservation. A broad range of soil and water conservation technologies is "on the shelf," and in most cases the techniques are well understood and the results are quite predictable. Basically, the improved practices work well—whether they be saltwater intrusion dikes, terraces, tree planting, composting to increase organic matter and soil fertility, or some other technique.

The key is getting farmers to implement them, and this is where the human element comes into play. In addition to "doing the job," the improved technology must provide an economic benefit, usually with a short- or medium-term payoff, if it is to be adopted. It also needs to be compatible with existing demands for labor and skill levels of farmers. Finally, farmers must be given an opportunity to learn about the technology and determine for themselves if it is appropriate for their particular conditions.

Two technologies were introduced in the lowlands of the Gambia: saltwater intrusion dikes and water retention dams (Table 8.1). Both were uniformly successful because they permitted uncultivatable land to be brought back into production for a crop, rice, that was of particular interest to the community, especially women, and because rice yields increased very significantly.

In contrast, contour plowing, grass waterways, and terraces introduced in the uplands were generally less successful. They resulted in much smaller yield increases, and the payoff for investing in their construction materialized only over the medium to long term. Also, they were usually constructed in millet, grain sorghum, and cowpea fields, and these crops are usually farmed less intensively than lowland rice. However, these technologies can prevent flooding and stop gully erosion. In villages where these problems were especially severe, the technologies were readily adopted.

The rock lines proved to be a successful technology in Mali. The concept was easy to understand, the technology was easy to learn, and it conserved moisture critical to higher grain yield. Farmers saw a rapid yield response in the first season after investing their labor to construct the barriers. Like many conservation practices, rock lines are most effective when implemented for an entire watershed rather than just a few farms or fields. This highlights the importance of having community or village organizations coordinate implementation of these techniques. It is often more difficult for villagers to learn how to organize themselves to construct rock lines on a sufficiently large scale than it is to learn the techniques of building the rock lines. This was the case in Mali, where inadequate village organization sometimes hampered widespread adoption of an otherwise successful technology.

The practice of stabling livestock and developing manure pits was less successful, and adoption was less widespread. This was largely because the practice is more appropriately targeted to livestock owners who are also active in crop production and want to improve soil fertility. In Mali this was not always the case.

The conservation technologies introduced under the two projects in Jamaica were quite different, as was their relative success. IRDP promoted the construction of bench terraces using heavy equipment, while HAP promoted the planting of perennial trees using manual labor. The former was expensive and complex; the latter was relatively inexpensive and simple. The former was clearly inappropriate, as some farmers actually lost productive land; the latter was familiar to most farmers, consistent with existing cropping patterns, and provided significant, short-term benefits. Under IRDP, many farmers constructed the terraces and other erosion control structures because of external incentives (cash payments), but did not maintain them because many of the technologies were inappropriate. Under HAP, farmers planted perennial trees on steep hillsides primarily to increase yields and cash income, but at the same time the techniques increased soil cover and reduced exposure to heavy rainfall, thereby reducing rainfall runoff and soil erosion.

In the Philippines, more than in most other countries, the introduction of the "right technology"—whereby farmers could produce crops without damaging the environment and natural resource base—was critical to success. SALT, the agroforestry hedgerow technique introduced by USAID, was clearly an appropriate technology. It stopped soil erosion, improved soil fertility, and reversed land degradation on the infertile, steep slopes of the nation's uplands. A key factor contributing to its adoption and spread was training beneficiaries in the principles of community organization. Another reason farmers adopted SALT was the lack of alternative opportunities for wage employment. When such opportunities were available, farmers generally did not invest the labor necessary to adopt the improved agroforestry practices.

In Nepal, no single technology was widely adopted. The improved practices that were introduced—composting, tree planting, gully erosion control, and stall feeding livestock—did not generate large economic benefits or yield increases. Instead, they contributed to a noticeable, but not dramatic, improvement in yields and reduction in erosion.

Table 8.1.
USAID-supported Interventions in Technological Change, by Country

Country	Intervention	Was It Successful?
the Gambia	Saltwater intrusion dikes; water retention dams	Yes
	Contour plowing; grass waterways; bench terraces	Somewhat
Mali	Rock lines	Yes
	Stabling livestock; using manure pits	Somewhat
Jamaica	Concrete bench terraces	No
	Perennial tree crops; improved practices	Yes
Philippines	Agroforestry hedgerow farming	Yes
Nepal	Composting; stall feeding; reforestation	Somewhat

Education and Awareness

In all five countries, the impact of environmental awareness campaigns—exhibitions, posters, technical bulletins—was difficult to assess. In general, there was little evidence that such campaigns had any effect on the rate of adoption of the technologies introduced under any of the projects (Table 8.2). Farmers adopted the conservation technologies not to avoid potential long-term negative effects of soil erosion, but to achieve short-term economic benefits.

On the other hand, word of mouth, site visits, and experiential learning were crucial in educating farmers about the specific technologies being introduced by USAID in each of the five countries. This was often done through training and institution building and, at the local level, by encouraging participation.

Table 8.2.
USAID-supported Interventions in Education and Awareness, by Country

Country	Intervention	Was It Successful?
the Gambia	Word of mouth; farm visits	Yes
	Posters; exhibits; radio broadcasts	No
Mali	Top-down, one-way extension messages	Somewhat
Jamaica	Extension service; parastatals; local management committees	Somewhat
	Posters	No
Philippines	Word of mouth; farm visits; training workshops	Yes
Nepal	Village-level meetings; plays; role playing; site visits	Somewhat

Institution Building

The extent to which institutions functioned well and local populations participated effectively helps to explain why some conservation programs were more successful than others. In the Gambia and the Philippines, USAID encouraged local participation and strengthened local communities, NGOs, and farmer associations (Table 8.3). These local groups proved to be important vehicles for disseminating the new technologies, constructing and maintaining the conservation infrastructure, distributing inputs, and marketing outputs. Similar efforts were made in Mali (village level organizations), Jamaica (local management committees), and Nepal (first panchayats [local councils], then user groups and NGOs). However, the effectiveness of this component of these three programs was limited. Even in the Gambia and the Philippines, where there was strong institutional development, there is considerable doubt about the sustainability of the programs because insufficient funds is crippling their continuation.

Policy Environment

Appropriate economic policies seemed to be more important in Mali and the Philippines than in the Gambia, Jamaica, and Nepal (Table 8.4). In Mali USAID was instrumental in reducing fertilizer subsidies, which gave farmers an incentive to use organic fertilizers, which were cheaper and more environmentally friendly than chemical alternatives. In the Philippines, USAID helped the government implement a significant policy shift under which individual farmers gained twenty-five-year rights to public land in upland areas, thereby assuring they would benefit from the conservation program. In the other three countries, the effect of economic policies on sustainable agriculture was either neutral (the Gambia, where prices were relatively unimportant because rice was consumed domestically and not sold in the marketplace), exogenous (Jamaica, where international market prices determined the profitability of export crops), or negative (Nepal, where the importance of appropriate government policy was not fully appreciated).

Table 8.3.
USAID-supported Interventions in Institution Building, by Country

Country	Intervention	Was It Successful?
the Gambia	Soil and Water Management Unit (SWMU) supported for thirteen years; competent advisors provided; trainees returned to good jobs; link between participation and benefits emphasized	Yes
Mali	Village-level organizations emphasized	Somewhat
Jamaica	Technical assistance provided to Ministry of Agriculture (MOA); local management committees (LMCs) created; link between participation and benefits not emphasized	Somewhat
Philippines	Training centers created; farmers and extension agents trained; NGOs strengthened; community participation emphasized; farmer associations created	Yes
Nepal	Initial emphasis on district level organizations; later, on NGOs and local user groups; training was provided	Somewhat

Table 8.4.
USAID-supported Interventions Concerning the Policy Environment, by Country

Countries	Intervention	Was It Successful?
the Gambia	None, but economic policy reforms had already been introduced by other USAID programs	Neutral
Mali	Policy reforms reduced the role of the public sector, increased market liberalization, and reduced the fertilizer subsidy	Yes
Jamaica	None, but economic liberalization and deregulation helped create a policy environment conducive to export crop production	Somewhat
Philippines	Certificates of stewardship ensured secure access to land	Yes
Nepal	Legal status was given to user groups to protect and encourage good management of forests on public lands	Somewhat

PROGRAM PERFORMANCE

The following sections examine the extent to which USAID programs were effective and efficient.   Also of interest is whether the programs were sustainable and replicable.

Program Effectiveness

Generally speaking, a program is effective if it reaches the population it intends to benefit and if the results are those anticipated and desired in the design of the activity.   The soil and water conservation activities supported by USAID in the Gambia were effective on both counts.   This was due in large measure to (1) the selection of comparatively simple, low-cost, and easy-to-maintain technologies; (2) the direct and almost immediate linkage between the problem (reduced productivity due to saltwater intrusion) and the proposed solution (construction of saltwater intrusion dikes); (3) the ability to demonstrate significant, short-term benefits to those participating in the activity; and (4) the willingness of community members to redistribute equitably reclaimed lands brought into production.   From 1983–1984 to 1992–1993, 1,611 hectares of lowland rice lands were rehabilitated, and soil conservation measures were applied to 1,920 hectares of upland area.   As a result, 140 villages and 29,529 people were positively affected.   Women, the rice growers in the Gambia, were the principal beneficiaries.

The 2 percent of Mali that is arable and suitable for farming was targeted under USAID's sustainable agriculture program.   From 1989 to 1992, 1,711 meters of rock lines and 19,740 meters of dikes were constructed.   In addition, since the program was premised on the belief that literacy was essential to project success, more than 500 literacy centers were established: 65 percent were for men, 20 percent for women, and the remainder for mixed-sex groups. Beyond that, there was no deliberate targeting of particular people or groups. The soil conservation practices were generally not adopted, except by farmer demonstrators.   The results of the literacy program were minimal.   In fact, the problem of agricultural unsustainability, which began in the 1970s with a major drought, has worsened since then as a result of continued rainfall shortages, population pressures, deforestation, and poor cultivation practices.

Although the majority of hillside farms in Jamaica are small (70 percent are under 2 hectares; 95 percent are under 4), HAP did not deliberately attempt to reach the smallest, or the poorest, farmers.   To the contrary, it attempted to reach those who had secure land tenure, were dedicated farmers, and were young (in a country where the average age of farmers is relatively high, fifty-five years).   As a result, more marginal farmers were often not beneficiaries.   All participants (over 9,500), regardless of income level or farm size (which averaged two-thirds of an acre), received the same benefits: enough seedlings and fertilizer to cover not more than one acre of land.   Neither the husband nor the wife benefited more than the other; instead, additional income generated under HAP was treated as family income and shared between the two.

The sustainable agriculture projects in the Philippines targeted impoverished rural households and ethnic groups living in one of the poorest regions of the country. These people, for the most part, had been overlooked by government programs. The technology that was introduced (SALT) required only limited financial resources and was available to any farmer with land to cultivate. In addition, the program generated benefits for neighboring farmers and landless residents, who were hired to help establish and, later, prune the hedgerows. The program also generated public benefits, such as reduced risk of flooding, that were not targeted to specific groups.

In Nepal, women and disadvantaged groups have a predominant role in decisions related to agricultural production and resource utilization. It was logical, therefore, to target these groups as project beneficiaries. Many formed user groups (equitably represented in terms of gender, caste, and ethnicity) in the course of implementing and managing the conservation activities. Anecdotal evidence shows that in the Pereni subwatershed, for example, farmers increased irrigated area from 45 to 180 hectares over a four-year period and also rehabilitated eroded soils.

Program Efficiency

Program efficiency assesses benefits in relation to costs. For a program to be efficient, benefits must, at a minimum, equal the return that could be earned on alternative investments elsewhere in the economy.

An economic analysis of the soil and water conservation program in the Gambia showed that during the thirteen-year project period the benefit-cost ratio was 0.76 to 1. Benefits were less than costs, indicating that the project was not economically viable over that time period. According to the analysis, the break-even year was 2006. At that point, benefits would just equal costs, and the benefit-cost ratio would be 1. When the analysis excluded the thirteen-year donor phase of the project, treating costs incurred then as sunk costs, and instead included only the fourteen-year period ending in 2006 (the break-even year), the benefit-cost ratio was 5.18 to 1. This means that each dollar expended on the soil and water conservation program would return more than 5 dollars, which, from the government's point of view, is very attractive.

In Mali, no attempt was made to assess the economic efficiency of the USAID projects. However, analyses show that construction of rock lines to reduce soil erosion and restore soil quality was financially viable from the farmer's point of view, depending on the means used to transport the rocks. To construct 100 meters of rock lines, it took forty days of labor using headloads, twenty-one days using carts, and ten days using trucks. If the rocks were transported by truck, construction of rock lines had a high internal rate of return

(IRR). But when more rudimentary modes of transport were used (carts or headloads), the IRR declined.

In Jamaica, HAP was judged economically feasible in 1987 when the project was designed. The estimated IRR was 9 to 22 percent, depending on assumptions concerning rates of adoption, commodity prices (mainly of coffee and cocoa), wage rates, and yield increases. However, yield increases for coffee had been overestimated by at least a factor of two. When IRRs were recalculated under the assumption that coffee yields were one-half those assumed in the 1987 analysis, estimated IRRs ranged from 6 to 18 percent, and estimated project benefits were cut almost in half.

SALT had not spread sufficiently in the Philippines to cover the costs of the projects. As of 1993, only about 2,000 hectares were being cultivated using SALT—out of 9.5 million hectares of public uplands where the technology could be applied. Assuming the benefits of SALT were $400 per hectare, a total of 41,250 hectares would have to be put under SALT cultivation to cover the costs of the two projects. However, $400 per hectare is a conservative estimate of benefits. If other benefits (reduced flooding, more stable watersheds, an improved opportunity to grow cash crops) were included in the analysis, fewer than 41,250 hectares would have to be cultivated using SALT in order to cover project costs.

The evaluation team in Nepal did not estimate the economic efficiency of the soil and water conservation program. Nonetheless, the team concluded that the program was not efficient, mainly because it depended on large-scale, costly engineering works. Also, it used a top-down approach to introduce the new technologies without involving the beneficiaries, and the technologies were not widely adopted. Since the infrastructure is now in place and the user-oriented approach is being used, the natural resource component of the follow-on project is likely to be more efficient.

Program Sustainability and Replicability

A final issue is whether or not the soil and water conservation programs were sustained after USAID assistance ended. USAID's soil conservation work in the Gambia is both sustainable and replicable. Farmers realized good returns to their labor investments, and there is solid evidence that they are maintaining their dams and barriers and even extending them wherever possible. The staff of the Soil and Water Management Unit, the main institution strengthened by USAID in the Ministry of Agriculture, has the technical capacity to continue to design the kinds of saltwater dikes and water retention dams that had such a positive impact. To do this, however, the unit will need continued funding from the Gambian government or donors. Although soil salinization problems are generally site specific, the technologies applied in the Gambia can be replicated elsewhere, such as in neighboring Senegal where similar conditions exist.

Similarly, the rock line technology introduced by USAID in Mali to conserve soil moisture can be successfully extended to other areas with similar soils, slopes, cropping patterns, and rainfall—both within Mali and in other nearby Sahelian countries. The positive returns to labor invested in building rock lines make it a financially sustainable technology for most farmers. However, it may not be institutionally sustainable at the village level. Conservation structures should be installed to cover fairly large areas, usually all or most of the sloping fields of the watershed. This requires villages to organize farmers to undertake this task. The capacity of villages to organize farmers, therefore, is a key determinant of whether or not the technology is replicated.

The improved soil conservation techniques used in Jamaica have been applied in many countries. The practices work well and are replicable under similar soil, climate, and cropping conditions. However, the long-term sustainability of these practices is questionable. This is not because they require a large investment; they do not. Rather it is because farmers require institutions to supply agricultural services, inputs, and markets. In Jamaica, these institutions at the local level tend to be ineffective and function poorly.

The technology developed in the Philippines can work well in many countries, particularly where steep slopes and acid, infertile soils are being converted from forest land to cropland. Moreover, farm level economics makes SALT profitable. The technology is replicable as long as there are viable institutions, such as an extension service, to introduce it and train farmers in its use. In the Philippines, NGOs were one of the most important institutions to perform this function. But NGOs or similar organizations may not operate in, or have the resources to extend SALT to, all areas of the country.

The techniques introduced in Nepal are simple and do not require large investments or complicated training programs. They are replicable both within the country and in other countries. In fact, all of the technologies used in Nepal are routinely applied elsewhere.

CONCLUSIONS AND RECOMMENDATIONS

Four management recommendations emerge from this synthesis of five country case studies on agriculture and the environment. Two of the recommendations are based on experiences and lessons learned common to all five countries. The other two recommendations are based on evidence found in only three or four of the countries.

1. *Positive economic benefits: Introduce conservation technologies that yield significant economic (as well as environmental) benefits in a relatively short period of time.*

- In the Gambia, rice production doubled and sometimes tripled—in one year—in areas where saltwater intrusion dikes had been constructed. Because the benefits from contour berms were typically less immediate and less appreciable, adoption of this technology was less widespread.

- In Mali, economic benefits resulted from adjusting policies that had *discouraged* adoption of sustainable agricultural technologies by keeping the price of chemical fertilizers lower than that of more environmentally friendly organic fertilizers.
- In Jamaica, farmers received immediate economic benefits (free seedlings, free fertilizer, and free technical advice)—which more than compensated for the three or four years it took for the seedlings to produce coffee or cocoa. Resuscitation of existing trees almost doubled yields within two years.
- In the Philippines, farmers abandoned the sloping agricultural lands technology (SALT) if it was not linked with an "economic engine" or profitable cash enterprise.
- In Nepal, conservation practices linked to increased rural incomes were more likely to be adopted than those that were not.

2. *Simple technology: Introduce conservation technologies that are easy to maintain, place minimal demands on labor, require few changes in existing practices, are simple, and are relatively inexpensive.*

- In the Gambia, the saltwater intrusion dikes satisfied most of these criteria; however, they were not simple.
- In Mali, rock lines and other conservation structures were simple and relatively inexpensive, as was organic fertilizer recycling; all of these measures complemented existing practices.
- In Jamaica, perennial tree crops planted under HAP were familiar to farmers and improved practices were simple to adopt, but the additional labor requirement proved to be a constraint. In contrast, the conservation technologies promoted under IRDP were complex, expensive, unfamiliar to farmers, and required changes in existing practices.
- In the Philippines, SALT was not a simple technology, but it worked because systematic training (including farmer-to-farmer training) ensured that farmers adopted the technology without committing errors that could lead to poor results.

3. *Utilize local institutions: Support and strengthen institutions and local organizations that supply inputs, technical advice, and markets to help ensure the sustainability of conservation programs.*

- In the Gambia, USAID stayed the course by supporting the Soil and Water Management Unit for thirteen years; however, lack of continued budgetary support will limit its ability to provide technical advice at the local level.
- In Mali, USAID supported village-level organizations and institutions, which provided the link among farmers, improved technology, and associated inputs farmers needed to apply the technology.
- In Jamaica, long-term sustainability of the conservation activities is questionable, largely because government institutions that supply inputs, technical advice, and markets lack the budget and the staff to do so efficiently; NGOs, however, are filling the gap.

- The same is true in the Philippines, where local NGOs and farmer organizations provide technical advice and inputs and will continue to so as long as they are adequately funded.
- In Nepal, local organizations and community participation helped keep the natural resource management programs in operation.

4. *Provide secure tenure: Support soil and water conservation programs only when intended beneficiaries have secure access to land.*

- In the Gambia, community members redistributed reclaimed land equitably to those who worked to construct and maintain the saltwater intrusion dams.
- In Jamaica, secure land tenure, one criterion used to select farmer beneficiaries, was especially important to ensure farmers would reap the benefits of planting and maintaining perennial tree crops long into the future.
- In the Philippines, "certificates of stewardship" provided individual farmers, community organizations, and small firms twenty-five-year rights to public land in designated upland areas. Farmers who did not own land received the landowner's assurance of at least medium-term access to the land.

Other general observations can be added to recommendations growing out of USAID projects outlined in this chapter. Care for the environment requires following sound economic policies of the *standard model* of Chapter 9. Failure to follow the model distorts price signals, often bringing low returns to agricultural output and perpetuating poverty. Growing populations of poor farmers and farm laborers beset with the vicissitudes of survival find it difficult to defer consumption from current needs to invest in durable long-term conservation structures and practices.

A small economic tax base per capita is unable to support proper pay for civil servants, so they are prone to corruption to supplement their income. Weak public institutions can ill resist domestic or foreign exploitation of indigenous timber or land-poor squatters exploiting the exposed fragile soils for agriculture once the land has been cleared. Poorly financed research and extension services are ill equipped to provide farmers with technical assistance to conserve soil or use pesticides safely. An unfavorable business climate and low public investment in human resources and infrastructure preclude having a vigorous agribusiness sector supplying modern farm inputs, marketing farm products, and supporting a high-yield commercial agriculture able to afford a sound environment. The list could go on, but the point is clear: Protection of the environment is possible only with sound overall economic and social policies in this era of rapid population growth in developing countries (see Southgate and Whitaker 1994).

Finally, appropriate environmental technology is not necessarily low-science technology. Modern conservation tillage technology conserves more soil than conventional plow tillage while maintaining output and profitability. Such technology often requires more pesticides than conventional tillage, but science is helping by introducing biological pest controls, by developing safer chemical pesticides, and by genetically engineering pest-resistant crop varieties.

The United States illustrates the potential for technology to reduce environmental degradation through conservation tillage and other means. Sheet and rill (water) erosion rates fell by two-thirds from the 1930s to the 1990s (Tweeten and Forster 1996). Also, yield-increasing technology allowed 1990s' food demand to be supplied using only one-third as many hectares (many of them safe rather than environmentally fragile) as would have been required using farming technology of the 1930s. Combining these yield and area effects, the conclusion is that supplying 1990s' food output with 1930s' technology could have raised erosion rates by nine times.

NOTE

1. New land is being made available for crop production mainly from forest clearing and, to a lesser extent, from land reclamation (including desalinization, irrigation, and drainage).

REFERENCES

Blaikie, P. 1985. *The Political Economy of Soil Erosion in Developing Countries*. New York: Longman Press.

Consultative Group on International Agricultural Research. 1988. "Sustainable Agricultural Production: Implications for International Agricultural Research." Report of the Technical Advisory Committee. Washington, D.C.: CGIAR.

Craswell, E. T. 1993. "Management of Sustainable Agriculture." In *World Soil Erosion and Conservation*, ed. D. Pimental. Cambridge: Cambridge University Press.

Lal, R., and F. J. Pierce. 1991. "The Vanishing Resource." *Soil Management for Sustainability*, 1–5. Ankeny, Iowa: Soil and Water Conservation Society.

Ministry of Foreign Affairs. 1993. *Sustainable Land Use*. Netherlands: Development Cooperation Agency.

Oldeman, L. R., V. W. P. van Engelen, and J. H. M. Pulles. 1991. "The Extent of Human-Induced Soil Degradation." Annex 5 of *World Map of the Status of Human-Induced Soil Degradation: An Explanatory Note*, ed. L. R. Oldeman, R. T. A. Hakkeling and W. G. Sombroek. Wageningen, Netherlands: International Soil Reference and Information Centre.

Southgate, Douglas, and Morris Whitaker. 1994. *Economic Progress and the Environment*. New York: Oxford University Press.

Tweeten, Luther, and Lynn Forster. 1996. "Looking Forward to Choices in the 21st Century." In *The Best of Choices*. Ames, Iowa: American Agricultural Economics Association.

9

Food Security

Luther G. Tweeten

INTRODUCTION[1]

The good news is that globally, more people are better fed than ever before. Over 1.5 billion people were added to world population between 1970 and 1990, while the number of chronically undernourished dropped 150 million persons.

The unfortunate news is that some 800 million people still chronically consume too little food for a healthy, active life. At least an additional quarter billion people periodically suffer inadequate food consumption as food accessibility is interrupted by unstable weather, prices, employment, and by pestilence such as drought, disease, and war. Asia has the greatest number of food insecure people, while Africa has the highest proportion of its people rated as food insecure (Reutlinger and Alderman 1980; FAO, 6). Asia is making considerable progress in reducing food insecurity; Africa is not. Worldwide, an estimated 18 to 24 million people die of hunger each year (Alamgir and Arora 1991, 2). Numbers are unreliable and probably underestimated. One reason is because many people die prematurely from diseases such as diarrhea and measles, which ordinarily are not fatal but cause death among persons weakened by undernutrition.

Demographers predict that the world population will approximately double from its 1995 level and peak at 11 billion people by the year 2100 (Lutz 1996). Growth will be largely in developing countries. Demand for food will expand with rising incomes as well as with more people, and it may triple by year the 2100 from the 1995 level. Providing that food supply in the face of environmental, natural resource, and other constraints will be challenging indeed.

Food security affects many dimensions of well-being. Women without adequate diets give birth to children with low birth weights and high mortality rates. Mothers cannot breast feed their babies properly. In children, inadequate food consumption can impair cognitive and neurological development, which in turn can reduce learning capacity, attention span, and school performance (AID 1982, ii). Adults without proper food intake have low productivity and low capacity to be food secure. These adults produce children with the problems described previously, completing the food insecurity cycle. *The ideal is for all people at all times to have physical and economic access to sufficient food to meet their dietary needs to have a productive and healthy life.*

OBJECTIVE

The objective of this chapter is to outline a framework for food security in developing countries. That framework is designed to

1. Enhance food security in developing countries receiving economic assistance, and
2. Provide a conceptual framework for donor policy to pursue food security through economic assistance programs.

This chapter establishes a conceptual framework for broad-based, sustainable economic progress to provide food security. It then turns to transitory food security and means to deal with it. The final section lists possible donor options for food security. Definitions and dimensions of food security are addressed next before outlining elements of a framework to promote food security.

Definition of Food Security

In April 1992, the Agency for International Development (AID 1992) adopted the following basic definition of food security: "when all people at all times have both physical and economic access to sufficient food to meet their dietary needs for a productive and healthy life." This definition, used in this chapter, is also used by the World Bank (1986a, 1), by the Food and Agriculture Organization (FAO) Committee on World Food Security (see Huddleston 1990, 72), and by the Food, Agriculture, Conservation, and Trade Act of 1990 (PL 101-624).

Dimensions of food security are shown in Figure 9.1. *Food availability* refers to the supply of food present from production, imports, or stocks. Policies such as buffer stocks, excess production capacity, and production practices (e.g., diversification, flexibility, drought-resistant varieties) are means to ensure food supply in the face of pestilence and unstable weather from year to year. *Food accessibility* refers to effective demand to acquire available food from earnings or as transfers from others. *Food utilization* refers to the human body actually making use of the nutrients in food that is consumed, properly digested, and absorbed.

Whereas food availability highlighted *supply* of food (from production, stocks, and imports) at the national level and production and inventory at the farm level, food accessibility highlights effective *demand* and purchasing power of consumers. Given that world supplies of food have been adequate every year in

Figure 9.1.
Some Dimensions of Food Security

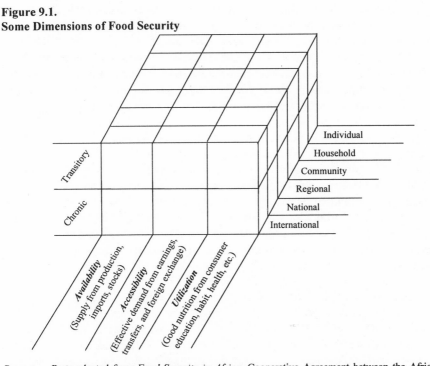

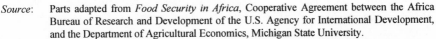

Source: Parts adapted from *Food Security in Africa*, Cooperative Agreement between the Africa
Bureau of Research and Development of the U.S. Agency for International Development,
and the Department of Agricultural Economics, Michigan State University.

recent decades to provide an adequate diet for every consumer but that millions of
persons have gone hungry for lack of buying power from earnings or transfers,
food accessibility is a felicitous concept appropriately emphasized in the preceding
definitions.

Ideally, food security means that all persons at all times *utilize* food necessary
for an active and healthy life.[2] People for whom food is available and accessible
but who fail to consume and absorb adequate nutrients experience food insecurity.
Given food accessibility, improper food utilization is the result of personal tastes,
culture, peer pressures, lack of knowledge, inadequate household processing and
storage, inadequate food labeling, misleading advertising, and physical and mental
illnesses.   Many of these causes are worthy of public concern.   The third
component, utilization, is included in Figure 9.1 to remind that consumer
education, information systems, health, and nutrition are components of food
security.

Food security may be viewed along other dimensions.   Issues at the world
level, such as internationally coordinated buffer stocks, can differ sharply from
issues at the individual or household level, such as the elderly or young being the
residual claimants on the family food supply (Figure 9.1).   Food security policies
at the community and regional level will be influenced by communication and

transportation linkages. Internationally, a food security strategy for developing countries cannot be properly devised without reference to trade, aid, commodity program, and stock policies of developed countries.

Adequate utilization implies adequate intake of vitamins, protein, minerals, and fiber as well as calories. Malnutrition in *developed* countries often is a very real problem of obesity from chronic excess calorie consumption. The focus of this chapter is food insecurity and undernutrition associated with poverty in *developing* countries.

Food security for all people at all times goes beyond transitory food supply or buying power shortfalls to encompass the much larger dimension of chronic food insecurity (Figure 9.1). For chronically food insecure people, food consumption is hardly ever adequate. Broadening the concept of insecurity beyond the uncertain, unexpected, or random setback recognizes that transitory food insecurity cannot be cleanly separated from chronic food insecurity. Individuals and nations troubled by chronic food insecurity are most prone to transitory food insecurity. Those with resources to avoid chronic food insecurity are likely to be able to purchase, borrow, save, or in other ways escape transitory food insecurity. Thus *food security is inseparable from poverty.*

The concept of chronic food insecurity recognizes dimensions of food availability, accessibility, and utilization over the long run. Policy for such a trajectory has few bounds. Because the food insecure are poor people who typically devote 60 to 80 percent of their income for food, food insecurity attends poverty. And because poverty is a function of the level and distribution of national income, food security cannot be separated from economic development. In short, food security encompasses disciplines ranging from nutrition at the individual level, to family economics at the household level, to all-weather road construction and maintenance at the regional level, to economic development policy at the national level, and to trade and aid at the international level. Hence this chapter addresses broader issues of economic development relating to food security.

Other dimensions of food security are revealing. USAID uses the term *food self-reliance* to refer to a nation's ability to produce food domestically and to import commercially the food it does not produce. Food self-reliance gets to the heart of development strategies to eliminate hunger because it recognizes the role of domestic income and foreign exchange on the demand side and domestic food production and food imports on the supply side.

The preceding definitions avoid defining food security as self-sufficiency, which normally varies through the demographic transition. The demographic transition has a *food transition* counterpart. In a primitive stage, society engages in subsistence production, autarky (no trade), and self-sufficiency. Famine and other pestilence are common in such societies. As development proceeds and health and nutrition improve, death rates fall and incomes rise, causing a sharp increase in food demand from population growth and income growth. A large proportion of additional income goes to purchase food as formerly poor people improve their diets. Resource requirements to feed a nation rise as demand shifts from direct consumption of grains and other plant products to meat. That is, it can take seven times as much resources to provide a given number of calories to people through beef than through direct consumption of grains. Thus, food production often does not keep pace with food consumption growth as development proceeds. Fortunately, developing countries experiencing rapid income growth generate export earnings used to purchase needed food from developed countries, which have sharply increased food production per capita.

Forces attending greater income—improved health enhancing chances of child survival, more resources for old age, declining value of children for work, high costs and time for schooling, and urbanization—all make for lower birth rates with development. As developing economies mature, food demand expansion slows as the population growth rate falls with lower birth rates and as a smaller proportion of added income is used to purchase food. Meanwhile, the supply of food expands as earlier investments in local agricultural research and extension finally pay off with improved practices and technology. Consequently, some developing countries become exporters as they become developed. This food transition may require decades of growth. Other formerly low-income countries, such as Japan, South Korea, and Taiwan, became less self-sufficient even as they became more food secure. Thus, economic development and the demographic transition bring food self-reliance but not necessarily food self-sufficiency.

Attempts at self-sufficiency can reduce buying power at the household level and economic development at the national level, reducing food security. Buying power, as measured by family or individual income, is closely correlated with food security, as measured by personal food consumption.

A recurring theme in this chapter is that food security has two principal components at the national level: (1) broad-based, sustainable economic progress relying on the private sector under supportive public policies to raise most people out of income and food insecurity; and (2) targeted food and other transfers to those who lack resources and income or other means for food security. A later section emphasizes policies for economic development to provide food security.

ELEMENTS OF A BROAD-BASED, SUSTAINABLE ECONOMIC DEVELOPMENT STRATEGY TO PROMOTE FOOD SECURITY

The principal source of food insecurity is poverty. Because the most cost-effective means to reduce poverty in developing countries is by increased productivity and buying power, the cornerstone of a successful food security strategy is economic development.[3] Some individuals and families are bypassed by the market, hence economic development is necessary but not sufficient for food security. Although economic development bypasses some, it provides the wherewithal to finance food imports and food and income transfers to those left behind. Given economic development, the sufficient condition to end food insecurity is the political will and administrative capacity for essential transfers.

Economic development to address food and income insecurity differs from conventional economic development in that it must be *broad based and sustainable* (BBS). It is *broad based* in that policies are designed to raise productivity and buying power of the entire population. Policies must avoid a dual agriculture focusing public sector resources to achieve productivity gains for large farms while neglecting smallholders (see especially Tomich *et al.*, Part 2). The latter constitute the great majority of farmers and have a proven record of responding to economic incentives and improved technology. Human resource development efforts such as public education must reach women, minorities, rural residents, and the poor as well as others. It is *sustainable* in that policies buying short-term gains at the expense of future growth (e.g., overexploitation of resources and excessive borrowing, money creation, and government operating account deficits) are avoided. It avoids the boom and bust policies of business and political cycles, which create instability and food insecurity. It is efficient, allocating resources where social payoffs are highest to raise income and living standards. It provides the economic base for transfer payments to food insecure people. The surplus produced by a strategy of BBS development provides an economic base to purchase foreign currency and food imports or to purchase domestic buffer reserves of stocks. The surplus provides the wherewithal to supply public goods such as agricultural research, infrastructure, and schooling services, which are efficient sources of future food and income streams. The surplus from economic development supports technology and practices to conserve soil and pursue other dimensions of an environmentally sound agriculture.

Too much emphasis on redistribution especially in the early stages of development destroys the surplus of savings and investment required for human, material, and technological capital formation and economic progress. A "pie" of income must exist before equity in the division of that pie can be pursued. Finding the proper mix of economic efficiency and growth versus equity and distributive justice is a challenge to any government. Food and other assistance from donor countries can make that trade-off less onerous. Technical assistance and policy analysis can help to identify equity-growth trade-offs for decision makers.

In short, the objective of moving all peoples at all times to a position of food security requires a combination of market-oriented development activities, safety nets redistributing food and income, and public and private actions designed to foster both.

Empirical Evidence of Food Security Promoted by Economic Development

That economic growth reduces food and income insecurity is apparent from long-term data for eleven developing countries, as reported in the *World Development Report 1990* (World Bank 1990, 48). Each percentage point increment in annual mean income growth reduced the proportion of persons in poverty by 2.3 percentage points over a 10-year period. The report succinctly concluded that "in short, growth reduces poverty" (World Bank 1990, 47). The report also concluded that the poorest of the poor participated in economic growth (p. 48).

The obverse, that food and income shortfalls especially disadvantage the poor, also is important to recognize. For example, because of the greater proportion of income spent on food and more elastic demand for food by low-income people, relative food consumption falls ten times as much for the poor as for the wealthiest 5 percent after a given reduction in food supplies (Mellor 1978). That setback for the poor detracts from their already low nutritional status.

In India, the four states with the fastest growth rates in their agricultural sectors reduced the proportion of the rural population in absolute poverty by over half in a twenty-year period (1963 to 1983) with similar weather at the beginning and the end. The states that did poorly in agricultural growth actually experienced an increase in the proportion of their rural population in poverty. Countries that have done well in agricultural development (e.g., Thailand, Indonesia, and Taiwan) have all experienced a radical decline in absolute poverty and hence have dramatically improved food security.

Studies show a close link between income and social indicators other than food security. Infant mortality rises with poverty (World Bank 1990, 31). The incidence of rural malnutrition declines significantly as gross national product increases to approximately $1,000 per capita based on data for eighteen low-income countries (Figure 9.2).

Empirical evidence is compelling that the poorest nations are in no position to undertake redistributions that successfully close food deficits. Of the thirty lowest income countries in 1988, only two had an average calorie supply of 2,300 or more per capita (World Bank 1991, 258). Transfers of at least 15 percent of current gross domestic product (GDP) would be needed to eliminate the poverty gap in Bangladesh (World Bank 1990, 50). Transfers of only 1.1 percent of current GDP would be required in Brazil, a country with greater income. Given the leakage of transfers for administration, to the middle class (to gain their political support), and to others, actual transfers would need to be much larger than indicated. Large transfers require taxes that reduce GDP. Real GDP (deadweight) losses from taxes and other market distortions required to finance transfers are massive in Egypt, for example, where transfers are a relatively high 7 percent of GDP (World Bank 1990, 50).

Role of the Private Sector in Promoting Food Security

Because the number of food insecure persons is so large and because national income is so low in many developing countries, food insecurity cannot be eliminated by food and income transfers. In the case of the able-bodied, development rather than transfers is the lowest-cost means to food security.

Figure 9.2.
Rural Malnutrition in Eighteen Low-Income Countries in the Mid-1980s

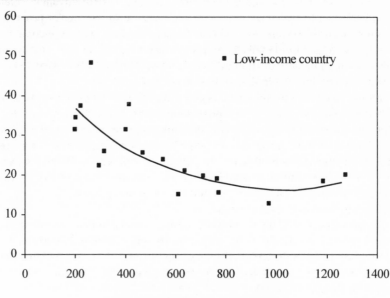

Percent of malnutrition

GNP per capita (1987 U.S. dollars)

Source: IFPRI 1990, 35.

Much of this chapter focuses on public policies for food security. That focus must not veil the larger fact that *most of the task of providing food security in developing countries will be accomplished by the private producers and marketers responding to price incentives set by supply and demand in markets*. A food security strategy not harnessing the efficiency of markets will fail. The private sector will make decisions whether to produce food or fiber for home consumption or the market, for the domestic market or for export, and for consumption or storage. It will determine whether to use labor-, land-, or capital-intensive production methods, whether to employ conventional or new technologies, and whether to borrow or lend. As explained later, the public sector can influence some of these decisions, but it cannot make them because the millions of decisions required daily even in a small economy would overwhelm public decision makers.

THE STANDARD MODEL

Providers of foreign assistance often are in a position to promote dialogue, educate, and support appropriate public policies in the developing world; hence knowing what is appropriate public policy to support the private sector is important to donors and developing countries alike.

The seminal economic revelation of the past five decades is the triumph of the *standard model* for prescriptive economic policy. The standard model is neoclassical microeconomics at its core but with a patina of monetarism and Keynesianism, recognizing the public role in providing sound macroeconomic policy essential for an efficient private sector.

It has triumphed not because of its neat conceptual foundation dating to Adam Smith and others, but because it works, as evident from experience ranging from Hong Kong to Chile. Meanwhile, competing systems have failed spectacularly, as evident from the experiences of Cuba, North Korea, and the Soviet Union. The compelling evidence for success of the standard model is more than anecdotal, and comes from numerous analytical studies (Agarwala 1983; Bale and Lutz 1981; Gwartney et al. 1996; Holmes and Kirkpatrick 1996; Sachs and Warner 1996; Zhao et al. 1991). Bruno et al. (1996) found that aggregate economic growth reduces poverty, and that rural economic growth appears to have a greater effect than urban economic growth on overall poverty reduction.

The standard model is deceptively simple. Its essential elements are so straightforward and few that they can be written on the back of an envelope. The model does not represent the end of economics—refinements will occur over time. Not all elements of the standard model need be fulfilled; even the economically most successful countries do not meet all requirements, but failure to honor key elements relegates countries to poverty and food insecurity. On the other hand, meeting the elements ensures economic growth to provide the wherewithal essential for food security, although rates of progress will differ among countries due to varied endowments of natural resources, institutions, and cultures (work ethic, entrepreneurial zeal, savings rate, etc.).

The overriding current issue is not what works but how to progress from current systems to the standard model. That requires knowledge of how to change dysfunctional attitudes and institutions, including political systems. No social or any other kind of scientist is much good at that, partly because the prescription for cultural and institutional change has neither the proper theory nor experience underlying the standard model (see Ruttan 1995). Some elements required for change were outlined in Chapter 2. Elements required for a successful economy are outlined in this chapter.

Worldwide experience provides telling evidence that a dynamic, growing economy capable of meeting food and other needs of people must rely mainly on the private sector, on markets, and the price incentive system for most economic decisions and activity. Markets work best where goods are rival, exclusionary, and transparent. Where these characteristics are sufficiently absent, the government is needed to provide public goods or direct incentives for the private sector to act in the public interest.[4]

Is there an optimal size of the public sector? The fast-growing newly industrialized economies of Asia devote one-fifth of their GDP for public sector spending versus about one-third for the United States and Japan, and nearly half for France and Germany. Tanzi and Schuknecht (1995) concluded that, compared to high public sector growth economies, the economies with the lowest rise in public spending from 1960 to the 1990s were more efficient and innovative, had faster employment and patent registration growth, and had smaller "black market" (illegal) sectors. The analysts did not find that relatively lower public outlays made a big difference in school enrollment, life expectancy, and infant mortality. Circumstances will vary from country to country, but a public sector ranging from one-fifth to one-third of GDP appears to be adequate for economic progress and food security. The percentage may be even less in early stages of growth. The choice of (1) a high safety net, large public sector, and slow growth versus (2) a low safety net and rapid growth is political as well as economic.

A role for the public sector is to provide public goods and correct externalities to help the private sector function more effectively. A relatively lean, modest-size, but effective public sector is essential for a well-functioning private sector. The public sector needs to perform well several activities for economic development.

Institutional Environment

Institutional environment refers to the formal and informal political, social, and legal arrangements that provide for property rights, production, exchange, distribution, and competition. Efficient institutions provide an environment where short- and long-term contracting and investing can be made and carried out in a manner that effectively conveys the wants of consumers to resource and product providers so that those wants can be met as fully as possible. That in turn is best served by a bureaucracy selected and trained for competence, credibility, predictability, integrity, and dependability. Rules of the game should not be arbitrary or capricious but need to entail low transaction costs in meeting the needs of society.

Unlike conventional institutional economics emphasizing macroinstitutions responsible for the political and legal rules of the game, the *new institutional economics* emphasizes modes of contract and organization determining or regulating activities at the firm, agency, and individual levels (North 1990; Williamson 1995). Some institutions, such as tribes, that were highly functional products of historic socioeconomic force become dysfunctional in a modern economy. The new institutional economics attempts to explain why progress has eluded countries such as the former Soviet Union despite impressive human capital and infrastructure. The answer lies in carryover of institutions and culture that served socialism and previous traditions but that are dysfunctional for democratic-capitalism. Much of the new institutional economics is not new but a recognition of the importance of transaction costs, morality, incentives, and heritage in explaining the behavior of institutions.

Public administration. Many food insecure countries have established institutional arrangements that seriously constrain the operation of both private markets and public agencies. For example, inappropriate policies and bureaucratic incentives have created rent-seeking public bureaucracies that impose prohibitively high transaction costs on private entrepreneurs and that are incapable of effectively providing needed public services. These inappropriate institutional arrangements have contributed heavily to economic, social, and political decline and food insecurity in many developing countries, but particularly in Africa. Appropriate laws and business codes dealing with fundamental aspects of liberalized markets, such as ownership, contracting, investment, commerce, and labor, (combined with effective technical and legal bureaucracies that efficiently and equitably apply them) provide an environment enabling the private sector and competitive market forces to work.

Security, stability, and order. A supportive legal and judicial system is essential to promote savings, investment, and capital formation in an environment where long-term private and public investments can be planned and carried through. Such a system can create incentives for productive commercial activity, individual initiative, freedom, and justice. Oppressive regulations protect monopoly and drive the private sector into an underground economy subject to exploitation and food insecurity.

Democracy is highly desirable but not essential for economic progress. Several nations in East Asia have had rapid growth under authoritarian rule, but leadership succession problems can destabilize such economies. Many countries can benefit from devolution of authority to local governments, which can provide essential community services and infrastructure and have taxing power to support those activities with a sense of community. Excessive military (or unproductive civil service) spending is especially burdensome because it reduces civilian investment and diverts the able-bodied from gainful employment.

Property rights. An institutional system of property rights with official commitment to respect private property (including that owned by foreign firms) fosters savings, investment, and capital accumulation. Property rights are critical for irrigation water as well as other real property. Chile, for example, has demonstrated the value of property rights to greater efficiency through marginal cost pricing of irrigation water. Foreign direct investment attracted by property rights can dwarf official development assistance in raising living standards and national income. Respect for property rights also reduces domestic capital flight to other countries.

Competition. A well-run economy avoids monopoly power of private or public firms; natural monopolies (where only one firm can operate to supply the market at low cost) are regulated as necessary. Openness to foreign trade and investment helps to protect against exploitation by concentrated domestic industries. Parastatals (state owned and operated industries) are best avoided. Free firm entry and exit and deregulated markets are useful objectives, with appropriate exceptions for health, safety, and environmental protection.

Sound Macroeconomic Policies

Globalized financial capital markets today endorse soundly run economies with capital inflow and doom poorly run economies with capital flight. Sound macroeconomic policies draw private foreign direct investment in plant, equipment, and people.

Fiscal responsibility. The operating account of government needs to be balanced. Deficits during recession must be offset by surpluses during better times. A capital account deficit (borrowing) is justified only where returns on investment are sufficient to leave a social dividend after paying interest and principal. The "operating account" refers to the central government, but sometimes central government fiscal policy cannot be separated from regional or state fiscal policy. An example is Brazil, where profligate state governments have caused national fiscal problems.

Monetary restraint. The most effective central banks are at arm's length from government and have one objective—price stabilization. To avoid inflation, the money supply needs to rise no faster than real output. (Modest inflation of say 3 percent per year may be advantageous to give wage and salary flexibility.) Sound fiscal policy reduces pressure on the central bank to create money and thereby induce inflation to finance government deficits. Positive real interest rates are important to mobilize savings and direct investment to priority uses. Prices and interest rates will signal proper scarcity values to markets only when freed from the "noise" of inflation and controls.

The widespread Macroeconomic Degradation Process, or MDP (Tweeten 1989), begins with a nation living beyond its means and culminates in a shortage of foreign exchange. Countries initiating the MDP accrue burdensome debt by incurring large operating account fiscal deficits in government and trade. They are attempting to live beyond their means. Large foreign debt absorbs considerable foreign exchange earnings to service debt rather than to purchase imports consistent with food security. When their capacity to borrow at home and abroad reaches limits, they print money. Excessive creation of money results in inflation, overvalued currency, and a shortage of foreign exchange. A resulting financial crisis is likely to bring structural adjustment, austerity, and food insecurity.

The MDP has two main phases: (1) an expansionary phase, while the nation is living beyond its means and perhaps benefiting food insecure people, and (2) a stabilization or structural adjustment phase of retrenchment to a sustainable economy. These two phases average lower economic growth, more instability, and greater food insecurity than would a sustainable macroeconomic policy.

Buffer stocks are discussed in the next section, but here we note that the most cost-effective national "buffer stock" for most developing countries is international trade. Imports and exports can adjust to prices to maintain food security. Unsound macroeconomic policies deny a country full use of that cost-effective food security tool. Food aid may be useful in the short run to ease the burden on the poor during structural adjustment to a sound macroeconomy that will provide self-reliance and food security in the long term.

Appropriate taxation.   Government services must be financed.   Deficit spending and printing of money cause inflation, a cruel tax to be avoided. Any tax system will influence market incentives and may retard growth; the challenge is to pay for public goods with minimum distortion while preserving some progressivity. Suggestions are to

- Tax "bads," such as cigarettes, alcohol, gasoline, waste effluent, and consumption in general, rather than "goods," such as savings and investment.
- Impose user fees to recover costs of public service. Examples are taxes on irrigation or municipal water, electricity, and the like—services too often subsidized and hence used wastefully.
- Tax company income at a uniform and moderate rate and personal income with a moderate top rate and as few exemptions and deductions as possible so the base is broad and average rate is low.
- Tax property as broadly and uniformly as possible, based on market value, and perhaps with mild progressivity at high levels for farmland if concentration of ownership is a social problem.
- Tax retail sales or value added. The value added tax, or VAT, requires considerable administrative capability and is not suited for many developing countries.   Its advantages are incentives for compliance (failure to report costs of "upstream" supplies raises taxes to the "downstream" firms) and low distortion of the economy because the tax falls on consumption. Food can be exempt from the VAT.
- Impose a uniform and low tariff on imports, if imports are taxed at all.

Export taxes are especially onerous and are best avoided because they often entail large deadweight costs (national income loss) that fall on domestic producers and destroy incentives. Property taxes have long been neglected in developing countries. They can entail less deadweight costs than export taxes and may encourage efficient land use.   If graduated, property taxes discourage concentration of land ownership, spread ownership among more families, and reduce disruption of productivity that can attend alternative redistribution efforts such as land reform discussed in Chapter 6.[5] Property taxes administered by local government can supply revenues to support local public infrastructure and social services.

Liberal Trade Policy

Open economy. A singularly ubiquitous attribute of successful economies is utilization of foreign markets. A World Bank study (1995) found that real wages stagnated in countries where exports increased the least but real wages increased about 3 percent a year in developing countries where exports as a share of GDP were above the median. An economy open to foreign trade and investment needs to be as free of market distortions as possible consistent with environmental protection and collection of taxes to support essential functions.   An open economy attracts foreign direct investment bringing not only capital but technology, managerial skill, access to world markets, and local employment.

Several developing countries in East Asia have developed rapidly by pushing exports, sometimes with state support, while restricting imports directly with tariffs or quotas or indirectly with undervalued currency or unwritten understandings among merchants. This neomerchantilist approach to development has faults: (1) Consumers, including workers, are denied the standard of living they have earned; and (2) dangerous trade frictions are generated by dumping abroad, causing foreign producers to seek trade protection. Foreign consumers gain from "dumping," and the world may tolerate infant industry protection in developing countries for a time. But trade is a two-way street, and developing countries need to open markets as quickly as feasible to promote higher standards of living and trade harmony.[6]

Properly valued foreign exchange. Fiscal responsibility and monetary restraint will help to avoid an overvalued foreign exchange rate and foreign exchange shortage—serious threats to food security. Overvalued currency saps the economic vitality of domestic producers but favors wealthy and politically powerful urban consumer elites. The exchange rate for a developed country can be established by the market. If pegged to hard currencies such as the dollar for stability, the exchange rate of a country will need to be adjusted periodically for domestic inflation relative to that of trading partners and also floated from time to time to avoid economic degradation.

Infrastructure

Road, bridge, seaport, airport, electricity, communication, and major irrigation facilities can be worthy public investments serving the private sector and food security. Provision of public infrastructure and social services (listed in the next subsection) need to be supported or guided by the public sector.

An efficient economy requires effective communication and transportation systems (see Chapter 4). Because these have "public good" properties, the private sector acting alone will not provide the optimal level. However, the public role often is best restricted to funding and regulation, while construction and day-to-day operation are provided efficiently by private firms.

Appropriate infrastructure makes private markets work better and raises national income. Such infrastructure serves food security by reducing the frictions of space and time. All-weather roads are essential to transport produce from food surplus to food deficit areas and to allow efficient commercial input supply and product marketing activities consistent with increasingly productive farm and nonfarm industries. Mobility enhanced by appropriate infrastructure helps entrepreneurs and workers take advantage of the best economic opportunities available in the country, thereby raising individual and national buying power and food security.

Services

World population will rise at a rate of approximately 80 million people per year to year 2000 and beyond. The additional population will need to be fed mainly through greater productivity of existing land and water. Africa is of special concern because 250 million Africans subsist on per capita incomes of less than $1 per day, 30 million preschool children are undernourished, and per capita food production is falling. Cereal imports of sub-Saharan Africa are projected to triple—from 9 million metric tons in 1990 to 27 million metric tons in 2020 (Rosegrant 1995, 30). Africa cannot afford such imports; the donor community will need to help finance imports to avoid severe food shortages.

While some concessional food aid will be unavoidable, a better use of donor funds is to promote agricultural development because nearly 90 percent of Africa's poor live in rural areas where the economic base is agriculture. The continent has no choice but to raise productivity of agriculture to achieve broad-based sustainable development.

African countries typically spend less than 0.5 percent of agricultural gross domestic product on agricultural research. This compares to 1 percent in higher-income developing countries and 4 percent in the United States—the latter typical of industrialized countries. Because a more productive agriculture is critical to achieve almost any objective (e.g., investment in human resources, infrastructure, safety net), a minimum target of 1 percent of the value of agricultural output in the short run to intermediate run and 2 percent in the long run is appropriate for low-income countries to invest in agricultural research (Pinstrup-Andersen, p. 105). A priority for donors is to help developing countries achieve those targets.

A major World Bank (1990) study of poverty concluded that countries most successfully reducing poverty promoted economic growth with policies encouraging efficient use of labor and *adding to human capital of the poor*. Services such as schooling, agricultural research, extension, information systems, commodity grades and standards, primary health care, and sanitary water supplies are needed (see Chapters 3, 5, and 7).[7] The public role extends beyond improving production through adaptive research, extension education, institution building, and technology transfer. For example, the extension service can work with individuals and private firms to improve food processing and marketing for better nutrition and for longer shelf life and home storage.

As noted in Chapter 3, agricultural research and extension in developing countries can have a very high economic payoff. Few developing countries can afford in-country basic research, but the payoff has been almost universally high from *applied* research emphasizing local adaptation of technologies from elsewhere. When encouraged to do so, the private input supply sector has strongly supplemented the public sector provision of agricultural research and extension to improve food production and marketing practices and technology. Jordan provides a good example, where private firms have shown initiative not only in importing new technologies but also in extending information to farmers necessary to evaluate and adopt improved inputs and techniques.

Information is essential to allocate food efficiently over time and space. Modern data collection, processing (e.g., with microcomputers), communication, and transportation systems help private markets to function better.   Price information helps consumers and producers make better decisions. Crop forecasts provide early warning of food shortfalls or surpluses.

Forecasts of crop production, consumption and food prices, and impending food shortages can raise the efficiency of markets. A free press and open political system also facilitate the flow of information and response. Information systems have "public goods" properties.   That means that private markets alone do not suffice, and a public role is justified.

Environmental Protection

Broad-based and *sustainable* economic development is threatened by environmentally unsound practices (see Chapter 8). Such practices result in soil erosion, salt buildup and waterlogging of irrigated land, deforestation, desertification, and species extinction. Some practices cause chemical contamination of food and water supplies and of field workers. Pressures on land and water resources to supply the food demands of growing but very poor populations intensify environmental problems in the developing world (see World Bank 1991, 61). The market alone will not care for the environment. But many developing countries lack the public resources required to educate producers or to provide controls and incentives for aligning private and social costs (benefits) essential for an environmentally sound agriculture. Weak public institutions cannot protect open access land, property rights, or logged forests from land-desperate farmers.

Sustainable agriculture is a term emphasizing an environmentally sound agriculture that can meet rising food needs in the long and short run (see Tweeten 1992). The approach attempts to capture the synergisms possible with a systems framework combining (1) integrated crop management (often employing forage legumes in crop rotations, alley cropping, etc. to reduce chemical fertilizer and pesticide use), (2) conservation tillage (often employing no-till or other residue management techniques to reduce soil erosion and conserve moisture), (3) integrated pest management (employing biological pest control and minimizing pesticide use consistent with "best management practices," and (4) crop-livestock systems to make better use of farming resources, including forage legumes, and to supply high-quality protein in the form of meat, milk, and eggs.

Given that expansion of cropland would severely damage the environment in many countries, sharply higher food needs must be met by raising crop yields in developed and developing countries. That requires modern science, including biotechnology, to improve varieties and judicious use of synthetic fertilizers and pesticides.

Market distortions can be corrected to reduce environmental degradation. For example, underpricing by government for logs taken from public forest lands invites excessive cutting for export by the private sector without proper attention to replanting or protection of fragile cutover lands from farm squatters. Underpricing of farm irrigation water (e.g., Egypt) and of synthetic fertilizers and pesticides (e.g., Indonesia) has degraded the environment. Overvalued currency and high taxes on crop exports (e.g., Tanzania, Uganda) have impoverished farmers. Combined with high population growth, poverty is a major cause of soil erosion and hence of food insecurity.

The aforementioned *standard model* says nothing of infant industry, agricultural commodity price support, and public employment policies. Cases can be found where governments have protected new industry from foreign competition until it became efficient enough to compete without subsidies in world markets (e.g., Taiwan and Korea), where crop procurement prices (minimal forward prices announced before plantings and guaranteed by government) encouraged investment in efficient agricultural production (e.g., Indonesia), and where food-for-work and other public employment measures built needed infrastructure at low cost (e.g., India). However, many governments have insufficient administrative capacity, political will, or discipline to operate such programs efficiently.

Most commodity price interventions either discourage farm production with commodity taxes and price ceilings or tax food consumers with excessive farm price supports. Economic progress and food security are, for the most part, best served by avoiding such policies.

In some cases commodity prices are held above market-clearing levels to benefit farmers. Weber et al. (1988, 1991) found that in Africa many small farmers are net purchasers of staples and are made more food insecure by high food prices. The disadvantage to small farmers of higher food prices is even more pronounced in Asia. Consumers, disadvantaged by high food prices, exceed the number of producers in every country.

In other cases, commodity prices are held below market-clearing levels to benefit consumers. The result is to reduce farm purchasing power and incentives to save and invest (in human, material, and technological capital) and to allocate resources to their best use consistent with opportunity costs. Farm production is discouraged and more affluent urban consumers are subsidized. The efficient policy is to allow border prices (world prices "backed up" to local markets) for traded goods. Nontraded goods (ordinarily neither exported nor imported) will, on the average, be priced by the market to cover costs of production determined by the value of resources in producing traded goods and services. Despite private storage, fluctuations in food prices arising sometimes from international markets burden the poor. Many governments take measures to reduce variation in domestic farm and food prices below variation in world prices. For countries desiring only to stabilize and not raise food prices, a policy proposal is made in a later section for reducing price instability without sizably misallocating resources.

Food security is likely to be enhanced by leaving to producers the decisions on cropping patterns between production for domestic food versus export markets. In the early 1980s, analysts (Epplin and Musah 1985, 25) estimated that the resources of a typical farm family in Liberia could access three times as much rice (the main staple food) by producing tree crops for export and purchasing imported rice rather than by producing rice for local consumption. Export cropping entails risks of possible interruptions, as later events in Liberia made all too evident. Producers anticipated risks and were diversifying production accordingly between producing rice for household consumption and tree crops for export well before civil strife began in the 1980s.

Export cropping and other diversification from food production is viewed by many as inconsistent with food security. But Staatz et al. (1990) noted that farmers in highly unstable and low-rainfall areas of northern Mali had as much food security as farmers in southern areas with more stable, higher rainfall. The north had adapted to uncertainty by diversifying income sources and relying more on the market for food supplies.

In conclusion, food security is served by a broad based, sustainable (BBS) and market oriented development policy. Such policy allows prices to reflect scarcity values and guide resource allocations while using targeted food assistance and broad-based growth policies, such as investments in human resources to target equity needs of the food insecure lacking resources, to meet basic needs.

The *standard model* for economic development provides considerable scope for trade-offs among goals of economic growth, equity, and stability. The appropriate trade-offs are best chosen by representative, informed governments. A useful rule of thumb for governments is to pursue policies and investments that raise real national income. Ordinarily, it is inappropriate to intervene in the operation of efficient, competitive markets to promote equity. But one component must be added to make necessary conditions sufficient for food security—a safety net. Thus the *standard model* in a BBS system is necessary but not sufficient for food security.

Food and Income Transfer Safety Net

A safety net is required for those unable to achieve a socially acceptable level of well-being by depending on the market, family, and other sources. Examples of vulnerable groups include landless peasants, small landholders, and the urban poor. These groups often have underdeveloped human resources and few material resources and therefore are prone to food insecurity.

The food insecure face a continuum of problems that can be addressed with programs ranging from developmental to straight redistributional. For example, food distribution programs can provide free food to the non-able-bodied poor and destitute, education programs can include school lunches that attract children to school and relieve food insecurity directly, and road-building programs can employ the food insecure and pay them with either food or cash for purchasing food. Targeted food assistance is the only option to provide food security for some, but public investment in schooling and infrastructure can be both equitable and efficient.

Safety net efforts can be public or private sector initiatives. Public efforts to address short-term food insecurity can promote development and need not be solely redistributional transfers. With proper advance planning, public works projects can be initiated to build or repair roads that raise private agricultural efficiency. Private voluntary organizations frequently provide early warning of famine and take the lead in distributing food supplied by the public sector.

Many people can be made food insecure in the short run by sound economic policies to restrain money supply, balance government budgets, downsize bureaucracy, privatize, and end a nation's living beyond its means. Here, a food safety net to help the disadvantaged can cushion structural adjustment pains. However, persons released from overstaffed government bureaucracies and state-owned enterprises usually have more human and material assets than the average worker, and most can adjust without assistance to more productive (if not more remunerative) private employment or business opportunities.

COPING WITH TRANSITORY FOOD INSECURITY

Transitory food insecurity is addressed in this section because it poses unique issues for foreign assistance. Transitory food insecurity potentially can be alleviated by BBS economic progress because growth makes stock reserves, imports, food transfers, and other coping strategies affordable in developing countries. Despite economic progress, however, many countries alleviating chronic food insecurity will be unable to cope with unforeseeable large transitory food shocks arising from drought, floods, pests, and armed conflict. Such shocks frequently cannot be foreseen or protected against. Food aid can be especially important to address transitory food insecurity if in-country food supplies are unavailable. This section addresses problems of and policies for transitory food insecurity.

Stabilizing Food Prices and Availability

People need to eat every day. But the ability to acquire food from current income or from current self-provisioning production fluctuates greatly over the seasons and from one year to the next. Seasonal fluctuations are fairly predictable. Annual fluctuations are random; at best only the probabilities of supply in future years are known.

Much private and public economic activity in low-income agricultural economies is devoted to stabilizing access to food. Subsistence farmers diversify crops and cultivation practices, they stagger planting times, choose cultivars resistant to climatic adversity, and spread harvests of various crops over as much of the year as feasible. They also store commodities. Similarly, market stabilization is fostered over time and space by *arbitrage*, defined as buying when and where prices are low and selling when and where prices are high. Obtaining proper access to food over time and space comes at significant cost, whether the stabilizing is done by the private or the public sector.

Seasonal Instability between Harvests

Daily consumption requirements and access to food are aligned within a season mostly because the private sector engages in a great deal of stabilization. Only poor people suffer from seasonal hunger. However, even they are not necessarily well served by government programs stabilizing access to food reserves on their behalf. Often, assistance that augments their human resource productivity and, thus, their overall annual income is more cost-effective.

Stabilizing Against Fluctuating Harvests

For a subsistence farming household, transitory food insecurity can mean having less than the usual food reserve in the granary, seeking outside employment, sharing food among families, and selling less market surplus. For people who purchase their food in the market, a major concern is how to cope with fluctuating and often unpredictable food prices due to the instability in national and international food production.

As in the case of seasonal food insecurity, the private sector plays a major role in reducing the instability caused by random events affecting food harvests in different years.[8] As much as 90 percent of all storing takes place on farms and in homes, even when countries hold sizable public stocks. Yet major differences exist between mechanisms for coping with seasonal and interyear transitory food insecurity. Brisk international trading is likely to be the more cost-effective buffer instrument in the case of the latter, while local storage and intracountry trade are more important for ensuring stable seasonal access to food. Different crops, often grown in different locations and subject to different growing conditions, can be substituted in human diets. Thus trade is a powerful and relatively low-cost option for stabilizing people's access to food everywhere if yields tend to average out among regions, people are not too isolated from each other, transport costs are kept low, and policy barriers are not erected against trade.

The most effective way for governments to contribute to the alleviation of transitory food insecurity is to promote economic development and efficient food markets. Development assures the purchasing power needed on a "rainy day" to acquire food from outside the affected region or from previously stored supplies. Well-functioning food markets are important because they lower the cost of transforming commodities in time and space, the basic prerequisite for stable prices. At present, markets rarely operate efficiently because of underinvestment in public infrastructure and because of restraint of trade—usually by governments and aggressively promoted by special interest groups. Therefore, until market efficiency is attained via policy/administrative reform, it may be desirable from a humanitarian perspective to consider some public intervention.

COST-EFFECTIVE PUBLIC ROLES IN STABILIZATION

In discussing public policies to address transitory food insecurity, it is important to distinguish between relatively mild, frequently occurring fluctuations in the access to food and sudden, unpredictable famines. The former are predictable in a probability sense. The latter are rare and are not predictable from historical data. Most recent famines occurred as a result of war, political upheaval, or other infrequent and unpredictable causes for which neither the public nor private sectors could make adequate food provision at affordable cost.

The next few paragraphs briefly review the efficacy of various public instruments for stabilizing prices and supplies beyond what could be expected from a well-functioning market. Before proceeding, two issues applicable to the implementation of stabilization by any method are examined: (1) the source of instability, and (2) the problem of porous borders. Policy responses such as buffer stocks, variable tariffs, and self-sufficiency also are addressed.

The Source of Instability

The widespread belief that unstable domestic food prices and supplies are mainly caused by fluctuations in domestic food production and stock operations is much oversimplified. For food security, a nation's agriculture matters more as a provider of individual buying power and earner of foreign exchange.

Any country today has the option of consuming food that is produced domestically or imported. This means that in a country that trades (poor countries caring for a stable food supply can hardly afford to do otherwise), the price and availability of food is determined by its border price, which in turn depends on the world price and the exchange rate.

The trend toward a more market-oriented global economy has conflicting influences on use of trade as a buffer stock. International prices of cereals have been relatively stable in recent history, in part because of American and European Union (EU) buffer stocks accumulated under commodity programs. America and the EU are likely to hold fewer buffer stocks after market reforms of the 1990s. Unlike in the past, however, the EU will do more to buffer world prices by transmitting world price signals to its producers and consumers. Freer trade allows greater sharing of supplies among countries. On balance, more open world agricultural trade markets following the Uruguay Round continue to make trade the best buffer stock.

Porous Borders

Whatever the instrument chosen for influencing the stability of food prices and supplies, a government unable to control the movement of commodities across its borders will have difficulty implementing a public stabilization agenda which differs from the "judgment of the market."

If commodities "leak" across borders—as is especially the case in small countries with long borders and modest-size enforcement agencies—any stabilization measure will be less effective and more costly than suggested by the usual calculations, which ignore the porosity of borders. One way of getting around this problem is for neighboring countries to synchronize their stabilization policies, which is unlikely to happen. It would be generally undesirable to seal borders and pursue an independent food security strategy even if it were possible. Free trade not only supplies food, it also constrains governments from pursuing costly market distortions which reduce real income and foreign exchange earnings essential to buy food.

Instruments for Stabilization

We now turn to three instruments of potential use to stabilize food supplies and prices. Each has shortcomings.

Variable Duties. As indicated earlier, markets ordinarily are best left to allocate without pricing interventions. Pan-seasonal and pan-regional pricing, which holds prices constant over the marketing year and among regions, interferes with arbitrage and is unwise. An importing country intent on stabilizing food supplies and prices can do so at minimal net Treasury or national income loss with a variable duty. The procedure is for the government to impose an import tax in years when the border (world) price is unacceptably low, and to pay an import subsidy when the border price is unacceptably high. The preferred method is to keep domestic prices within a band of a certain percent (20 percent, for example) above and below a moving average of world price. Because the tax collected when border prices are low and the subsidy paid when border prices are high tend to offset each other over time, the budgetary and economic cost of such a stabilization policy can be low. A similar scheme could be applied to a food exporter to help stabilize domestic prices.

The record of the European Union variable levy is not encouraging because, unlike the preceding proposal, domestic prices were supported consistently at high levels at great cost to domestic consumers and foreign producers. But carefully formulated variants of the preceding approach have been used with varying degrees of success in Chile, Papua New Guinea, Côte d'Ivoire, and South Korea (Knudson and Nash 1988, 4).

Before the scheme is attempted in developing countries, the main questions are

1. Can the program be administered to avoid corruption and waste?
2. Will governments use a biased reference border price resulting consistently in either subsidies or taxes?
3. Will governments master the self-discipline to operate and maintain a stabilization fund?
4. Can borders be controlled to prevent exports when domestic price is below the border price and to prevent illegal imports when domestic price exceeds the border price?

5. Can the procedure avoid exporting instability to other countries, creating more unstable world food prices?

Without attempting to address these questions in any detail, we note that foreign assistance can play a positive role by influencing governments to discard costly and ineffective stabilization schemes. Foreign assistance (financial and food aid, bilateral and multilateral aid) can be provided in countercyclical fashion— more in years when the aid-receiving countries need more budgetary resources and foreign exchange to subsidize food prices and less in other years when taxing is in order and foreign exchange is less needed.

Buffer stocks. For developing countries, buffer stocks are a costly instrument for interyear stabilization. Stocks often have to be held for several years and storage facility costs accrue even when the storehouses are empty. Because private entrepreneurs usually face high risk, they require a premium return on their resources to justify holding buffer stocks. There is much uncertainty about the timing and the profitability of the operation. Timing of purchases and sales to cover storage costs is made difficult by unpredictable domestic harvests and foreign markets. Fluctuating exchange rates and government trade policies sensitive to political considerations add to the uncertainties.

Studies (Gardner 1979; Makki et al. 1995; Pai and Tweeten 1991; Reutlinger et al. 1976) which simulate the profitability of an investment in interyear buffer stocks in an open, free market repeatedly show that they are not profitable except when they are held on a small scale, in which case they provide only modest stabilization. Private traders hold few buffer stocks.

So the important question remains: Is potential instability in the access to food a legitimate concern for public intervention? Alexander Sarris, Don Gunasekere, and Brian Fisher (in Reinsel 1993) provide evidence that governments operate buffer stocks no better than does the private sector.

Modest-size buffer stocks are useful to respond to unexpected food shortages before imports arrive.[9] Beyond that reserve, storing money is cheaper than storing commodities. Money earns interest; buffer stocks cost interest, depreciation of facilities, and spoilage. Except for a country under the threat of military embargo, a developing country takes no more risk by depending on supplies from foreign markets than by relying on its domestic production and domestically held buffer stocks (World Bank 1986a).

One argument in favor of buffer stocks is that grain rather than money must be stored, irrespective of cost considerations, because it is difficult to master the discipline to save and accumulate foreign exchange in years of good harvests. There is some justification for holding buffer stocks if a country's food price instability depends more on domestic availability and demand and less on the border price. Such is the case for "nontraded goods" characterized by a large gap between the import and export price so that the country's comparative advantage suggests self-sufficiency over a wide range of border prices. The most likely reasons for a large gap between the import and export price are geographic isolation, poor road and port facilities, underdeveloped markets, and price interventions. The appropriate long-term solution is to overcome as many of these constraints as possible. It is useful to recognize that many nontraded goods are perishable and hence not easily or cheaply stored.

National food self-sufficiency. Countries unwilling or unable to rely on trade as an instrument for stabilization can deliberately limit their options to self-sufficiency. Previous sections noted the high cost of relying on national buffer stocks or excess production capacity in the form of resources chronically committed to food production in excess of those needed in a more stable environment. In a normal year, the surplus output (from the effort to be sure of producing enough) results in depressed prices and production incentives. The consequence may be less production and food shortages in future years. These measures and price supports erode a country's financial resources to import or in other ways adjust to a short domestic crop.

An alternative available in most countries is early warning systems that improve ability to make import arrangements and appeal for foreign aid before food shortages become severe. Attention must be given to assuring sufficient port capacity to handle much larger than usual imports.

Government and external assistance agencies can play some role in stabilizing the food supply, particularly in the case of sudden breakdowns of the normal source of food supply. But far more important for reducing transitory food insecurity and avoiding famines is the creation of conditions whereby all people have stable and sufficient purchasing power and well-performing food markets. These conditions will not be achieved in many countries; hence, there is no alternative to massive periodic relief operations, preferably with more attention than in the past to cost effectiveness and to international cooperation among donors. *However, it is unwise for countries to grow dependent on "emergency" food aid; instead, countries need to follow policies that ordinarily avoid food crises.* Of course, food aid should not be denied when people face famine. As a general rule, the appropriate instruments for assuring stable food supplies even to disaster-stricken populations are trade (imports) and modest stocks sufficient only until food imports can arrive. This presumes discipline in the management of fiscal policy and of foreign exchange by developing countries' governments and accessible international commodity and financial markets for borrowing and saving.

THE SAFETY NET, TARGETED ASSISTANCE, AND FOOD AID

This section addresses three remaining food security issues: (1) the height of the safety net, (2) whether to target transfers, and (3) whether to monetize the food aid used to support the safety net.

Height of Safety Net

Food security often is best served in the long run by lower birth rates, in the intermediate run by economic development, and in the short run by food transfers. The market will help make many decisions, such as food crops versus export crops, or farm versus nonfarm industrial growth, but the market will not determine an appropriate safety net level of food or other transfers. That decision is best made by people through representative political processes. A role of donors can be to provide awareness of trade-offs so that countries can make sound decisions and, given the approach selected, work toward cost-effective use of the food and other aid to achieve equity, efficiency, and stability.

A safety net set too low helps no one. On the other hand, a food safety net set too high absorbs donor and host nation resources, cutting off opportunities for economic growth and self-reliance. Food must not be subsidized to the point that its low cost and ready availability cause it to be wasted or fed to animals. The shared striving for security has held families and communities together in developing countries. Too high a safety net can undermine the family as well as economic incentives. Attempts by government to provide a food safety net by price controls or other market distortions are often counterproductive.

Targeting

No developing country can afford across-the-board food subsidies; targeting is essential. Targeted transfers are appropriate for each stage of development. At the lowest income stage, transfers to severely food-deficit families can be targeted informally by health, education, church, and private voluntary organization workers who identify the food poor. At the second stage, targeting may be by fair price shops stocking foods acceptable to the poor but avoided by more well-off consumers. At a higher stage of development, food stamps or cash transfers may be income conditioned. The appropriate delivery system also depends on circumstances. For example, fair price shops have worked better in Asia than in Africa or Latin America.

Monetize Food Aid

This chapter emphasizes BBS economic development for food security. Policy reform, infrastructure, human resource development, and agricultural research and extension are central. None of these is most readily promoted by food aid. Food aid becomes fungible (useable for any purpose) if it is monetized (sold in the market for local currency).

The first rule of foreign aid is that food aid is inappropriate to a country that is exporting food. In such circumstances food aid discourages food production of the aid recipient and diminishes commercial food exports of the donor. If people are starving in a country exporting food, the proper role of donors is to work for policy reform and to purchase local food supplies for distribution to the needy.

Food aid per se has special value because it is sometimes available when other aid is not, and it is vital to respond rapidly to emergency food needs. For the latter, accessible food reserves must be drawn upon on short notice for direct distribution to people starving because local food is unavailable. Turning from transitory to chronic food insecurity, food aid (or food entitlement coupons redeemable elsewhere) can be directly distributed by health clinics to at-risk groups, such as pregnant and lactating women and their infants, and by schools in lunches for low-income students.

Although food aid can sometimes be used to fund needed public works when a country is short of food, it is ordinarily inappropriate for the state to be the employer of first resort or last resort. The state needs to employ individuals only as necessary to provide needed public services efficiently. Even these services often can be provided more efficiently by private suppliers—with public regulation and support as necessary.

For most purposes the most efficient route to food security is to monetize food aid. Even for a public food aid safety net where donor-supported food aid is available, it is generally more cost effective to sell the imported food at the port city, and then buy local foods in the interior to serve the nutritional needs and tastes of the local safety net recipients at low transport or other cost.

Because untied cash aid can be used to purchase food or any other component of a food security strategy giving a higher payoff than food aid, it follows that cash aid is more valuable than food aid (at face value) for food security. Food aid has often been more available, however, in part because $1 of food aid effectively has cost the American government less than $1 given that the alternative is to pay American farmers not to produce. Also, taxpayers and voters in donor countries often support food aid because they feel it is less likely than cash aid to be lost to corruption or other types of waste in countries receiving aid.

The American government is likely to hold less reserve grain stocks or diverted acres in the future, thereby raising the cost of food aid. Still, Americans will likely continue to be more willing to give food than other types of foreign aid. In short, food aid may be less valuable than unspecified cash aid, but the availability of food aid and opportunities to monetize it for serving critical needs make it useful.

CONCLUSIONS

Food security depends on food availability, accessibility, and proper utilization. Annual global food output has grown on average by nearly 0.5 percent per capita since 1950. Thus, the world has had sufficient *aggregate* food supplies to provide all people with an adequate diet; global food availability has not been the problem. The lack of food accessibility at the individual and household level has been far more serious. Accessibility has been constrained by lack of buying power by people with too little human, material, and technological capital to produce enough food or income to feed themselves, and by inability of others to provide sufficient food transfers to them. Some individuals with access to food do not utilize food properly because of illness, ignorance, or culture. Thus nutrition, education, and health programs are important means of improving utilization.

This chapter outlines the *food security synthesis* for poor developing countries:

1. The principal cause of transitory and chronic food insecurity is poverty. People with adequate buying power overcome the frictions of time (e.g., unpredictable, unstable harvests from year to year) and space (e.g., local food shortages) to be food secure.
2. Poverty can be overcome through broad-based, sustainable, economic development.
3. The most effective and efficient means to economic development is to follow the *standard model*, which assures an economic "pie" to divide among people and among functions such as human resource development, infrastructure, family planning, a food safety net, and environmental protection. The standard model is applicable to any culture and provides a workable prescription for economic progress ensuring buying power for self-reliance and food security in any nation. Eventually, in conjunction with family planning it brings zero population growth.
4. Failure to follow the standard model traces partly to economic illiteracy but mainly to *political* failure. Individuals and groups with power and authority often lose with political change — even if current policies are egregiously incongruent with the public interest. Economic distortions bestow economic rents on those in authority who dispense licenses and enforce regulations. Parastatals provide employment for friends and relatives of power brokers. Hence bad public policy carries powerful momentum.
5. Political failure is inseparable from *institutional failure*. The triumph of special interest politics at variance with the public interest occurs when institutions are weak and poorly structured. Institutional change is required to adopt the standard model. Food insecurity and economic stagnation are not so much the result of limited natural resources, environmental degradation, or lack of a workable economic growth model. Rather they are the result of misguided public policies, which in turn are the product of weak institutions and corrupt governments serving special interests.
6. Poorly structured, inadequate institutions often trace to *cultural factors* such as tolerance of the public for unrepresentative, corrupt, incompetent government, indifferent to the broad-based involvement of citizens in government. Government leaders often view their position as an opportunity for personal aggrandizement rather than to be a servant of the public interest. Socioinstitutional change and hence the standard model adoption are blocked by cultural characteristics which provide a fertile climate for governments not representing the public interest.
7. The challenge of food security for our time is socioinstitutional change. How to bring about such change deserves attention by the best minds in economics, sociology, political science, and other disciplines. Several approaches have been used with only limited success to bring socioinstitutional change. Tweeten (1989, 1992) has worked on the Agricultural Policy Analysis Project, and Mellor (1978, 1990) has worked with the International Food Policy Research Institute to educate leaders of developing countries for policy change. The World Bank and IMF try to buy change. Some laissez faire advocates call for no outside interference so that severe economic failure will motivate domestic policy reform in food insecure countries. These approaches have had the least success in South Asia, sub-Saharan Africa, and the former Soviet Union— regions most in need of reform. Change seems to occur only when a nation's leaders and people become fully committed to the policies that bring economic progress and food security.

This chapter did not address the causes and cures for a frequent source of food insecurity: violence. Violent conflict is often rooted in tribalism, ignorance, and hatreds persisting for generations in culture. Social scientists have not been of much help in dealing with cultural issues. Most feel that culture, like families, should be celebrated, not changed. When culture, like families, becomes dysfunctional to the point of bringing killing and starvation, however, intervention is warranted.

Developed countries can do much to promote food security, and efforts will be most successful in developing countries following the standard model. The most important policy of industrial countries is open markets to developing country exports. Market access is important not only in primary commodities but also clothing, textiles, footwear, processed foods, and other products into which developing countries diversify as development progresses. (The importance of diversified income sources to food security has been noted.) Other important facilitators of growth, in addition to direct aid, include basic research and holding emergency food reserve buffer stocks—efforts which developing countries cannot afford. Basic research on biotechnology and other processes that raise yields and reduce dependence on synthetic pesticides can foster new green revolutions in developing countries. In addition, governments of developed countries need to give attention to special food reserves for responding quickly to food shortages that inevitably emerge from time to time in developing countries.

Global trade liberalization, which developed countries have led but for which developing countries also need to take initiative, has much to offer food security in all countries. According to estimates in the *World Development Report 1986* (World Bank 1986b, 131), global liberalization of agricultural commodity programs and border protections would reduce the coefficient of variation in the world price of wheat from 0.45 under 1985-type conditions to 0.10 after liberalization, and in rice from 0.31 under 1985-type conditions to 0.08 after liberalization. In the 1990s, trade liberalization was attended by commodity program liberalization, reduced acreage and grain stock reserves, and less foreign aid by industrialized countries. Thus the net impact on price stability and food security of trade liberalization depends on many factors.

NOTES

1. This chapter draws on a *Food Security Discussion Paper* (PN-ABK-8833) released in May 1992, prepared for U.S. Agency for International Development under supervision of the International Science and Technology Institute. Tweeten was team leader. The contributions of team members John Mellor, Shlomo Reutlinger, and James Pines are gratefully acknowledged for the original discussion paper and to this chapter.

2. Some analysts (see Lowdermilk 1992, 4) have included *utilization* with availability and accessibility dimensions of food security. According to Lowdermilk, adequate utilization "rests upon the adequate health and nutrition of the individual." The term *food utilization* for purposes of this chapter has dimensions of food consumption and absorption.

Proper food consumption means eating an adequate diet. Those who consume adequate diets may not absorb available nutrients because of digestive and other health problems.

3. Food poverty is defined as persons falling below the FAO/WHO (World Health Organization) calorie requirements, which vary by circumstance but average approximately 2,300 calories per person. This is also the food security threshold discussed later.

4. Because of public sector tendencies for rent-seeking, corruption, incompetence, and weak links between demand for public needs and the supply of those goods, the benefit of doubt needs to be for the private sector to operate in the many gray areas where goods and services could be viewed as either public or private. In many instances, such as natural monopolies, the public sector can take bids and oversee public goods and services actually delivered by private firms (e.g., garbage, electricity).

5. Although widely used in many developed countries for a century or more, property taxes have been unsuccessful in most developing countries. Thus graduated property taxes may be unworkable, and land reform also has severe limitations (Chapter 6). Alternatives are more promising. With economic development, opportunities for more equitable distribution of wealth are much greater with human resource development than with land reform. Land initially is a major portion of wealth, but it becomes increasingly unimportant as economic development proceeds. A vision of future potential for developing countries is provided by the example of the United States. Some 70 to 95 percent of the $16 trillion estimated U.S. asset wealth was human capital in 1990 (Carlson 1991, 4–5). *Farm real estate accounted for only $600 billion or 4 percent of that wealth.* Thus in the long run, broad-based economic development offers vastly more opportunity for equitable distribution of wealth through access to education, training, basic health and sanitation services, and other human capital formation opportunities than through land reform. Human resources account for about two-thirds of wealth in Latin America, Africa, and South Asia.

6. The pitfalls of excessive protection against imports is illustrated by sub-Saharan Africa whose market share of world exports fell from 3.1 percent in 1955 to 1.2 percent in 1990. The drop is not explained by nontariff of tariff barriers imposed by other countries on Africa's exports—duties averaged less than 1 percent (Yeats et al., 39). Rather, a problem is sub-Saharan Africa's barriers to imports from other countries, which raised costs of Africa's exports by raising costs of inputs imported to produce products for export. Africa finds exporting more difficult when it protects itself from imports. Over one-third of all sub-Saharan Africa imports face nontariff barriers, more than eight times the average for fast-growing exporters and for high-income non-OECD countries. Its tariffs average 26.8 percent, more than three times rates of fast-growing exporters and four times the OECD average (Yeats et al., 41). While OECD countries reduced tariffs nearly 40 percent in the Uruguay Round, sub-Saharan Africa's tariffs hardly changed. The anti-trade bias of sub-Saharan Africa is reinforced by domestic policies such as inadequate investment in roads.

7. Provision of services and infrastructure often interact in promoting food security. Food supplies depend heavily on women in developing countries. Time for that critical task is expanded when provision is made for sanitary water supplies close to home. Tree planting to provide firewood close to home also can free more time for family members to be food secure. Agricultural extension can often help communities organize to provide such services and infrastructure.

8. Buffer stocks are for interyear stabilization, *seasonal* stocks are for seasonal (within-year) stabilization between harvests, and *pipeline* stocks are minimal stocks in transit and on shelves for markets to function.

9. The International Monetary Fund (IMF) has sought with limited success to facilitate borrowing by food-short developing countries to finance imports. The IMF's Compensatory Financing Facility (CFF) and the Food Financing Facility were set up to help countries troubled by export shortfalls and high import prices. The STABEX program of the European Community for Africa, Caribbean, and Pacific countries also was designed to help. The IMF Food Facility was an extension of CFF, making medium-term credit available for excess cereal imports not offset by export earnings. Loans for cereal imports were available for up to 100 percent of the IMF quota for a period of five years, with two years' grace, at an interest rate of 7 percent (Alamgir and Arora 1991, 173).

Not much use has been made of the Food Facility. During 1981–1987 only seven countries benefited from it. Only two (out of forty-two) least developed countries drew on it (Alamgir and Arora 1991, 176). The Compensatory and Contingency Financing Facility (CCFF) of the IMF, set up in 1988, offers other possibilities, but with its focus only on countries implementing IMF-supported adjustment measures, it too is unlikely to be used widely by developing countries.

REFERENCES

Agency for International Development. May 1982. "Nutrition." A.I.D. Policy Paper. Washington, D.C.: USAID.

———. April 1992. "Definition of Food Security." A.I.D. Policy Paper Determination No. 19. Washington, D.C.: USAID.

Alamgir, Mohiuddin, and Poonam Arora. 1991. *Providing Food Security for All*. Ithaca: New York University Press for International Fund for Agricultural Development.

Agarwala, R. 1983. "Price Distortions and Growth in Developing Countries." Staff Working Paper No. 575. Washington, D.C.: World Bank.

Bale, M. D., and E. Lutz. 1981. "Price Distortions in Agriculture and Their Effects: An International Comparison." *American Journal of Agricultural Economics* 63: 8–22.

Bruno, Michael, Martin Ravallion, and Lyn Squire. 1996. "Equity and Growth in Developing Countries: Old and New Perspectives on the Policy Issues." Policy Research Working Paper 1563. Washington, D.C.: World Bank Policy Research Department.

Carlson, Keith. September/October 1991. "The U.S. Balance Sheet: What is it and what does it tell us?" *Review* 73: 3–18. St. Louis: Federal Reserve Bank.

Epplin, Francis, and Joseph Musah. 1985. "A Representative Farm Planning Model for Liberia." In *Proceedings of the Liberian Agricultural Policy Seminar 1985*. Report B-23. Stillwater: Agricultural Policy Analysis Project, Department of Agricultural Economics, Oklahoma State University.

Food and Agriculture Organization of the United Nations (FAO). 1996. "Food Security and Nutrition." Technical Background Document 5 for World Food Summit. Rome: FAO.

Gardner, Bruce. 1979. *Optimal Stockpiling of Grain*. Lexington, Mass.: Lexington Books.

Gwartney, James, Robert Lawson, and Walter Block. 1996. *Economic Freedom of the World: 1975-1995*. Vancouver, Canada: Fraser Institute. London: Institute of Economic Affairs.

Holmes, Kim, and Melanie Kirkpatrick. 1996. "Freedom and Growth." *The Wall Street Journal*, Monday, December 16, A12.

Huddleston, Barbara. July 1990. "FAO's Overall Approach and Methodology for Formulating National Food Security Programs in Developing Countries." In *Food Security in Developing Countries*, ed. Simon Maxwell, 72–80.

International Food Policy Research Institute. 1990. *IFPRI 1990 Report*. Washington, D.C.: IFPRI.

Knudson, Odin, and John Nash. May 1988. "Agricultural Price Stabilization and Risk Reduction in Developing Countries." Mimeo. Washington, D.C.: World Bank.

Lowdermilk, Melanee. January 17, 1992. "Review of FY 1991 API Reports: Food Security." Memorandum. Washington, D.C.: AFR/ARTS/FARA/FSP/AID.

Lutz, Wolfgang. 1996. "Global versus Local Approaches to Population, Development, and Environmental Analysis." Presented to American Association for the Advancement of Sciences Meeting in Baltimore, Maryland, February 10. Laxemburg, Austria: International Institute for Applied Systems Analysis.

Makki, Shiva, Luther Tweeten, and Mario Miranda. 1995. "Wheat Buffer Stocks and Trade in an Efficient Global Economy." IATRC Working Paper No. 95-6. St. Paul: International Agricultural Trade Research Consortium, University of Minnesota.

Mellor, John. October 1978. "Food Price Policy and Income Distribution in Low-Income Countries." *Economic Development and Cultural Change* 27: 1–26.

———. 1990. "Ending Hunger: An Implementable Program for Self-Reliant Growth." In *The World Food Crisis: Food Security in Comparative Perspective*, ed. J. I. Hans Bakker. Canada: Canadian Scholars' Press.

———. 1992. "Agriculture." In *Handbook of Economic Development*, ed. Dominick Salvatore and Enzo Grilli. New York: Fordham University.

North, Douglass. 1990. *Institutions, Institutional Change, and Economic Performance*. New York: Cambridge University Press.

Pai, Dee-Yu, and Luther Tweeten. 1991. "Farm Income Enhancement Versus Stabilization in a Wheat Buffer Stock Policy." Proceedings of Farm Income Enhancement Conference. Columbus: Department of Agricultural Economics and Rural Sociology, Ohio State University.

Pinstrup-Andersen, Per. "Toward a Consensus for Action." In *A 2020 Vision for Food, Agriculture, and the Environment*, 104-8. Washington, D.C.: International Food Policy Research Institute.

Reinsel, Robert, ed. 1993. *Managing Food Security in Unregulated Markets*. Boulder, Col.: Westview Press.

Reutlinger, Shlomo and Harold Alderman. 1980. "The Prevalence of Calorie-Deficient Diets in Developing Countries." *World Development* 8: 406.

Reutlinger, Shlomo, David Eaton, David Bigman, and David Blom. 1976. "Should Developing Nations Carry Grain Reserves?" In *Analysis of Grain Reserves, A Proceedings*, ed. David Eaton and W. Scott Steele, 12–38. Washington, D.C.: ERS, U.S. Department of Agriculture.

Rosegrant, Mark. 1995. "Who Will Go Hungry?" In *A 2020 Vision for Food, Agriculture, and the Environment*, 29–37. Washington, D.C.: International Food Policy Research Institute.

Ruttan, Vernon. 1995. *United States Development Assistance Policy: The Domestic Politics of Foreign Economic Assistance*. Baltimore, Md.: Johns Hopkins University Press.

Sachs, Jeffrey, and Andrew Warner. July 1996. *Sources of Slow Growth in African Economies*. Cambridge, MA: Harvard Institute for International Development.

Staatz, John, Victoire D'Agostino, and Shelly Sundberg. 1990. "Measuring Food Security in Africa: Conceptual, Empirical, and Policy Issues." *American Journal of Agricultural Economics* 72: 1311–17.

Tanzi, V., and L. Schuknecht. December 1995. "The Growth of Government and the Reform of the State in Industrial Countries." IMF Working Paper. Washington, D.C.: International Monetary Fund.

Tomich, Thomas, Peter Kilby, and Bruce Johnston. 1995. *Transforming Agrarian Economies*. Ithaca, N.Y.: Cornell University Press.

Tweeten, Luther. December 1989. "The Economic Degradation Process." *American Journal of Agricultural Economics* 71: 1102–11.

———. 1992. "The Economics of an Environmentally Sound Agriculture." In *Research in Domestic and International Agribusiness Management*, ed. Ray Goldberg, Vol. 10. Greenwich, Conn.: JAI Press.

Weber, Michael, John Staatz, and John Holtzman, Eric Crawford, and Richard Bernsten. 1988. "Informing Food Security Decisions in Africa: Empirical Analysis and Policy Dialogue." *American Journal of Agricultural Economics* 70: 1044–52.

Weber, Michael, John Staatz, and Lawrence Rubey. 1991. "Targeted Consumer Food Subsidies and the Role of U.S. Food Aid Programming in Africa." PN-ABG-831. Washington, D.C.: Agency for International Development.

Williamson, Oliver. 1995. "The Institutions and Governance of Economic Development and Reform." In *Proceedings of the World Bank Annual Conference on Development Economics*, 171–97. Washington, D.C.: World Bank.

World Bank. 1986a. *Poverty and Hunger: Issues and Options for Food Security in Developing Countries*. Washington, D.C.: International Bank for Reconstruction and Development.

World Bank. 1986b (to 1995). *World Development Report 1986 (to 1995)*. New York: Oxford University Press.

Yeats, Alexander, Azita Amjadi, Ulrich Reincke, and Francis Ng. December 1996. "What Caused Sub-Saharan Africa's Marginalization in World Trade?" *Finance and Development* 33:38–44.

Zhao, Fenkum, Fred Hitzhusen, and Wen Chern. 1991. "Impact and Implications of Price Policy and Land Degradation on Agricultural Growth in Developing Countries." *Agricultural Economics* 5: 311–24.

Index

About the Editors and Contributors

RAISUDDIN AHMED is Director of the Markets and Structural Studies Division at the International Food Policy Research Institute (IFPRI). He has been working at IFPRI since 1976, first as a research fellow and then as a division director. Before coming to IFPRI, he served in the government of his native Bangladesh as deputy chief of the Agriculture and Water Resources Division of the Planning Commission and as Chief Agricultural Economist of the Ministry of Agriculture. He has been involved in research on agricultural marketing and pricing policies, agricultural diversification, and agricultural technology policies in Asia and Africa. He has also been examining the effects of infrastructure on agricultural productivity, rural employment, and rural income distribution. Dr. Ahmed has provided leadership in conducting a number of field research projects in Vietnam, Bangladesh, Pakistan, and Senegal. He has published numerous journal articles, country economic reports, research monographs, book chapters, and books. Dr. Ahmed received a M.A. in economics and a Ph.D. in agricultural economics from Michigan State University, an M.S. in agricultural economics from the American University in Beirut, and a B.S. in agricultural sciences from Dhaka University.

CYNTHIA DONOVAN is currently a Rockefeller Foundation Social Science Research Fellow with the West Africa Rice Development Association (WARDA) posted at the Sahel station in Saint Louis, Senegal. She recently completed a study on the effects of food aid on market development in Mozambique for her doctoral dissertation with Michigan State University. Previously, she has undertaken research and training concerning price policy, market information systems, market development, and cooperative development. Her current research involves the productivity of resource use in irrigated rice cultivation and the farm-level constraints to efficiency. She was a research analyst at IFPRI from 1987 to 1990 during which time this research on infrastructure was conducted.

LAWRENCE KENT is a Senior Development Economist with Development Alternatives, Inc. His expertise is in rapid economic field research, small enterprise and agricultural policy, and project design and evaluation. He has worked in development since 1985 as an economist and agricultural extension agent, conducting field research, analyzing economic data, and implementing projects for USAID, the World Bank, the United Nations, and a variety of NGOs in Africa, Asia, and Eastern Europe. From 1994 to 1995, he served as DAI's representative in the Balkans, while working for a policy research firm in Bulgaria.   Mr. Kent speaks fluent French and conversational Spanish, Mauritanian Arabic, Russian, and Bulgarian. He has a Master of Public Affairs degree from Princeton University.

VIRGINIA A. LAMBERT is a rural sociologist and social scientist.   She managed the technical assistance component of the Gender in Economic and Social Systems Project at Development Alternatives, Inc. She is a land tenure and agricultural development specialist with twenty years of experience   in Latin America. She has used both quantitative and qualitative methodologies in designing, implementing, and evaluating land tenure, rural employment, and women in development projects for USAID missions. She has also managed research programs and technical assistance projects. Ms. Lambert is fluent in Spanish. She has a M.S. in rural sociology from the University of Wisconsin.

DONALD W. LARSON is a professor in the Department of Agricultural Economics at The Ohio State University. He has consulted for USAID and the World Bank in the areas of agricultural credit and rural finance, informal and microenterprise finance, and marketing and price policy, and he has written extensively in these areas. Having worked in Colombia and Brazil, he has a speaking knowledge of Spanish and Portuguese; he also has a reading knowledge of French. Dr. Larson holds a Ph.D. in agricultural economics from Michigan State University.

DONALD G. McCLELLAND is an economist with twenty-four years of experience with USAID. He worked sixteen years with the Agency's policy office as policy advisor and economic analyst for food and agriculture; two years with USAID/Kenya as mission economist; and six years with USAID's central evaluation office, focusing on natural resources and the environment and food aid. He has served as Team Leader (or economist) on numerous overseas consultancies, has served on the United States Delegation at several international conferences sponsored by the United Nations, and he has articulated USAID food and agriculture policy at various domestic and international meetings. He has designed and managed policy-oriented economic research. His writings include USAID policy papers and policy determinations, evaluation reports, and analytical studies. Dr. McClelland's Ph.D. is from the University of Pennsylvania.

RICHARD L. MEYER has worked in the field of rural finance and economic development in developing countries for twenty-two years as a faculty member in the Department of Agricultural Economics at The Ohio State University. While at OSU, he has led contracts and cooperative agreements funded by USAID, and he has been a consultant to USAID, FAO, IFAD, and the World Bank. He has written many articles, book chapters, and other publications and has made several presentations at professional meetings on rural finance, agricultural credit, deposit mobilization, economic development, and rural transportation. He has taught courses in agricultural finance and economic development. He has led research projects in Brazil and Thailand and conducted research in the Philippines, Bangladesh, Portugal, Ecuador, Ghana, and The Gambia. Dr. Meyer holds a Ph.D. in agricultural economics from Cornell University.

JAMES F. OEHMKE is a Associate Professor and Liberty Hyde Bailey Fellow in the Department of Agricultural Economics and the African Studies Center at Michigan State University. He received his Ph.D. in economics from the University of Chicago. For the past fifteen years Dr. Oehmke has been involved in the analysis of research, development and technical change, both in developed and developing countries. He is an editor of the book *The Economics of R&D Policy* (Praeger 1985), and has published numerous journal articles, bulletins, and staff papers on technical change in agriculture.

MITCHELL A. SELIGSON is a professor in the Department of Political Science at the University of Pittsburgh. He is a leading authority on land tenure, agrarian reform, and political participation, with over twenty-three years of research and consultancy experience. Dr. Seligson has designed and evaluated USAID projects focused on strengthening participation in local government, determining the impact of land titling projects, and assessing agricultural sector dynamics. He has completed consultancies on the future of land tenure, legislative strengthening, and the impact of remittances on small enterprise development. Dr. Seligson has published nine books, seventy-seven articles, and fifty-two conference papers regarding political participation, agrarian development, land tenure, revolutions and regime transitions, political culture, democratization, and income inequality. He speaks Spanish fluently and holds a Ph.D. in political science from the University of Pittsburgh.

SCOTT SIMONS currently heads the Economic Policy Support Unit in Malawi's Ministry of Agriculture and Livestock Department. This unit was created to support transition of Malawi's agricultural economy from one characterized by pervasive government controls to a market-based economy. The unit focuses on design and implementation of policies related to liberalizing agricultural input and output markets, parastatal reform, and privatization in the agricultural sector. Prior to that, Dr. Simons was Director for Economics and Policy Analysis at Development Alternatives, Inc. He has also been an advisor in Kenya's Ministry of Planning and National Development. Dr. Simons is an economist with policy and planning experience in agriculture, in natural resources, and in macroeconomics. He has worked in over 15 countries, principally on the African continent, and mostly in the area of policy reform. Other research subjects have included: sources of productivity growth, development of marketing systems, environmental impacts of agriculture, and formal and informal credit markets. Dr. Simons speaks French and Swahili. He holds a Ph.D. in agricultural and natural resource economics from the University of Maryland.

LUTHER G. TWEETEN is Anderson Professor of Agricultural Marketing, Policy, and Trade in the Department of Agricultural Economics at The Ohio State University. His research interests are in agricultural development, policy, trade, marketing, and rural development. He is author or co-author of seven books and over five-hundred journal articles and published papers. He has broad international experience in Asia and Africa. He is a Fellow and former President of the American Agricultural Economics Association. His experience includes a distinguished professorship at Oklahoma State University and visiting professorships at Stanford University, University of Florida, and University of Wisconsin.

ISBN 0-275-95815-9

90000>

EAN

9 780275 958152

HARDCOVER BAR CODE

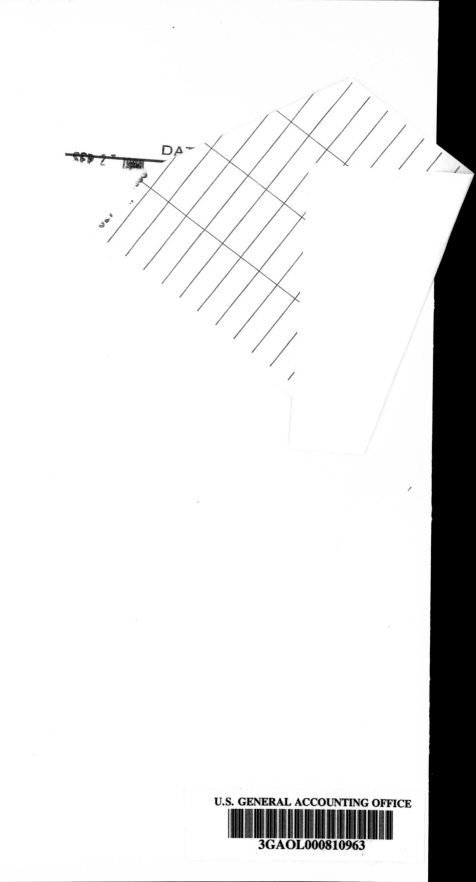

DA

SEP 2